Second Edition

Mentoring The Stars:

A Program for Volunteer Board Leaders

Cynthia Nowicki Hnatiuk, EdD, RN, CAE
Vice President, Organizational Development
Anthony J. Jannetti, Inc.
Pitman, New Jersey

Mentoring the Stars: A Program for Volunteer Board Leaders
Second Edition

Author
Cynthia Nowicki Hnatiuk, EdD, RN, CAE

Managing Editor: Linda Alexander
Cover Design: Darin Peters
Director of Creative Design & Production: Jack M. Bryant

Second Edition
ISBN 978-0-9795029-8-9

Publication Management:
Anthony J. Jannetti, Inc
East Holly Avenue Box 56
Pitman, NJ 08071-0056
Phone: 856.256.2300
Fax: 856.589.7463
Web site: www.ajj.com

Anthony J. Jannetti, Inc. (AJJ) is an association management, marketing, and publishing company serving the health care industry and specialty nursing associations. Jannetti Publications is a division of AJJ, and publishes such high-quality nursing journals as *Nursing Economic$, MEDSURG Nursing, Pediatric Nursing,* and *Dermatology Nursing,* as well as other educational and professional products and services. Visit www.ajj.com for more information.

Printed in the United States of America

Hnatiuk, C.N. (2009). *Mentoring the stars: A program for volunteer board leaders.* (2nd Ed.). Pitman, NJ: Anthony J. Jannetti, Inc.

Contents

Mentoring the Stars: A Program for Volunteer Board Leaders

Foreword

Mentoring the Stars: A Program for Volunteer Board Leaders

Every association on the globe was created for the same basic reason: a group of people realized that they could solve common problems, address common needs, and accomplish common goals together better than any one of them could do alone.

So, we should not be surprised when "competent" board members [see page 12] chuckle when they hear, "Our association is unique." Their experience in other places has exposed them to a variety of conditions and dynamics common to associations. The competent board member is able to see precedents in that experience.

"Expert" board members [see page 13], however, are more likely to smile and nod in agreement. The sum total of their experience has provided them with the wisdom of evolving insight. They have come to understand that, while it is unlikely that any association will encounter a problem or opportunity not previously encountered by another, no two associations have ever exhibited exactly the same combination of realities.

Mentoring the Stars is at least **three** books in one. First, it provides a well-reasoned framework for consenting adults to empower each other to increase their ability to contribute to a common purpose to which they are committed. It carefully blends the best research available about the unique character of nonprofit voluntary enterprise with the proof of actual experience. In the most practical of terms, Dr. Nowicki Hnatiuk identifies "the right things to do" and describes "the right ways to do them."

Mentoring the Stars represents an original collection of intelligence. Its pages define the competencies needed to lead in the context of voluntary organizations. Associations have a complex organizational environment where we must persuade, because we cannot order and do not enjoy the power of command. For those with the will to govern well, this book describes how to deploy essential principles of persuasive leadership: (1) Learn to ask people for their opinions before you decide; not afterwards; (2) Learn to help people understand what they need to be thinking about, without telling them what to think; and, (3) Learn to spend as much time "working on" the enterprise as you spend "working in" it.

Mentoring the Stars is also an exquisite orientation for members and staff new to the leadership dynamics of nonprofit voluntary membership organizations. It provides the content, focus, and mechanism for associations that care about their future to continuously promote effective governance. The tools provided for the unique mentoring approach inherent in the text's design will be useful to all. The content aggregated in the text represents the essence of knowledge anyone serious about engagement with a voluntary membership organization should possess.

Mentoring the Stars is a brilliant aggregation of the attributes of the character and culture of associations that achieve success. With clarity and conciseness, it captures the essence of what "not just good" but "great" leadership practices. For the well-traveled association leader, it's a practical self-assessment that provides the opportunity for continuous self-refection and improvement.

Glenn Tecker
President and CEO
Tecker Consultants LLC

Preface

Mentoring the Stars: A Program for Volunteer Board Leaders

Mentoring the Stars: A Program for Volunteer Board Leaders is a unique approach to mentoring new members or leaders of volunteer association boards of directors or executive boards. Executive board members are truly the stars of their associations. They have often dedicated countless volunteer hours as well as their special expertise to achieve the highest status in the association – a member on the executive board. It is a great honor to achieve this level of success, yet along with this honor comes apprehension and fear. Many executive board members have not held positions at this level before and are uncertain of what to expect and whether their skills and abilities will match up with what is needed at this level. Often it takes at least one year for new board members to perform competently in their roles.

Now in its second edition, this Mentoring Program has proven success in helping new board members more quickly attain the skills and competencies necessary to function as effective members of their association's executive leadership team. It is unique in that it combines a self-directed learning approach with the benefits of a mentoring relationship. The eight chapters of this book provide the content for new board members to learn about their roles and responsibilities. Suggestions for linking with an experienced board member, or mentor, are also provided as a means for enhancing and reinforcing learning.

Mentoring Program Benefits

- Associations will have an effective and organized method to assist new board members in assuming responsibility for learning and becoming competent in their roles.
- New board members will attain the competencies of an executive leader through the knowledge gained from this book and establish a mentoring relationship with an experienced board member.
- Experienced board members will have a systematic and comprehensive way to help new board members transition to their board role.
- Associations will use the program's content and tools for ongoing board development.

In an ideal situation, the association will include this Mentoring Program as a component of its board development plan. The board would select appropriate, experienced board members, or mentors, to facilitate the program and assist new board members in learning their roles and responsibilities. Both new board members and mentors would receive this book and interactively proceed through its contents. Associations are encouraged to refer to the tips to use this Mentoring Program successfully found on page VIII.

For new board members and mentors, the first chapter provides detailed information on how to most effectively use the book and get the most out of the mentoring program. It is recommended that both new board members and mentors read

Chapter 1. It contains a self-assessment tool for new board members to evaluate their learning needs and determine which chapters of this book will meet those needs (see Tool 2 in the Chapter 1 Tool Kit). The first chapter also contains a self-assessment tool for mentors to assess their mentoring skills (see Tool 4 in the Chapter 1 Tool Kit).

Mentoring Program Plan

Once new board members assess their learning needs, they are encouraged to discuss them with their mentor and jointly develop a Mentoring Program Plan (see Tool 5 in the Chapter 1 Tool Kit). As new board members complete their selected chapters of this book, they are encouraged to respond to the learning assessment at the end of each chapter and discuss their thoughts and learning with their mentor. This interaction helps them to reinforce and apply their learning to real-life situations.

Chapter Selection

For this program to be most applicable and timely, new board members should complete those chapters that are most applicable to the activities they are engaged in at the present time. For example, if board members are planning to attend their first board meeting, they would most likely benefit from completing Chapter 8, **Effective Meetings**. If the budget will be discussed at the upcoming meeting, they would also benefit from reading Chapter 7, **Budget and Financial Management**. The value of the self-study portion of this book is that it can be accessed and used at the time the new board members need to learn the information.

This book is designed to be user-friendly with easy readability, practical information, assessment tools, and numerous tables containing tips for becoming a successful board leader. Pages are designed with space for writing thoughts, notes, and questions. **You may also go online to www.ajj.com/mentoring to access the tables and tools (use password MTS2E989).** Associations, mentors, and new board members are encouraged to use the content and tools in ways that are most applicable to their needs. The tools may be printed and used for assessments and discussion. Associations may assign chapters for the entire board to read as a board development initiative.

Most of this book's content is simple. The theoretical information is sufficiently balanced with practical, immediately usable material. While some information may not be new, board members are encouraged to open up their minds and realize they are at a different point in their lives/careers. Previously learned information may take on new meaning when a person assumes a new role or position.

Whether you are a new board member or an experienced board member fulfilling the role of a mentor, you will learn how to enhance your skills as executive board leaders. ***Mentoring the Stars*** was developed from numerous sources, including my own experiences as an organizational development specialist, a former president of a professional association, and a staff executive.

Good luck in your role as an executive board leader!

Cynthia Nowicki Hnatiuk

Tips for Using this Mentoring Program Most Effectively

1) Upon election or appointment of new board members, the association should carefully select experienced board members to serve as mentors to new board members. Chapter 1 provides tips on how to match new board members with appropriate experienced board members.

2) Provide a copy of the ***Mentoring the Stars*** book to each new board member and each mentor.

3) Encourage mentors and new board members to progress through the Mentoring Program by developing and adhering to the Mentoring Program Plan, found in the Tool Kit at the end of Chapter 1. Request periodic feedback on the progress made. Encourage mentors and new board members to bring their questions to the board and share various components of their learning.

4) Evaluate the outcomes of the Mentoring Program for new board members, mentors, and the association using the the Tool Kit at the end of Chapter 1.

5) Determine ways to recognize/reward completion of the Mentoring Program!

6) Use the chapters, tools, and tables to assess and provide board development activities for the entire board.

Download the Chapter Tools, Figures, and Tool Kits online at www.ajj.com/mentoring — Use password MTS2E989

Cynthia Nowicki Hnatiuk, EdD, RN, CAE, is vice president for organizational development at Anthony J. Jannetti, Inc., an association management company specializing in management of professional nursing associations. Cynthia is a registered nurse who has many years of leadership, organizational management, staff education, and publishing experience.

Cynthia is the executive director of the Academy of Medical-Surgical Nurses, the American Academy of Ambulatory Care Nursing, and the Medical-Surgical Nursing Certification Board. She has previously served as the executive director of the Dermatology Nurses' Association, the Dermatology Nursing Certification Board, the National Association of Orthopaedic Nurses, the Orthopaedic Nurses Certification Board, and the National Federation for Specialty Nursing Organizations.

As a volunteer leader, Cynthia is a past president of the American Society of Plastic Surgical Nurses and the Plastic Surgical Nursing Certification Board. At the time of this publication, she served on the American Society of Association Executives (ASAE) CAE Commission.

While serving as an executive director, Cynthia works with board chairpersons to develop and provide leadership development activities for board members and volunteer leaders. She obtained her doctorate in adult education from Nova Southeastern University in Fort Lauderdale, FL. Cynthia received her master's degree in nursing from the Medical College of Ohio and her bachelor's degree in education from the University of Toledo. She is a member of ASAE and is a certified association executive (CAE).

Acknowledgments

I would like to thank several individuals who have helped to make this book possible. First, to the many volunteer leaders with whom I have worked. They have taught me so much and have used the first edition to enhance their board roles. Linda Alexander, the managing editor, provided numerous creative ideas and countless hours of outstanding copy editing, and helped all of us to keep on track. Jack Bryant, the art and design expert, brought his creativity to the awesome formatting and production of the book. Darin Peters provided his artistic talent to the design of the front and back covers. Thank you to Tony Jannetti, the publisher and my boss, for his unending support of both editions of the book. And, to Harve Hnatiuk, my husband, for his patience and love as I researched and wrote this second edition. I was very fortunate to have this wonderful team!

Cynthia Nowicki Hnatiuk, EdD, RN, CAE
Vice President, Organizational Development
Anthony J. Jannetti, Inc.
East Holly Avenue Box 56, Pitman, NJ 08071-0056
cyndee@ajj.com

Chapter 1

Mentoring: A Guide for the Mentor And Mentee

Key Points

- ★ Definitions (mentee, mentor, mentoring, mentoring program, mentoring relationship, and volunteer association)
- ★ Mentoring
- ★ Matching Mentors and Mentees
- ★ Foundations of Mentoring
  - Adult Learning Principles • Novice to Expert Continuum
- ★ Phases of the Mentoring Relationship
- ★ Characteristics of Successful Mentoring
- ★ Mentee Role
  - Benefits for the Mentee
- ★ Mentor Role
  - Ideal Mentor Qualifications and Characteristics
- ★ Potential Problems with Mentoring
- ★ Balancing a Volunteer Position with Other Responsibilities
- ★ Mentoring Program Plan
- ★ Developing Expectations
- ★ Evaluating the Mentoring Relationship

Download the Chapter 1 Tables, Figures, and Tool Kit online at www.ajj.com/mentoring — Use password MTS2E989

Tables & Figures

- ★ Table 1-1 Adult Learning Principles
- ★ Figure 1-1 Novice to Expert Continuum
- ★ Table 1-2 Guiding Novice Board Members
- ★ Table 1-3 Characteristics of Advanced Beginner to Expert Stages
- ★ Table 1-4 Phases of the Mentoring Relationship

Tool Kit

- ★ Tool 1-1 New Board Member Guide to the Mentoring Program
- ★ Tool 1-2 New Board Member Self-Assessment
- ★ Tool 1-3 Mentor Guide to the Mentoring Program
- ★ Tool 1-4 Mentor Self-Assessment
- ★ Tool 1-5 Mentoring Program Plan
- ★ Tool 1-6 Mentee Evaluation of the Mentoring Program
- ★ Tool 1-7 Mentor Evaluation of the Mentoring Program

Being new to a volunteer executive board is an exciting experience, yet it also elicits fear and anxiety. Individuals who have been elected or appointed to board positions have most likely demonstrated success or achievement within the association, another association, or their work setting. While they bring these experiences to the association, they most likely have not been prepared for "being on the board." This is a new experience with new expectations and new ideas to be learned.

The purpose of this chapter is to discuss the concept of mentoring and how a mentoring program can help new board members more quickly and effectively acclimate to the role of a board member. This chapter will help both the mentor and mentee understand the mentor concept, functions and responsibilities of each role, and how to get the most out of the relationship. The information presented is applicable to a variety of settings and situations in addition to a volunteer association and a board member role. Therefore, mentors and mentees may use this information in other areas of their lives.

A critical element of an association's success is its ability to recruit top talent and make sure that these leaders integrate well into the association through formal and informal structures. Many new board members lack formal board or executive leadership experience or education. They have a difficult time identifying with their new administrative peers while at the same time they feel alienated from their grassroots colleagues. It takes time to accept a new identity as an executive leader.

This chapter will educate both mentors and mentees on creating and maintaining a successful mentoring relationship. It provides the foundation for the *relationships* between mentors and mentees. The remaining chapters will provide *specific* information to assist new board members in learning their board roles and responsibilities.

Definitions

A few terms that will be used throughout this chapter are: mentee, mentor, mentoring, mentoring program, mentoring relationship, and volunteer association or organization.

Mentee - The new board member who engages as a learner in the mentoring program.

Mentor - An experienced board member who helps the new board member learn the roles and responsibilities and the culture of the association.

Mentoring - The process in which a seasoned executive board member influences, advises, coaches, facilitates learning, and oversees the development of a new board member.

Mentoring Program - A program that provides new board members an organized mechanism to learn their roles and responsibilities, and the direction and culture of the association.

Mentoring Relationship - The relationship between the mentee and mentor that is created and nurtured throughout the mentoring process.

Volunteer Association or Organization - The terms *association* and *organization* will be used interchangeably throughout this book. They refer to a voluntary, organized group, primarily a not-for-profit entity, whose aim is to serve the interest of its members. An association serves individual members (professional associations), companies (trade associations), or philanthropic associations (foundations, charities). The group is governed by a volunteer executive board or board of directors.

Mentoring

The literature is abundant with thoughts about mentoring. Mentoring is a reciprocal and collaborative learning relationship between two, sometimes more, individuals with mutual goals and shared accountability for the outcomes and success of the relationship. It is a process where the more experienced person assists in the learning and development of the less experienced individual. Traditional views of mentoring describe it as a relationship that occurs spontaneously and is based on a chemistry between two people. Over the last decade or so, facilitated mentoring programs have emerged where the mentor-mentee dyad has been selected, paired, or matched by others rather than by the individuals themselves (Zachary, 2005).

This mentoring program challenges the traditional view of mentoring. It is uniquely designed to blend the knowledge that mentees gain through self-directed learning activities, such as reading this book, with the benefits of a mentoring relationship in which mentors assist in taking the written word a step further to application and real meaning. This program is especially suited for associations whose board members are often separated by time and space. Distance or e-mentoring becomes possible through technology.

The design of this mentoring program is a proactive development process for helping new board members develop and enhance their leadership skills over a period of time. Since it normally takes at least one year or more to learn the role of a board member, this program is meant to shorten the learning curve and hasten individual and organizational learning.

"A successful relationship is even more beneficial when the individuals involved like each other, understand their responsibilities, have a mutual desire to build a relationship, realize they both have something to offer and learn from the other, and share the goal of excellence in board service."

Matching Mentors and Mentees

Planned mentoring programs such as this must be supported by the association's top leaders. Instead of waiting for prospective mentees and mentors to find one another, the association is encouraged to proactively create an avenue for new board members to link up with appropriate partners. The board has the responsibility of matching the new board member with an appropriate mentor. Providing a good fit between the mentee and mentor can either make or break the relationship and the ultimate success of the mentoring program. A successful relationship is even more beneficial when the individuals involved like each other, understand their responsibilities, have a mutual desire to build a relationship, realize they both have something to offer and learn from the other, and both share the goal of excellence in board service.

A good fit between the mentor and mentee occurs when mentors are caring, compassionate, genuine, and willing to disclose information about themselves and about what they know. Mentees, on the other hand, need to be open to accept feedback and be willing to learn more about themselves and their expected role. Matches are often more likely to be successful when mentors and mentees are involved in selecting their partners. However, mentoring relationships can be successful when the two individuals are selected by others such as a selection or mentoring team.

Successful matching of the mentor and mentee can occur when the association has developed matching guidelines. These guidelines may be based on skills, expertise, availability, learning/facilitation style and fit, experience, interpersonal skills and behavior, professional interest, personality, accessibility, education background, gender, willingness/interest, availability, and compatibility. Sometimes boards have one or a few new members and only a few available mentors. The above guidelines can be helpful in making the most appropriate match.

A successful mentoring program has many benefits for the association. It encourages stability and continuity in the association, as well as increased productivity, increased quality of service, vitality, and reduced costs. The association will have a smoothly functioning leadership team and more satisfied, knowledgeable, and competent board members who are able to steer the association into the future. Boards that offer a mentoring program embrace individual and organizational learning, and provide a value-added benefit of board service.

"A successful mentoring program encourages stability and continuity in the association, as well as increased productivity, increased quality of service, vitality, and reduced costs."

Foundations of Mentoring

Inherent in the mentoring concept are two important foundational concepts — principles of adult learning and the novice to expert continuum. While these concepts will be most beneficial in helping mentors be effective in their roles, they can also be helpful for mentees to gain a better understanding of the mentor role. It is likely that mentees will become mentors to new board members in the future.

Adult Learning Principles

The mentoring relationship involves the mentee as an adult learner engaged in a life experience that presents new opportunities for growth and development. The astute mentor is knowledgeable of adult learning principles and applies them to the mentoring relationship as a development process.

Mentoring is a partnership between the mentor as teacher and the mentee as learner. The quality of this partnership determines the true value of the learning experience. As adult learners, mentees assume responsibility for their own learning and behavior. As teachers, mentors act as guides and facilitators of learning.

The partnership must be based on the belief that the learner is at the center of any significant adult learning activity. Learners must be involved in all phases of the learning process - needs identification, planning, participation, and evaluating the learning outcome. As facilitators of adult learning, mentors approach mentoring as a development sequence which requires an awareness of the mentees' learning needs and their stages on the learning curve. In considering mentees as unique adult learners, mentors must be flexible and willing to make adjustments in the learning experience based on the mentees' maturity and learning styles. Effective mentoring becomes a continuous learning process that is a synthesis of events, experiences, thoughts, observations, feedback, and analyses.

Further adult learning principles that are beneficial to the mentoring relationship are included in Table 1-1 (next page).

Table 1-1
Adult Learning Principles

- Adults need time to learn at their own pace.
- Adults have unlimited potential for growth and development.
- Moving from the simple to the complex gives the adult a sense of achievement.
- Learning involves moving from dependency on the teacher/facilitator to increasing self-directedness, but at different rates for different people.
- The learning environment is characterized by physical comfort, mutual respect and trust, freedom of expression, and acceptance of differences.
- Learning must be based on learners' needs. Facilitators help learners diagnose the gap between what they know and what they need to know or do.
- Adults are motivated by the desire to immediately use or apply their new knowledge or skills. When learners need to do something now that they do not know how to do, they have a "readiness to learn." This is what is meant by the "most teachable moment."
- Adults are responsible for their own learning and take an active role in the learning process.
- Adult education is learner-centered. It begins with the learners and where they are, and takes into consideration what will be meaningful for them.
- Adults are what they have done. They have a deep investment in the value of their life experiences. Adult education includes and builds upon the life experiences of the learners.
- Learning should begin at a level equal to the learner's comprehension level.
- Adult education fosters critical reflective thinking.
- Problem posing and problem solving are fundamental aspects of adult education.
- Adult education is concerned with the development of the whole person, including their attitudes, feelings, and emotions.
- Learning can happen anywhere.
- Learning is enhanced by repetition.
- Much significant learning is acquired through doing.
- A positive or negative self-concept can promote or inhibit learning respectively.
- Stress reduces one's ability to learn.
- Learners need to know how they are progressing on their learning goals. This is accomplished through self-evaluation and feedback from others.

Source: Cohen, 1995; Knowles, 1980; Lindeman, 1961; Rogers, 1979.

Novice to Expert Continuum

As we begin a new role, we find ourselves at a novice level. Through experience we learn and progress to higher levels of performance. Most of us have moved along the novice to expert continuum perhaps several times in our lives. We've reached the expert level only to realize our life circumstances or goals change, and we find ourselves a novice once again. Since we've been there before, we know the stages and hopefully can progress more quickly along the continuum.

Returning to a novice stage can be frustrating for new board members. They may have been an active member in the association for a number of years and know the association well, or they may have been a successful chairperson or other leader. When they ascend to the board level, things change. The board member realizes that volunteer service at the executive level involves steering the association and creating its strategic direction. The role requires a new skill set and for many new board members, a return to the novice level. This mentoring program will help you accelerate through the novice to expert continuum.

Benner's (1984) Novice to Expert model explains how the acquisition of new skills requires a progression through stages or levels, and discrete capabilities distinguish the stage of development reached. There are five levels that one passes through in the acquisition and development of a skill: novice, advanced beginner, competent, proficient, and expert. This model fits perfectly with the stages of growth for new board members. As they learn their new roles and grow, they progress along the novice to expert continuum (see Figure 1-1).

Figure 1-1
Novice to Expert Continuum

Novice ➡ Advanced Beginner ➡ Competent ➡ Proficient ➡ Expert

New role or situation

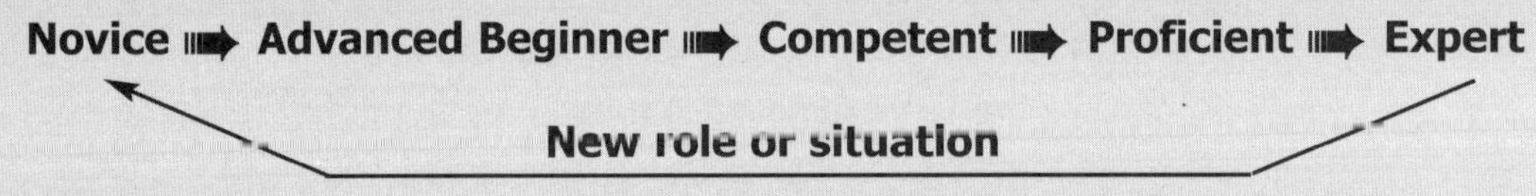

When we are faced with a new role or situation, we most often begin as novices and progress along the continuum. Since no one is an expert at everything, we often find when we change positions or roles, we move from expert back to novice.

Source: Benner, 1984; Nowicki, 1998.

Novice. When new board members take on new and unfamiliar roles, they often begin at the novice stage. Novice board members use rules and facts to guide their actions. They adhere to these rules without consideration for the context of the situation. These rules are limiting since no rule can tell the novice which tasks are most relevant in an actual situation and when it is acceptable to make exceptions to the rule. Novice board members are unable to view situations as a whole, rather they see the individual parts. It is difficult or near impossible for them to put all the parts together and see the big picture. They are concerned with the tasks at hand and cannot do more than one thing at a time.

Situation: A novice board member was assigned to be the board liaison to a committee tasked with revising a printed resource directory. The committee was nearing completion of its work. Concurrent with the committee's work, the association began using new technology that easily converted print materials into a Web-based format. When the novice board member reported the committee's progress to the board, a board member asked if the directory would be a Web-based product. The novice board member responded, "I never thought about suggesting a Web-based directory. I was told the resource would be in the traditional print format." The novice board member was operating "by the rules" according to the assignment that was given to the committee. The novice was unable to see that the context changed and she could have suggested a Web format knowing that this new technology was available. Novice board members do not know when it is acceptable to make an exception to the "rule."

Novice board members greatly benefit from structured learning activities, such as this mentoring program, which combine written information with the benefits of a mentor. The mentor's influence and guidance can assist novice board members in the ways identified in Table 1-2 (next page).

> ***"The board member realizes that volunteer service at the executive level involves steering the association and creating its strategic direction. The role requires a new skill set and for many new board members, a return to the novice level. This mentoring program will help you accelerate through the novice to expert continuum."***

Table 1-2
Guiding Novice Board Members

- Make introductions to individuals on the board and within the association.
- Take the novice board members to formal and informal meetings and have debriefing sessions afterwards. This includes board meetings.
- Offer guidance in the customs/culture of the association.
- Provide information and serve as a resource for the association's mission, goals, and practices.
- Publicly praise novice board members' accomplishments and abilities.
- Exhibit exemplary board member behavior.
- Demonstrate an ability to get things done.
- Make recommendations for advancements/projects.
- Recognize and encourage potential.
- Provide support in times of personal crises or problems.
- Assist in plotting a career path within the association or profession.
- Contact novice board members at agreed-upon time intervals to provide support and check progress.
- Monitor the novice board members' progress.
- Assist in making decisions through listening, support, and feedback.
- Allow and encourage independence when ready, while continuing to provide the proper amount of guidance.
- Use adult learning principles (see Table 1-1).
- Share appropriate life experiences to personalize and enrich the mentoring experience, especially situations that occurred in the role of a board member. Describing mistakes made in a humorous way can be especially helpful ("You wouldn't believe what I did/said...").
- Encourage novice board members to take risks, make mistakes, and learn from them.
- Agree to a no-fault termination of the relationship when the time is right.

New board members need specific direction more often during the novice stage than at any other point along the continuum. As novices, new board members need and appreciate direction from their mentors. For example, in preparation for their first board meeting, it is very helpful for mentors to give specific instructions on how and when to:

- Prepare a board report, including how to use the reporting form with good examples.
- Make travel arrangements, if appropriate.
- Prepare what to bring to the board meeting and how to dress.
- Prepare for the meeting itself (e.g., reading the board book/packet to get the most out of the meeting, reviewing the agenda, and discussing the politically correct things to say and not to say, etc.).

Source: Nowicki, 1998.

Advanced Beginner to Expert. Novice board members continue to experience the real world and progress to the advanced beginner stage and beyond. The characteristics of the advanced beginner to expert stages are depicted in Table 1-3 (next page).

Often new board members who have worked their way up through the association find it difficult to begin their executive roles as novices. They want to feel and be seen as competent immediately upon taking office. It is uncomfortable knowing one does not have a firm grasp of a new role, especially when one has advanced to such a high level in the association. Both new board members and mentors must realize there are developmental stages to pass through before one actually reaches a high level of performance. This is normal and patience is the key to maintaining control of the situation. Not only do mentors need to be patient with new board members, but new board members must be patient with themselves as well.

New board members quickly become successful in their roles when they listen actively to what is going on, get involved in board activities (even if they are not fully contributing), and are willing to be sponges, soaking up as much learning as possible. Mentors can best help their mentees by using adult learning principles to help them learn, grow, and progress through the novice to expert stages. Knowing the characteristics of these stages helps to understand the development process and realize the time and commitment needed to progress to the next levels. Patience and a willingness to share and learn are the keys.

"Both new board members and mentors must realize there are developmental stages to pass through before one actually reaches a high level of performance. This is normal and patience is key to maintaining control of the situation."

Table 1-3
Characteristics of Advanced Beginner to Expert Stages

Advanced Beginner

Advanced beginners demonstrate marginally acceptable performance. They have encountered enough real situations to realize there is recurrent meaning in the components of the situation. Board members at the advanced beginner stage need assistance in determining priorities because they cannot readily sort out what is significant in complex situations. Their work centers on organizing and completing tasks. They become anxious when they feel they are losing control of the task environment. They are concerned with the current situation with little regard for the past or future. They rely on protocols or procedures to guide their actions and believe the protocols are appropriate for all contexts.

Advanced beginner board members are often working at the edges of their safety and knowledge. They are fully responsible for their actions, while at the same time feel largely dependent on more experienced individuals such as the mentor. Guidelines and applicable examples are helpful for them.

Competent

As advanced beginners gain confidence through experience with actual situations, they move to the competent level of performance. Competent board members begin to see their role in terms of long-range plans or goals. They focus their energy on accomplishing what they planned and controlling the activities and events in the situation. They are able to differentiate between important and insignificant components of a situation. Competent board members are able to set priorities.

They feel responsible for and emotionally attached to the decisions they make. Decisions are analytical and they are invested in the outcome. Successful outcomes can be very satisfying, while unsuccessful outcomes are not easily forgotten. Since competent board members are emotionally invested in their decisions, it is important at this stage to encourage them to talk about their feelings and anxieties and verbalize the questions they have.

The competent stage is characterized by not needing help, putting tasks in order, and planning based on goals and predictions. The competent board member's abilities to view the whole situation may be hampered by their emphasis on structuring their work by specific plans and goals. They may lack speed and flexibility. However, it is at this stage that competent board members feel they have mastered their roles.

Proficient

With continued practice and experience, competent board members move to the proficient stage. This stage is characterized by the ability to recognize the big picture and think systematically. Proficient board members are guided by their experience to anticipate what to expect in a given situation and how to modify their plans to respond to these events. Systems thinking improves their decision making ability.

Proficient board members are able to organize and analyze, interpret and understand, and manipulate the environment to respond to the situation at hand. Their actions are now ordered by the situation as it unfolds rather than by preset plans. Proficient board members read situations well and are able to set priorities. Leaving things out is no longer a worry because they are confident in their ability to notice the important things and filter out those that are unimportant.

Table 1-3 (continued) Characteristics of Advanced Beginner to Expert Stages
Proficient (continued) It is often at the competent and proficient stages that board members leave the board or they may decide to run for another term on the board. These individuals can be very valuable to the association because of the level of skill and expertise they possess. Those who leave the board, while it may be a loss to the board, are often given significant roles or projects within the association. Those who continue on as board members can contribute their advanced knowledge and expertise to challenge and help the board itself advance and achieve a higher level of performance.
Expert Proficient board members may make the transition to the expert stage, although not all individuals will attain expert status. This may be a matter of choice or a matter of ability. Experts function much differently from the other stages of development. When things are running smoothly and experts find themselves in familiar territory, they are immediately and directly able to grasp the situation. Important aspects of a situation stand out, and they are able to readily dismiss those that are unimportant. They know when they have a firm grasp of the situation and when they don't. Expert board members are often great historians and can explain why decisions were made in the past. They are often a rich source of information and quite capable of providing sound advice to the board. Expert board members possess a sense of intuition about certain situations as a result of extensive experience. Experts are quick and skillful in their actions. They zero in on problems and are fluid, flexible, and highly proficient. They are able to manage a variety of tasks or activities at the same time. They display a sense of calmness and control. Experts selectively filter information and pass on the important aspects to appropriate individuals. Experts no longer rely on rules to govern their practice. It is often difficult for experts to explain the thinking process they use in reaching a decision. They no longer think in steps or increments. Often the expert board member is not the best teacher for the novice because it is difficult for the expert to explain decisions or actions in enough detail for the novice to grasp and learn.

Source: Benner, 1984.

Phases of the Mentoring Relationship

The mentoring relationship can be characterized in three phases – beginning, middle, and closing. The characteristics of each phase are depicted in Table 1-4 (next page).

Table 1-4
Phases of the Mentoring Relationship

Beginning Phase

Characteristics

Mentors and mentees focus on interpersonal relationship building through establishing trust and nonjudgmental acceptance, articulating expectations of the relationship and each other, engaging in meaningful dialogue, determining well-defined learning goals, and initiating relevant self-disclosure. Mentees tend to put mentors on a pedestal and emulate behaviors. Mentors feel rewarded by the mentor role and value and nurture the development of the mentees. Both may discuss reasons for being on the board and exchange resumes/CVs.

Middle Phase

Characteristics

A safe and positive psychological climate is established and nurtured. Mentors request detailed information from the mentees and offer specific suggestions about current plans and progress in achieving goals. Mentees feel enhanced self-esteem due to the coaching and progress made. Mentees develop and confirm new skills. This phase is characterized by a high degree of interaction and intellectual exchange. Mentors progressively suggest new avenues for learning, then move toward tactics for solving new and more complex situations and problems. As the relationship builds, feedback (positive, but especially negative) is given and taken in a more comfortable and growth-producing way. Mentors encourage less and less reliance and the mentees become more autonomous in their roles.

Closing Phase

Characteristics

The formal part of new board member mentoring comes to closure as the content in this book has been discussed and new board members begin to feel comfortable functioning on their own. Since most associations have a one-year cycle of activities, new board members are much more equipped to see the bigger picture after their first year on the board. Mentors encourage the mentees to reflect critically on outcomes, goal achievements, and future plans. Mentors motivate mentees to take risks, make decisions without certainty of the results, overcome difficulties in the journey to reach their career goals, and become independent adult learners. Mentees achieve greater autonomy and become empowered. Both may mutually seek to dissolve the relationship. They may alternate between feelings of loss and liberation. Mentors remain interested and stay in touch with the mentees to provide continuing support and a safety net if needed. Mentors may feel they have shared everything they know and are proud of the mentees. As separation occurs, the relationship may transform into a friendship or peer mentoring in which both individuals take turns in mentoring each other through their board and life experiences. Mentoring that progresses and ends on a positive note will be memorable throughout the lives of both mentors and mentees. Mentees may themselves become mentors some day. Both partners and the association reflect on the success of the mentoring relationship, share best mentoring practices, thoughtfully consider any stumbling blocks and what was learned from them, determine ways to improve future mentoring, and celebrate the successes.

Source: Adapted from Cohen, 1995; Fields, 1994.

Characteristics of Successful Mentoring

Successful mentoring relationships must be built on trust, openness to self-disclosure, affirmation, and willingness and skill in giving and receiving feedback. Although the old cliché states "trust must be earned," a positive mentoring relationship needs to begin on the right foot – that is, both individuals trusting each other unless or until something happens to erode that trust. Establishing an early psychological foundation of *trust* is a prerequisite to promoting meaningful reflection and self-disclosure in future interactions.

> ***"The mentor and mentee must offer constructive feedback, positive and negative, to assure that common needs and goals are being met."***

Self-disclosure is another characteristic of a successful relationship. Both the mentor and mentee must be willing to share things about themselves, including those situations that may not have been pleasant experiences. The mentee must reveal vulnerable and weak areas so the mentor may provide support and guidance. The mentor must be willing to share personal mistakes since these real situations can provide valuable learning experiences for the mentee. Sharing mistakes in a humorous way can help alleviate some of the fear and anxiety the mentee may be experiencing.

Another characteristic is *affirmation*. The mentor must believe that the mentee will be successful and repeatedly make statements that affirm the mentee's knowledge and expertise. The mentor must believe in the mentee's capacity for success even though the mentee may be unaware of it. It is equally helpful for the mentor to show respect for the mentee's past, present, and future accomplishments.

The fourth characteristic of a successful relationship is *willingness and skill in giving and receiving feedback*. This is important for both the mentor and mentee since one of our greatest learning opportunities occurs through the feedback we give to and receive from others. Both individuals must offer constructive feedback, positive and negative, to assure that common needs and goals are being met. They need to know how the other is doing in the relationship to determine their future direction. It is most helpful if, early in the relationship, the mentor and mentee agree on how to give each other feedback.

The mentor will be faced with the difficult decision of when it will be appropriate to provide the mentee with negative constructive feedback. In the beginning of the relationship, both individuals may be strangers. Confrontation is difficult enough when two people have an established relationship. The implications of confrontative behavior at the beginning of a relationship must be carefully weighed. Timing on the part of the mentor is critical. Confrontative feedback too early in the relationship when the mentee primarily needs support can be unproductive and detrimental to the relationship.

> *"To get the most out of this program, the mentee should read this book, respond to the thought-provoking questions after each chapter, and enter into a mutually accountable relationship with the mentor."*

The mentee also needs to provide feedback to the mentor so the mentor is aware of the behaviors that are contributing to the success of the relationship and those that need to be altered. Mentors who have achieved success in their own lives learn more about themselves and their own competency through feedback from mentees.

Mentoring fosters mentee competence through mutual respect, trust, and admiration. The mentor brings to the relationship knowledge and expertise. The mentee brings enthusiasm and a desire to learn. Through a common vision and purpose, they blend together their qualities and create a synergistic relationship which helps each rise to a level higher than either could do alone. Let's take a closer look at the roles of the mentee and mentor.

Mentee Role

Mentoring doesn't just happen. It involves a significant expenditure of time and energy on the part of the mentor and especially the mentee. To get the most out of this program, the mentee should read this book, respond to the thought-provoking questions after each chapter, and enter into a mutually accountable relationship with the mentor. The program is time consuming, but the end result is intended to produce a well-prepared, productive, and successful board member who provides significant contributions to the team that leads the association. Successful mentees are willing to assume responsibility for their own learning and growth. They seek challenging assignments and responsibilities. While they are receptive to feedback and coaching by the mentor and other board members, they also are willing to constructively give feedback. If they are not receiving the feedback they need or desire, mentees assert themselves and ask for it.

New board members are elected/appointed to their positions because they have most likely demonstrated accountability for former responsibilities within the association. The demonstration of accountability, or living up to promises and commitments, needs to continue especially since board members serve as leadership role models to the association's members. Mentees also learn to achieve a balance between their own independence and reliance on the mentor. Over time, the independence will most likely dominate and the relationship will change.

After spending time with a mentor, mentees often feel refueled and inspired to make a difference in their associations. Other benefits of mentoring for the mentee include:

- Increased self-confidence
- Enhanced leadership skills
- Accelerated cultural acclimation
- Advancement opportunities
- Stress reduction
- Improved networking ability
- Political savvy
- Legal and ethical insight

"Mentors are personable, approachable, reasonable, and competent individuals who are committed to helping mentees achieve the success of which they are capable."

Mentor Role

Mentors are willing and committed to assist in the developmental growth of the mentee. This involves a reasonable amount of time and personal investment over an extended period of time. It is not unusual for mentors to believe they don't have enough time to spend on the mentoring relationship. However, the time invested is time well spent for both individuals and the association as a whole.

The mentor's primary purpose is to help the mentee learn the ropes, their role, the political environment, and the culture of the association in a formal, yet informal way. The mentor encourages the mentee to progress through the chapters in this book and is available to discuss each chapter's content. Therefore, the mentor needs to be familiar with the book's content. Frequent communication offering affirmation and support will help the mentee progress through the program in a timely manner.

The mentor may wear many hats such as teacher, supporter, protector, facilitator, counselor, guide, model, nurturer, predictor, coach, door-opener, idea-generator and bouncer, feedback-giver, eye-opener, energizer, standard-prodder, problem-solver, and challenger. These roles may sound like a tall order to fill, and they are. However, they demonstrate the importance of the mentor role. To be most effective in this role, mentors must have clear perceptions about themselves and how they are or are not able to wear all of these hats.

Mentors are the guides in establishing the criteria by which a successful relationship is developed and evaluated. They create a warm and accepting environment that allows the mentees to control the relationship, while at the same time permitting the mentees to be themselves and voice relevant concerns and needs. Mentors are not distant and idealized role models. Rather, they are personable, approachable, reasonable, and competent individuals who are committed to helping mentees achieve the success of which they are capable.

Effective mentors are confident enough in their own knowledge, skills, and successes that they do not perceive mentees or their accomplishments as threatening. They are committed to seeking situations that will benefit the mentees' development. They also praise the mentees' accomplishments and publicize them to others. Mentors often recommend their mentees for significant projects or promotions.

Mentors bring experience and wisdom. They provide their mentees with insights that would otherwise have been gained only through trial and error. They ask a lot of questions, especially "why?", which encourages mentees to stop and reflect on situations and potential alternatives. Mentors are good at linking together different bits and pieces of their mentees' lives, such as work and home, thoughts and feelings, successes and failures. They try to look at the bigger picture and the future. At times, this may be difficult for mentees because their focus is on the here and now. This type of mentoring can lead to breakthroughs or peak experiences, creating memorable occasions that last for decades.

Ideal mentor qualifications and characteristics include:

- Commitment to the mission and goals of the association
- Knowledge of the association and how to lead at the executive level
- Strong interpersonal skills
- Exemplary leadership skills
- Willingness to assist in the mentee's growth
- Willingness to learn from the mentee
- Personal power and charisma
- Ability to think strategically
- Ability to share credit and successes

- Ability to help the mentee learn from mistakes
- Ability to embrace diversity
- Patience
- Willingness to take risks and share lessons learned
- Accountability — living up to expectations and meeting deadlines
- Time/availability
- Personable and approachable
- Respect and consideration of the mentee

Mentors benefit from the mentoring relationship by learning, acquiring insight, and meeting challenges alongside their mentees. Mentors receive much satisfaction in seeing another person grow and be successful, knowing they played a part in making it happen. Mentees can affirm their mentors' abilities in making a difference and contributing to the future of the association. Since new board members are in most instances the high achievers in the association, mentors can gain a great deal of satisfaction in "mentoring the stars."

"Since new board members are in most instances the high achievers in the association, mentors can gain a great deal of satisfaction in 'mentoring the stars.'"

Potential Problems with Mentoring

Mentoring, just like any type of relationship, can have its problems or drawbacks. If the mentoring relationship is forced, it can fuel discontent, anger, and resentment. There is no guarantee that two people on a blind date will like each other even if a computer dating program matches them perfectly. The same is true of mentoring. Sometimes people are in different stages of personal development. Other times the mentor-mentee match simply doesn't work. It is no one's fault as not all chemistries are compatible. Personality clashes may exist. Sometimes one partner grows faster than the other or in a different direction and a strain on the relationship may occur.

One common problem that occurs is the lack of follow up and commitment to sustain the relationship. Volunteer leaders, especially those who rely on distance mentoring for a majority of their relationship, may not keep their commitments to stay in contact with each other. Their intentions are good, but other priorities interfere.

Other problems with mentoring include mentors who overburden the mentee with work and responsibilities and vice versa. Mentees may become a clone of the mentor and lose their individuality. Mentees may feel mentors are supervising their work too closely or perhaps being neglectful when mentees need their assistance. Mentees may also become too dependent on mentors. An unfavorable incident may occur in which the mentor or mentee feels betrayed or let down. Jealousy and personal or ethical disagreements may also strain the relationship.

"Prior to entering into a mentoring relationship, both parties should agree to a no-fault separation if one or both individuals realize the relationship is not working effectively."

Gender issues may arise between mentors and mentees of the opposite sex. Differences in communication styles can create misunderstandings. Women may manage conflict differently than men. They may delegate authority and make decisions differently. These differences may cause the relationship to separate rather than to build. Perceptions by others may cause problems if rumors begin that a romantic relationship is developing between the mentor and mentee.

Mentors or mentees who are experiencing failure may cause one another to feel guilty or embarrassed because they are associated with each other. If the mentor fails or falls out of favor with the association, the mentee, through association with the mentor, may also fall out of favor.

A final problem with mentoring is the case of toxic mentors. These are mentors who are detrimental to the success of the mentee. They can be described as avoiders, dumpers, blockers, and destroyers (Darling, 1985).

- Avoiders are mentors who are either unavailable or inaccessible to the mentee.
- Dumpers throw the mentee out to the wolves to either sink or swim.
- Blockers actively block the mentee's progress by refusing requests, withholding information, or blocking the mentee's development with overbearing supervision.
- Destroyers are criticizers who tear down the mentee in various ways.

Both mentors and mentees can learn from the problems that others have encountered in the mentoring relationship. If signs of these problems are beginning to develop in the relationship, both individuals have a responsibility to confront the situation and actively plan a resolution or dissolution. *Prior* to entering into a mentoring relationship, both parties should agree to a no-fault separation if one or both individuals realize the relationship is not working effectively.

Balancing A Volunteer Position with Other Responsibilities

There may be times when the mentor can have a significant role in helping the mentee achieve and maintain balance in their lives. Taking on a volunteer position often has time commitments that some board members are not prepared for. In fact, some associations encourage members to run for office and tell them, "You really won't have to do much, just attend a few meetings." For most boards, nothing is farther from the truth. Whether this is the case or not, mentors can help their mentees by talking about maintaining balance in their lives.

A productive board member is one who is focused and able to meet the board's and the association's expectations. Having the passion and time to actively contribute are dependent on what board members have on their plates. Some people over-commit, thinking they can do it all. Sometimes board members begin to disengage in their board work, stop participating or sporadically participate, or underperform. The mentor can assist in identifying these instances with their mentees and entertain a helpful discussion. Some board members get themselves in over their heads and do not want to disappoint anyone by not fulfilling all of their responsibilities. They often need "permission" to step aside either temporarily or permanently. It is better for them, and often better for the association as well.

Values and life circumstances sometimes compete. We may find ourselves out of balance and our energy reserves are drained. Working in a situation where we have to expend much more energy than we have just to keep up puts a drain on us. Often we simply are not doing any good for anyone, especially ourselves. As soon as we lose our balance, we need to realize it and try to regain it as soon as possible

The mentor may help the mentee regain balance just by talking through observations and the mentee's ability to maintain a body, mind, and spirit balance. Strategies for regaining balance in the mentee's life can be helpful in getting them back on track. Or, deciding to take a leave of absence or resign their position may be the best decision for all involved. This decision is never easy, but the mentor can have a significant role in making this transition as painless as possible.

"After reading this chapter, mentors and mentees should initiate and discuss their relationship. Formulating expectations of the relationship and of each other can be a particularly powerful way of planning for the success of the relationship."

Where to Go From Here?

Mentees are encouraged to refer to Tool 1-1, New Board Member Guide to the Mentoring Program, found in the Tool Kit at the end of this chapter, for specific steps to progress through the mentoring program. Mentees are encouraged to complete Tool 1-2, New Board Member Self-Assessment, also found in the Tool Kit. Mentors are encouraged to use Tool 1-3, Mentor Guide to the Mentoring Program and to complete Tool 1-4, Mentor-Self-Assessment.

Mentoring Program Plan

The mentor and mentee should mutually develop the Mentoring Program Plan. Tool 1-5 in the Tool Kit will be very helpful as a guide in developing the plan. It includes goals, expectations, a communication agreement, a timetable for completion of the chapters of this book, and periodic progress checks and evaluation.

Developing Expectations

Mentors and mentees should initiate and discuss their relationship. They should begin to learn about each other by exchanging resumes/curriculum vitae and discussing pertinent life experiences. Formulating expectations of the relationship and of each other can be a particularly powerful way of planning for the success of the relationship.

Expectations are the perceptions of the way we should behave in our roles or positions. In other words, expectations define what to do under various circumstances. Developing clear expectations can build a strong relationship. It also provides a framework for behaviors that are acceptable and unacceptable. Unclear expectations can break down communication and trust, essential elements of the mentoring relationship.

Some of us think we know what others expect of us without having to discuss our expectations. In most cases, this is not true. After all, if others do not know what you expect of them, how will they ever meet your expectations? Once expectations are developed, the mentor and mentee must agree to meet those expectations. Developing expectations will help to confront problems head on. While confrontation is usually not easy, clearly stated expectations help to take some of the pain out of confrontation because the person has essentially broken an agreement that he or she has made.

Expectations are statements of expected behaviors. They are a) observable, b) achievable and stated in a positive way, c) reviewed frequently for currency, and d) important, meaningful, and real to both the mentor and the mentee.

You may be thinking, "What does an expectation look like?" Below are some examples.

I expect my mentor to:

- Be committed and share in the responsibilities of the relationship.
- Encourage me to take risks, support me in these endeavors, and help me learn from my mistakes.
- Encourage my progressive independence, but continue to provide guidance and feedback as needed.
- Keep all information we discuss confidential unless otherwise agreed.

I expect my mentee to:

- Be willing to try new ideas, make mistakes, and learn from the experience.
- Accept my guidance and feedback in the constructive manner in which it is given, but be willing to challenge my thinking and ideas.
- Work diligently in progressing through the Mentoring Program Plan to become an effective and successful leader in the association.
- Keep all information we discuss confidential unless otherwise agreed.

Evaluating the Mentoring Relationship

Mentoring is primarily a close personal relationship and a process of working together as partners to achieve mutually agreed upon goals. This relationship and process should be carefully monitored on a regular basis to ensure its effectiveness or to resolve conflicts or problems before they are detrimental to the relationship.

Throughout the mentoring program, the mentee and mentor should determine set intervals to check on the progress of the mentoring process. They should provide feedback to each other on the strengths of the program, quality of the interpersonal dynamics, progress made to date, areas for improvement, and future direction. The results of these feedback sessions should be communicated to the executive board at periodic intervals such as at board meetings.

In addition to periodic feedback during the mentoring program, both the mentor and mentee should evaluate the strengths and limitations of the overall mentoring program. Benefits for the mentors, mentees, and the association can be determined along with recommendations for improvement of the program (see Tools 1-6 and 1-7 in the Tool Kit at the end of this chapter). Once this book is completed, the formal mentoring program goals should have been achieved. However, this does not mean the mentoring relationship must end. Hopefully, the relationship will continue for as long as both individuals agree to the need for and value of it.

"New board members can more quickly and effectively learn their new roles through a mentoring relationship with experienced board members. This mentoring program is unique in that it blends the knowledge gained by mentees reading this information with the benefits of a mentoring relationship with experienced board members."

Summary

As members of an association's leadership team, new board members can more quickly and effectively learn their new roles through a mentoring relationship with experienced board members. The design of the mentoring program presented in this book is unique in that it blends the knowledge gained by mentees reading this information with the benefits of a mentoring relationship with experienced board members.

This chapter discussed various tips for both the mentee and mentor to create and sustain a successful relationship. A self-assessment tool for mentees will help new board members in evaluating their learning needs and determining which of the following chapters to complete. A self-assessment tool for the mentor will help experienced board members evaluate their mentoring skills in preparation for the mentor role.

To benefit most from this chapter and this book, the mentee and mentor are encouraged to develop the Mentoring Program Plan to set direction for the relationship. New board members are encouraged to read those chapters that will meet their learning needs and engage in dialogue with their mentors after reading each chapter. A successful mentoring experience will result in numerous benefits for new board members, their mentors, the board as a whole, and, ultimately, the volunteer association.

Talking about the value and outcomes of the mentoring program with the board, other current and prospective volunteer leaders, and members, increases its visibility and importance. It fosters a mentoring culture that permeates the association and enhances leadership succession – future leaders become aware that mentoring will be available to them as they consider a future board role.

CHAPTER 1 TOOL KIT

Mentoring: A Guide for the Mentor And Mentee

The following tool kit contains resources that have been mentioned throughout this chapter.

- ★ Tool 1-1 New Board Member Guide to the Mentoring Program
- ★ Tool 1-2 New Board Member Self-Assessment
- ★ Tool 1-3 Mentor Guide to the Mentoring Program
- ★ Tool 1-4 Mentor Self-Assessment
- ★ Tool 1-5 Mentoring Program Plan
- ★ Tool 1-6 Mentee Evaluation of the Mentoring Program
- ★ Tool 1-7 Mentor Evaluation of the Mentoring Program

Download this Tool Kit online at www.ajj.com/mentoring — Use password MTS2E989

Tool 1-1
New Board Member Guide to the Mentoring Program

The following steps are suggestions for progressing successfully through the mentoring program. Place a check in the column once you have completed each step.

(✓) when completed	Activities
	1. Schedule time to begin the mentoring relationship with your mentor. Exchange resumes and discuss significant life experiences. Get to know each others' areas of expertise.
	2. Begin to develop the Mentoring Program Plan (see Tool 3 in the Tool Kit). Read the components of this plan and begin to prepare your responses in preparation for joint development of the program plan with your mentor.
	3. Complete the New Board Member Self-Assessment (see Tool 4 in the Tool Kit). This assessment will help to determine which chapters of this manual you want to complete and establish them in priority order. If there are chapters for which you feel confident in meeting the objectives, you may choose not to read those chapters. However, you may choose to "test" your knowledge of those chapters by reviewing the "Learning Assessment" at the end of the chapter.
	4. Jointly develop the Mentoring Program Plan with your mentor.
	5. Begin reading and completing the chapters of this book. Remember, you will want to readily apply your learning to an actual situation. Schedule the completion of those chapters that will be most helpful to you at appropriate times in the development of your role. For example, for your first board meeting, you will most likely want to read the chapter on Effective Meetings. If the budget will be discussed at this meeting, you will want to read the Budget and Financial Management chapter.
	6. After reading each chapter, except Chapter 1, complete the Learning Assessment at the end of the chapter. This assessment is designed to help you reflect upon and assimilate the information and knowledge gained. The true benefit of the mentoring relationship occurs when you discuss the Learning Assessment with your mentor.

Tool 1-1 (continued) New Board Member Guide to the Mentoring Program	
(✓) when completed	**Activities**
	7. Communicate, communicate, communicate with your mentor! Combined with the information in this book, this is the best chance you have of becoming a successful board member.
	8. Remember to periodically check the progress of the relationship and the Mentoring Program Plan.
	9. Communicate the progress of your mentoring program to the executive board.
	10. When this formal part of the mentoring program has concluded, discuss with your mentor the effectiveness of this program on your role as a new board member, along with the program's strengths and areas for improvement. Communicate this information to the executive board. Also, go back to your self-assessment (see Tool 4 in the Tool Kit) and complete the post-mentoring column to determine your progress in the mentoring program.
	11. Celebrate the success of your partnership and your accomplishments!

Tool 1-2
New Board Member Self-Assessment

The purpose of this tool is to provide a self-assessment of your knowledge and the skills necessary to be an effective board member. Major content areas for each of the chapters in this book are listed in the left column. Read each of these content areas and assess your degree of knowledge or skill in that area. Circle the degree to which you have the knowledge and skills using the scale below. To get the most out of this assessment tool, complete the tool now before you assume your role as a new board member. Then, when you have completed this book and your formal mentoring program, complete this tool again to determine your progress.

Scale:
4 = Have adequate knowledge and skills in the content area
3 = Have some knowledge and skills in this area, but need a review.
2 = Not sure of my knowledge and skills in this area.
1 = Have little to no knowledge or skills in the content area

After you have scored all content areas for the 8 chapters, go back and look at those with a score of 3 or less. These are the areas that you will want to review in this book. For those chapters with several scores of 2 or 1, add the chapter to your Mentoring Program Plan.

Chapter 1 - Mentoring: A Guide for the Mentor and Mentee		***Pre-Mentoring Program***	***Post-Mentoring Program***
To what degree do you have the knowledge and skills of the following?		*Knowledge & skills prior to this program*	*Knowledge & skills after completing this program*
1.1	Definitions of the terms mentee, mentor, mentoring, mentoring program, mentoring relationship, and volunteer association	4 3 2 1	4 3 2 1
1.2	How to match mentors and mentees	4 3 2 1	4 3 2 1
1.3	Foundations of mentoring: Adult learning principles and the novice to expert continuum	4 3 2 1	4 3 2 1
1.4	Phases of the mentoring relationship	4 3 2 1	4 3 2 1
1.5	Characteristics of successful mentoring	4 3 2 1	4 3 2 1
1.6	Mentee role and benefits of a mentoring relationship	4 3 2 1	4 3 2 1
1.7	Mentor role and ideal qualifications and characteristics of a mentor	4 3 2 1	4 3 2 1
1.8	Potential problems with mentoring	4 3 2 1	4 3 2 1
1.9	Balancing volunteerism with other responsibilities	4 3 2 1	4 3 2 1
1.10	Evaluating the mentoring relationship	4 3 2 1	4 3 2 1
1.11	Developing mentor and mentee expectations	4 3 2 1	4 3 2 1
1.12	How to develop a Mentoring Program Plan collaboratively with a mentor	4 3 2 1	4 3 2 1

Tool 1-2 (continued)
New Board Member Self-Assessment Page 2

Chapter 2 - Board Roles and Responsibilities	***Pre-Mentoring Program***	***Post-Mentoring Program***
To what degree do you have the knowledge and skills of the following?	*Knowledge & skills prior to this program*	*Knowledge & skills after completing this program*
2.1 Benefits of board service	4 3 2 1	4 3 2 1
2.2 Why associations exist	4 3 2 1	4 3 2 1
2.3 Three primary roles of a board	4 3 2 1	4 3 2 1
2.4 Responsibilities of an executive board	4 3 2 1	4 3 2 1
2.5 Board member competencies	4 3 2 1	4 3 2 1
2.6 Importance of a board member position description	4 3 2 1	4 3 2 1
2.7 Ethical and legal responsibilities of board members	4 3 2 1	4 3 2 1
2.7.1 Ethical standards and culture	4 3 2 1	4 3 2 1
2.7.2 Fiduciary responsibilities	4 3 2 1	4 3 2 1
2.7.3 Confidentiality	4 3 2 1	4 3 2 1
2.7.4 Conflict of interest	4 3 2 1	4 3 2 1
2.7.5 Antitrust	4 3 2 1	4 3 2 1
2.7.6 Sarbanes - Oxley Act	4 3 2 1	4 3 2 1
2.8 Ways to minimize risk and liability	4 3 2 1	4 3 2 1
2.8.1 D&O and other insurances	4 3 2 1	4 3 2 1
2.8.2 Avoiding personal liability	4 3 2 1	4 3 2 1
2.9 What can go wrong with boards	4 3 2 1	4 3 2 1
2.9.1 Board behavior challenges	4 3 2 1	4 3 2 1
2.9.2 Reasons for unsuccessful boards	4 3 2 1	4 3 2 1
2.10 Ways to build an effective board	4 3 2 1	4 3 2 1
2.11 Characteristics of effective board members	4 3 2 1	4 3 2 1
2.12 Ways new board members can become credible and effective in their roles	4 3 2 1	4 3 2 1
2.13 Conducting a board evaluation	4 3 2 1	4 3 2 1

Tool 1-2 (continued)
New Board Member Self-Assessment Page 3

Chapter 3 - Governance and Leadership	***Pre-Mentoring Program***	***Post-Mentoring Program***
To what degree do you have the knowledge and skills of the following?	*Knowledge & skills prior to this program*	*Knowledge & skills after completing this program*
3.1 Characteristics of effective governance	4 3 2 1	4 3 2 1
3.2 Differences between leadership and management	4 3 2 1	4 3 2 1
3.3 The leadership process (how leaders lead)	4 3 2 1	4 3 2 1
3.4 Characteristics of an effective leader	4 3 2 1	4 3 2 1
3.5 Creating synergy	4 3 2 1	4 3 2 1
3.6 Importance of systems thinking when governing an association	4 3 2 1	4 3 2 1
3.7 Elements of empowerment and levels of authority	4 3 2 1	4 3 2 1
3.8 How to avoid micromanagement	4 3 2 1	4 3 2 1
3.9 Inspiring and motivating volunteers	4 3 2 1	4 3 2 1
3.10 Board liaison role	4 3 2 1	4 3 2 1
3.11 Using the situational leadership model when working with volunteers	4 3 2 1	4 3 2 1
3.12 Use of charters or communication briefs when delegating work	4 3 2 1	4 3 2 1
3.13 Governance through mission, values, vision, and culture	4 3 2 1	4 3 2 1
3.14 Governance documents (strategic plan, articles of incorporation, bylaws, organizational chart, policies, and position descriptions)	4 3 2 1	4 3 2 1
3.15 Roles of officers, committees, and staff in governing an association	4 3 2 1	4 3 2 1

Chapter 4 - Decision Making	***Pre-Mentoring Program***	***Post-Mentoring Program***
To what degree do you have the knowledge and skills of the following?	*Knowledge & skills prior to this program*	*Knowledge & skills after completing this program*
4.1 Making simple and complex decisions	4 3 2 1	4 3 2 1
4.2 Roles of critical and creative thinking in decisions	4 3 2 1	4 3 2 1
4.3 Systems thinking in the decision making process	4 3 2 1	4 3 2 1
4.4 Consensus-decision making	4 3 2 1	4 3 2 1
4.5 Knowledge-Based Decision Making model	4 3 2 1	4 3 2 1
4.6 Process for decision making on issues of strategic importance	4 3 2 1	4 3 2 1
4.7 Simple decision making process	4 3 2 1	4 3 2 1

Tool 1-2 (continued)
New Board Member Self-Assessment Page 4

Chapter 4 - Decision Making (continued)	***Pre-Mentoring Program***	***Post-Mentoring Program***
To what degree do you have the knowledge and skills of the following?	*Knowledge & skills prior to this program*	*Knowledge & skills after completing this program*
4.8 Employing self-discipline during decision making	4 3 2 1	4 3 2 1
4.9 Decision making techniques (brainstorming, nominal group technique)	4 3 2 1	4 3 2 1
4.10 Handling tension, anxiety, and other challenges in decision making	4 3 2 1	4 3 2 1

Chapter 5 - Teamwork and the Board-Staff Partnership	***Pre-Mentoring Program***	***Post-Mentoring Program***
To what degree do you have the knowledge and skills of the following?	*Knowledge & skills prior to this program*	*Knowledge & skills after completing this program*
5.1 Definitions of team, teamwork, and team development/team building	4 3 2 1	4 3 2 1
5.2 Advantages of working together in a team	4 3 2 1	4 3 2 1
5.3 Basic elements of a team	4 3 2 1	4 3 2 1
5.4 Five stages of team development	4 3 2 1	4 3 2 1
5.5 Roles of team leader and team members	4 3 2 1	4 3 2 1
5.6 Evaluating one's skills as a team member	4 3 2 1	4 3 2 1
5.7 Problems that may occur with teams	4 3 2 1	4 3 2 1
5.7.1 Groupthink	4 3 2 1	4 3 2 1
5.7.2 Subgroups	4 3 2 1	4 3 2 1
5.8 Steps for building a team	4 3 2 1	4 3 2 1
5.9 Expectations of team members and a team leader	4 3 2 1	4 3 2 1
5.10 How to evaluate the effectiveness of teamwork	4 3 2 1	4 3 2 1
5.11 Importance of developing a board and staff partnership	4 3 2 1	4 3 2 1
5.12 Guiding principles for an effective board and staff relationship	4 3 2 1	4 3 2 1
5.13 Board chairperson and staff executive partnership and roles	4 3 2 1	4 3 2 1

Tool 1-2 (continued)
New Board Member Self-Assessment Page 5

Chapter 6 - Strategic Thinking and Planning	Pre-Mentoring Program	Post-Mentoring Program
To what degree do you have the knowledge and skills of the following?	Knowledge & skills prior to this program	Knowledge & skills after completing this program
6.1 Definition and importance of strategic thinking and planning	4 3 2 1	4 3 2 1
6.2 Importance of values, mission, and vision to the strategic planning process	4 3 2 1	4 3 2 1
6.3 Six steps of the strategic planning process	4 3 2 1	4 3 2 1
6.3.1 How to prepare for a strategic planning process	4 3 2 1	4 3 2 1
6.3.2 Scanning the internal and external environments	4 3 2 1	4 3 2 1
6.3.3 Analyzing data collected from environmental scanning	4 3 2 1	4 3 2 1
6.3.4 Determining strategic priorities	4 3 2 1	4 3 2 1
6.3.5 Developing goals, objectives, strategies, and action plans	4 3 2 1	4 3 2 1
6.3.6 Implementing the strategies	4 3 2 1	4 3 2 1
6.3.7 Evaluating the strategic plan and the process used to create it	4 3 2 1	4 3 2 1

Chapter 7 - Budget and Financial Management	Pre-Mentoring Program	Post-Mentoring Program
To what degree do you have the knowledge and skills of the following?	Knowledge & skills prior to this program	Knowledge & skills after completing this program
7.1 Board's fiscal responsibility	4 3 2 1	4 3 2 1
7.2 Treasurer's role	4 3 2 1	4 3 2 1
7.3 Budget and finance committee roles	4 3 2 1	4 3 2 1
7.4 Association's budget process	4 3 2 1	4 3 2 1
7.5 Purposes and components of financial statements (operating budget, statement of assets, liabilities and fund balances (balance sheet), statement of revenues and expenses, interim reports, and statement of cash flows)	4 3 2 1	4 3 2 1
7.6 Financial reserves	4 3 2 1	4 3 2 1
7.7 Board's role with investments	4 3 2 1	4 3 2 1
7.8 Financial audits and reviews	4 3 2 1	4 3 2 1
7.9 Meaning of an association's tax exempt status	4 3 2 1	4 3 2 1
7.10 Signs of financial distress	4 3 2 1	4 3 2 1
7.11 How to evaluate the soundness of an association's financial status	4 3 2 1	4 3 2 1

Tool 1-2 (continued)
New Board Member Self-Assessment Page 6

Chapter 8 - Effective Meetings	***Pre-Mentoring Program***	***Post-Mentoring Program***
To what degree do you have the knowledge and skills of the following?	*Knowledge & skills prior to this program*	*Knowledge & skills after completing this program*
8.1 Reasons for holding a meeting	4 3 2 1	4 3 2 1
8.2 Pre-meeting considerations	4 3 2 1	4 3 2 1
8.2.1 Purpose and value of an agenda	4 3 2 1	4 3 2 1
8.2.2 Consent agenda	4 3 2 1	4 3 2 1
8.2.3 Selecting participants, meeting time, and site	4 3 2 1	4 3 2 1
8.2.4 Conference call considerations	4 3 2 1	4 3 2 1
8.2.5 Standing meetings	4 3 2 1	4 3 2 1
8.3 Conducting a meeting	4 3 2 1	4 3 2 1
8.3.1 Establishing ground rules	4 3 2 1	4 3 2 1
8.3.2 Role of the chairperson	4 3 2 1	4 3 2 1
8.3.3 Role of the meeting participants	4 3 2 1	4 3 2 1
8.3.4 Consensus decision making	4 3 2 1	4 3 2 1
8.3.5 Parliamentary procedure	4 3 2 1	4 3 2 1
8.3.6 Handling challenging situations and behaviors in meetings	4 3 2 1	4 3 2 1
8.3.7 Groupthink	4 3 2 1	4 3 2 1
8.4 Executive or closed session	4 3 2 1	4 3 2 1
8.5 Components of meeting minutes	4 3 2 1	4 3 2 1
8.6 Effective ways to conclude meetings	4 3 2 1	4 3 2 1
8.7 Evaluating meetings	4 3 2 1	4 3 2 1

Tool 1-3
Mentor Guide to the Mentoring Program

The following steps are suggestions for assisting your mentee in progressing successfully through the mentoring program. Place a check in the column once you have completed each step.

(✔) when completed	Activities
	1. Ensure that your mentee receives a copy of this book, *Mentoring the Stars.*
	2. Schedule time to begin the mentoring relationship with your mentee. Exchange resumes and discuss significant life experiences. Get to know each others' areas of expertise.
	3. Read Chapter 1 of *Mentoring the Stars.*
	4. Review the Mentoring Program Plan (see Tool 5 in the Tool Kit). Begin thinking of ways you can assist your mentee in developing this plan. List some expectations you have of your mentee.
	5. Complete the Mentor Self-Assessment (see Tool 4 in the Tool Kit). This assessment will help to determine your mentoring strengths and areas for improvement. The references and additional readings at the end of the book may be used as a learning resource to enhance your mentoring skills.
	6. Jointly develop the Mentoring Program Plan with your mentee. Use the results of the mentee's New Board Member Self-Assessment to guide in the development of the plan. Remember, mentees will learn best when they can readily apply their learning to an actual situation. Encourage the mentee to schedule the completion of those chapters that will be most helpful at appropriate times in the development of the role. For example, for the first board meeting, the chapter on Effective Meetings will be very helpful. If the budget will be discussed at this meeting, the mentee will want to read the Budget and Financial Management chapter as well.
	7. Communicate, communicate, communicate with your mentee! Your support, guidance, and progress checks will strengthen the ultimate success of this new board member.
	8. Remember to periodically check the progress of the relationship and the Mentoring Program Plan.
	9. When this formal part of the mentoring program has concluded, discuss with your mentee the effectiveness of this program on their role as a new board member, along with the program's strengths and areas for improvement. Communicate this information to the executive board.
	10. Celebrate the success of your partnership!

Tool 1-4
Mentor Self-Assessment

The purpose of this tool is to provide a self-assessment of the mentor's skills. Complete and use the tool to evaluate strengths and areas for improving your mentor effectiveness. Read each mentor behavior and, using the scale below, circle your assessment of your skills in each area. After scoring the behaviors, look at those areas in which you circled an 'S' or 'L'. These are your areas for improvement. Begin developing your personal development plan to increase your mentoring effectiveness. You may consider discussing your areas for improvement with a person who has successfully functioned in the mentor role.

Note: If you have functioned as a mentor before, base your responses on past experience. If you have not previously functioned as a mentor, your responses should be based on how you have helped others learn and how you would most likely interact with a mentee.

Scale:
E= Experienced S=Some Experience, Could Learn More L=Little to No Experience and Need to Learn

Mentor Behaviors	Skill Assessment
1. I encourage mentees to express their honest feelings about their experiences. I maintain a nonjudgmental, but supportive attitude.	E S L
2. I initiate periodic progress reports to determine mentees' perceptions of their learning and progress toward goal achievement.	E S L
3. I refer mentees to other board members or individuals who may offer information and guidance in areas that I may not have the expertise.	E S L
4. I use eye contact when meeting with mentees.	E S L
5. I share my life experiences, especially as a board member, to help mentees learn from practical experience.	E S L
6. I encourage mentees to refer to the association's mission and values when communicating and making decisions.	E S L
7. I encourage mentees to gather all the facts and define the problem before attempting to solve a problem.	E S L
8. I ask probing questions and encourage mentees to reach their own conclusions and solve problems while providing helpful support. I try not to solve problems for them.	E S L
9. I link mentees with learning resources (human and material) to expand their knowledge and skills.	E S L
10. I encourage mentees to challenge the way things have always been done and "color outside the lines."	E S L
11. I point out inconsistencies in mentees' rationale for their actions and assist them in clearly thinking about their behaviors.	E S L
12. I encourage mentees who are upset or discouraged about a mistake, failure, or negative experience to identify what went wrong, determine reasons why and what could be done differently next time, and to learn from the experience.	E S L

Tool 1-4 (continued)
Mentor Self-Assessment Page 2

Mentor Behaviors	Skill Assessment
13. I provide negative feedback privately and at times when I think mentees are ready or able to constructively receive this information.	E S L
14. I provide negative feedback to mentees by a) making a positive comment, b) stating the undesired behavior/action, c) discussing ways to correct the situation and/or ways to improve in the future, and d) ending on a positive note of affirmation of the mentees' skills and abilities.	E S L
15. I assist mentees in viewing and managing change as a positive opportunity for growth.	E S L
16. When mentees are in a position to institute change, I encourage them to involve all individuals who will be affected by the change and attempt to obtain their "buy-in" prior to instituting the change.	E S L
17. I encourage mentees to continually assess their learning needs and provide guidance in meeting those needs.	E S L
18. I try to stimulate mentees to critically think about the long-range implications of their actions and goals.	E S L
19. I provide step-by-step guidance and direction to mentees when they are performing a task they have never done before. I provide feedback on their performance afterwards.	E S L
20. I look for situations, projects, or advancement opportunities for mentees to gain experience and demonstrate their expertise.	E S L
21. I guide mentees' actions in a way that is politically correct within the association.	E S L
22. I assist mentees to identify and make appropriate decisions about situations that pose ethical dilemmas.	
23. I communicate my concerns when the mentees' verbal and nonverbal behavior is not in agreement.	E S L
24. I share personal examples of difficulties and how I overcame them, either in my personal life or in my experiences within the association, as a method to provide insight and learning for mentees.	E S L
25. I express my personal confidence in mentees' abilities to succeed and their competence as adult learners.	E S L
26. I confront mentees with the reality of potential consequences in a direct, but supportive, manner if they are avoiding dealing with problems or not demonstrating accountability in fulfilling their board member responsibilities.	E S L
27. I encourage mentees to use me as a sounding board when handling difficulties. I listen and allow mentees to vent their feelings and frustrations. I then help mentees in exploring ways to deal effectively with their difficulties.	E S L
28. I am proud of my mentees' successes and publicly praise them for their accomplishments.	E S L

Tool 1-4 (continued)
Mentor Self-Assessment Page 3

Mentor Behaviors	Skill Assessment
29. I discuss with mentees the importance of their roles as role models and leaders of the association. I encourage mentees to display a positive attitude and a confident manner when interacting with fellow board members and the association's members.	E S L
30. I encourage mentees to actively participate in board meetings, assist in making effective decisions through consensus, and support the decisions of the board.	E S L
31. I encourage mentees to provide me with feedback about how I am doing as a mentor and how I am contributing, or not contributing, to their learning.	E S L
32. I establish with the mentees expectations or ground rules for our relationship. I periodically review these expectations with mentees to determine how well we are meeting them.	E S L
33. I discuss and clarify my role as a mentor as often as needed.	E S L
34. I encourage mentees to become progressively independent, but remain available as a coach and a facilitator of their continued learning.	E S L
35. I recognize and value the expertise that mentees bring to the relationship. I am open to learn from my mentees.	E S L
36. I assist mentees in developing reports or presentations, and provide constructive opportunities for them to rehearse any presentations they may need to give to the board or the membership.	E S L
37. I discuss with mentees potential problems or critical issues that may be discussed prior to board meetings so mentees can begin to think about their reactions and responses during these discussions.	E S L
38. When faced with making decisions for the association, I encourage mentees to critically think about what is best for the membership and the future of the association.	E S L
39. When engaging in dialogue and decision making, I encourage mentees to separate facts from feelings, interpretations, and opinions.	E S L
40. I can be trusted with sensitive information and I maintain confidentiality.	E S L
41. I lead a balanced life, making time for important interests including board service.	E S L

Source: Adapted from Cohen, 1995.

Tool 1-5
Mentoring Program Plan

New Board Member ____

Mentor ______________________________ Date ________________

The purpose of this plan is to set and provide continued direction for the progress of this mentoring program. The plan is developed collaboratively by the mentor and mentee. The mentee's self-assessment results should be used as baseline data to determine the mentee's learning needs. This tool serves as a guide to develop goals and expectations, a method of communication, and a timetable for completion of the chapters of this book. Complete your responses to each of the sections.

★ **GOALS:** What do you both want to achieve with this mentoring program? What do you want your outcomes to be?

★ **EXPECTATIONS:** What are your expectations of each other?

I expect my mentor to...

I expect my mentee to...

★ **COMMUNICATION AGREEMENT:** By what method(s) and how often will you communicate with each other?

Tool 1-5 (continued)
Mentoring Program Plan

★ **TIMETABLE FOR COMPLETION OF CHAPTERS OF THE MENTORING PROGRAM:** Use the mentee's self-assessment to determine which chapters need to be completed, in what priority, target date for completion of reading by the mentee, and target date for mentee and mentor to discuss the chapter's content.

Chapter by Priority	Date to Complete Chapter	Date for Discussion

★ **EVALUATION 1:** Determine periodic points at which you will discuss the progress of the mentoring program and the relationship. Develop future actions and renegotiate this plan as needed.

★ **EVALUATION 2:** Upon completion of the formal mentoring program, the mentee will complete the third column of the New Board Member Self-Assessment tool. The mentor and mentee will then discuss the strengths of the program, areas for improvement, and future direction. The mentor and mentee will communicate this evaluation to the executive board.

Tool 1-6
Mentee Evaluation of the Mentoring Program

DIRECTIONS: The purpose of this tool is for the new board member to evaluate the mentoring program after completing this book and/or the mentoring relationship has concluded. Circle your responses and answer the open-ended questions. When completed, discuss any significant thoughts and suggestions with your mentor and the board.

SCALE:
5=Strongly Agree 4=Agree 3=Neutral 2=Disagree 1=Strongly Disagree

1. The content of the book assisted me in learning my role as a board member	5 4 3 2 1	5 4 3 2 1
2. The content of the book helped me to structure my discussions with my mentor	5 4 3 2 1	5 4 3 2 1
3. The learning assessments at the end of each chapter were a valuable reflection and reinforcement of my learning	5 4 3 2 1	5 4 3 2 1
4. My mentor provided the guidance I needed to progress effectively throughout this program	5 4 3 2 1	5 4 3 2 1
5. The mentoring program was a valuable way to prepare me for my role as a board member	5 4 3 2 1	5 4 3 2 1

6. What did you most appreciate about the mentoring you received from your mentor?

7. What would you have liked your mentor to do that she/he did not?

Tool 1-6 (continued)
Mentee Evaluation of the Mentoring Program

8. How might you be a great mentor based on what you learned from your mentor and this mentoring program?

9. What parts of the mentoring program provided the best learning experiences?

10. What parts of the mentoring program could be improved?

11. Other comments? Thoughts?

Good luck in your role!

Tool 1-7
Mentor Evaluation of the Mentoring Program

DIRECTIONS: The purpose of this tool is for the mentor to evaluate the mentoring program after the new member completes this book and/or the mentoring relationship has concluded. Circle your responses and answer the open-ended questions. When completed, discuss any significant thoughts and suggestions with your mentee and the board.

SCALE:
5=Strongly Agree 4=Agree 3=Neutral 2=Disagree 1=Strongly Disagree

1. The content of Chapter 1 assisted me to learn/clarify my role as a mentor	5 4 3 2 1
2. The content of the mentoring program book helped the new board member and me to structure our discussions	5 4 3 2 1
3. The learning assessments at the end of each chapter were a valuable reinforcement of the mentee's learning	5 4 3 2 1
4. I was able to assist/guide my mentee effectively throughout the mentoring program	5 4 3 2 1
5. The mentoring program was a valuable way to prepare the mentee for her/his role as a board member	5 4 3 2 1

6. How did this program help you enhance your mentoring relationship with your mentee and your mentoring skills?

7. What parts of the mentoring program provided the best learning experiences?

Tool 1-7 (continued)
Mentor Evaluation of the Mentoring Program

8. What parts of the mentoring program could be improved?

9. Other comments? Thoughts?

Chapter 2

Board Roles and Responsibilities

Key Points

- Why Do Associations Exist?
- Board Effectiveness
- Three Primary Roles of a Board
- Board Responsibilities
- Board Member Competencies
- Board Member Position Description
- Ethical and Legal Responsibilities
  • Ethical Standards and Culture • Code of Conduct/Ethics • Legal Responsibilities and Considerations • Fiduciary Responsibilities • Confidentiality • Conflict of Interest • Antitrust • Sarbanes-Oxley Act
- Minimizing Risk and Liability
  • Volunteer Protection Act • Insurance • Avoiding Personal Liability
- What Can Go Wrong with Boards
  • Board Behavior Challenges • Unsuccessful Boards
- Building an Effective Board
- Characteristics of Effective Board Members
- Guidelines for Becoming an Effective Board Member
- Board Evaluation

Tables

- Table 2-1 Board Responsibilities
- Table 2-2 Board Member Competencies
- Table 2-3 Tips for Avoiding Personal Liability
- Table 2-4 Guidelines for Becoming an Effective Board Member

Mentoring Opportunity

- Learning Assessment

Download the Chapter 2 Tables and Learning Assessment online at www.ajj.com/mentoring — Use password MTS2E989

Welcome to the Board!

"Congratulations! You have taken on a tremendous responsibility and there are many members who are counting on your ability to effectively lead the association. You will find that your board tenure will be one of the most enriching experiences you will encounter."

Most people, at some time in their lives, volunteer for an activity or a project. Professional, trade, and philanthropic associations exist primarily because of the countless volunteer efforts of their members. While volunteerism in the United States remains quite strong, changing demographics, changing values, and competing demands on time present challenges to associations whose existence depends heavily on volunteer support.

In any given association, different kinds of activities attract various people with differing personalities and areas of interest and expertise. This is the value of diversity within associations. If all of us knew and liked the same things, how boring it would be.

You have been selected to be a vital part of your association's leadership team. Congratulations! You have taken on a tremendous responsibility and there are many members who are counting on your ability to effectively lead the association. You will find that your board tenure will be one of the most enriching experiences you will encounter. You will be excited and stimulated, and frustrated at times, and you will give a lot and receive many rewards. You will meet individuals and experience situations that will add new dimensions to your life. You will encounter learning opportunities that most people will not experience in a lifetime. So, open up your mind, be willing to learn, and enjoy your journey as a new board member.

Your board service will provide you with opportunities to:

- Explore the future of your profession or industry
- Experience the processes of environmental scanning and strategic planning
- Enhance critical thinking and decision-making skills
- Hone in on financial management skills and resource allocation
- Create cutting-edge approaches to advance the future of the association
- Enhance leadership development in others and yourself
- Share a passion for your profession and association
- Model leadership qualities at the highest level
- Build a community and culture that rallies around the association's mission and vision
- Make a difference

Why Do Associations Exist?

Volunteer associations exist primarily to serve their members and enhance the quality of their professional life. These volunteer associations provide special and needed programs and services to their members. The most important person in the association is the individual member. This needs to be kept foremost in the minds of executive leaders. Decision making must be based on doing what is right or in the best interest of the association and its members.

"Collectively, the members of an association are the owners of it. While board members are usually a subset of the ownership, they are also given the power to act as trustees on behalf of the owners."

Individual members of an association are important because they contribute ideas, labor, and money. Members participate at varying degrees and in various ways in the association's activities. Some simply pay their dues. Others become actively involved in the association's activities – attending programs, speaking, moderating programs, conducting telephone campaigns, and chairing committees, to name a few. Members recruit other members to the association and they contribute valuable ideas and insights.

No matter what the individual member's contribution, it must be valued. Sometimes it is easy to get discouraged because all some members want to do is pay their dues and nothing else, while the "rest of us" work hard to run the association. It is important to keep in mind that everyone is at a different point in their lives. Such life activities as work, career, family, going back to school, or other personal situations surface and take priority in our lives, and there is little time to contribute to anything else. Paying our dues is at least helping the financial status of the association.

Collectively, the members of an association are the owners of it. Ownership, in this sense, does not mean the members own actual stock as in a for-profit company. Rather, members contribute to the financial viability and have a vested interest in the association. We want them to feel a sense of ownership. While board members are usually a subset of the ownership, they are also given the power to act as trustees on behalf of the owners. Board members have a fiduciary responsibility for the integrity of the way the board is governed. The board is responsible for its actions, its own development, its work design, its own discipline, and its performance (Carver, 2006).

Board Effectiveness

As important as boards of directors are, many of them do not govern well. There are several reasons for this, including inadequate preparation to function as an executive leader. Many people are elected to executive boards because of their accomplishments within the association. Perhaps they have been chairpersons of committees, speakers, chapter presidents, or project managers. While they have been successful in these roles, their experiences, most likely, have not prepared them to be leaders at an executive level. Project management skills are important, but these are not the same skills needed to lead an association.

> ***"Many people are elected to executive boards because of their accomplishments within the association. Perhaps they have been chairpersons of committees, speakers, chapter presidents, or project managers. While they have been successful in these roles, their experiences, most likely, have not prepared them to be leaders at an executive level."***

Inadequate preparation to be a board member is not the "fault" of the individual member. Board training and literature on how to be an effective board member are not readily accessible unless you know where to acquire such materials. Therefore, orientation and education activities, such as this mentorship program, can be vital to the initial and ongoing development of a successful board member and, ultimately, a successful board.

The following information provides a brief overview of the responsibilities of the board and competencies of individual board members. The remainder of this book contains more detailed information that will help the new board member in meeting the responsibilities and competencies outlined in this chapter.

Three Primary Roles of a Board

The roles of the board can be described in three broad categories:

Setting Direction - This includes setting direction for the association, establishing policies and strategies to guide this direction, and defining outcomes to be achieved with clarity and consensus on what success will look like.

Ensuring Resources - Once direction is established, the board ensures that adequate resources, both human and financial, are in place for the operations, programs, and services offered by the association. The board provides cultural oversight to ensure that volunteer and staff work is synergized and based on trust and shared accountability.

Evaluating Performance and Outcomes - Monitoring and evaluating the implementation and outcomes of the association's work and processes is an important role in ensuring that goals and objectives are achieved and value is received by members.

Board Responsibilities

Within the three broad roles of the board, there are 10 board responsibilities. These responsibilities are described in Table 2-1.

Table 2-1 Board Responsibilities
1. Be mission driven.
2. Establish strategic direction.
3. Maintain linkage with the owners.
4. Make sound decisions.
5. Create and sustain value through effective programs and services.
6. Ensure and manage resources effectively.
7. Ensure organizational learning.
8. Assure executive performance.
9. Form and maintain linkages with other organizations.
10. Assess board and organizational performance.

Source: Nowicki, 1998.

1. Be Mission Driven

The board's fundamental responsibility is to assure that everyone directly and indirectly involved with the association's activities knows and lives its mission. Decision making, goal setting, and discussions about the association's future must be congruent with the mission. The mission is the driving force and the reason the association exists. The mission articulates the association's purpose, goals, and the primary constituents served. It serves as a guide to organizational assessment, planning, decision making, programs and services, and setting priorities in a world with numerous competing demands for scarce resources (Ingram, 2003).

The mission statement is often displayed in a variety of prominent places to create a constant presence of its importance. It may be included in newsletters, journals, brochures, stationery, etc. The mission statement itself should be reviewed periodically to determine whether it continues to meet the demands of an ever-changing environment.

"It is the board's responsibility to establish the strategic direction of the association and lead others in fulfilling that direction."

2. Establish Strategic Direction

It is the board's responsibility to establish the strategic direction of the association and lead others in fulfilling that direction. Most boards scan the internal and external environments and develop long- and short-range plans for moving the association into the future. The board is responsible for thinking strategically, establishing a strategic plan, and periodically evaluating progress on the goals and outcomes of the plan. The strategic plan should have enough structure to help the board focus its energies, but be flexible enough to allow for modifications as needs and priorities change.

To fulfill its mission and direct the association strategically, the board formulates and adopts policy. Policy is a governing principle, a framework for carrying out the work. It is a way for the board to maintain control while delegating functions to others. Implementation activities can and should be delegated to staff, committees, or task forces. Periodic reports from the workforce, such as those required for board meetings, document progress on achieving the strategic goals.

The board is responsible for communicating the strategic direction to the membership and providing periodic progress reports. It is important that members know what is going on and how they are receiving value for their investment. More information on strategic planning is available in Chapter 6 – Strategic Thinking and Planning.

3. Maintain Linkage with the Owners

The board can never lose sight of its members and their needs. It establishes linkages with its owners. The board members' behavior demonstrates that they are acting as moral trustees for the owners. The board gathers evidence of the owners' concerns, needs, demands, and fears. They view members as rich contributors of specialized knowledge and experience. Maintaining contact with the members can be accomplished through one-on-one interactions, interviews, focus groups, open forums with the board, and invited presentations at meetings. Advances in technology have greatly enhanced the board's ability to communicate frequently with members. The board must initiate the effort to listen, ask for feedback and suggestions, and engage in dialogue with the members.

Most associations have at least one annual meeting that is attended by a significant percentage of members and potential members. Often during these meetings the board spreads itself very thin with board, committee, and other types of meetings. Few boards set time aside to establish or reestablish linkage directly with the grassroots members, prospective members, and other stakeholders. This is a prime opportunity to connect with a significant number and variety of individuals.

"When making collective decisions, the most important questions to ask and answer are: "What is best for the members?" "What is best for the association?" and "How will this decision contribute value to the members?""

4. Make Sound Decisions

One of the most critical responsibilities of the board is to make decisions that are knowledge-based and in the best interest of the association. Board members must weigh all the facts, clearly define problems and situations in which decisions are needed, ask critical questions, generate various alternatives, make the necessary decisions, and determine appropriate follow-up measures. High-functioning boards engage in open, candid dialogue. These board members have the courage to speak up especially if things do not seem right. Often, others have the same concerns or questions, but not the courage to voice them. Once the issue is placed on the table, others often open up with the same or similar concerns.

When making collective decisions, the most important questions to ask and answer are: "What is best for the members?" "What is best for the association?" and "How will this decision contribute value to the members?" Decisions that are made by asking these questions are often the right decisions because they take into account the persons and the reasons for which the association exists. Further, decisions should be made to act, not to react, and the focus should be to succeed, not to avoid failure.

Good decisions are often the result of much dialogue and deliberation. Once a decision is made, the board agrees to accept the decision or at least agree to live with it and support the decision, especially outside of the boardroom.

5. Create and Sustain Value Through Effective Programs and Services

Through strategic thinking and planning, the board determines the programs and services to be offered by the association. The board is then responsible for assuring that these programs and services are meeting the association's mission and are perceived by the owners as adding value to their membership investment. As new ideas for programs and services are proposed, the board must critically question whether these ideas are consistent with the association's mission. It is equally important to determine how these new ideas fit into the overall picture of where the association is, where it is headed, and what resources are available.

> *"The board is responsible for generating income sources and managing expenses to ensure the financial viability of the association and its programs."*

6. Ensure and Manage Resources Effectively

Providing adequate resources to accomplish the association's goals and activities, and to ensure its viability, is an essential board responsibility. One of the association's most important assets is its human resources, including volunteers and staff. The board must carefully select competent individuals, provide clear direction to them, recognize their achievements, and monitor their outcomes. A responsible board will empower these individuals to do their work and not allow itself to become involved in too much operational detail and micromanage the association or its workforce.

An association is only as effective as the resources it has available to meet its goals. One important board responsibility is to manage the financial resources effectively. Owners expect their boards to protect accumulated interests and ensure that income and expenses are managed properly. The board is responsible for generating income sources and managing expenses to ensure the financial viability of the association and its programs. It is also responsible for adopting and monitoring the association's budget, financial status, investments, and insurance program.

7. Ensure Organizational Learning

For most associations, providing learning opportunities for its members and stakeholders is a key component of its mission. Equally important is the board's role in ensuring that continuous learning occurs among its workforce, both volunteers and staff. Opportunities for board and senior staff development are provided through formal and informal board development activities, board orientation, volunteer leader development, and leadership mentoring programs. Experiential learning occurs while leaders are actually doing their work as long as the work is meaningful, has clear outcomes, and is enjoyable. Most board members and other volunteer leaders have not had the experiences provided through associations. Therefore, they learn on the job. Coaching and mentoring by experienced leaders is critical to their continuous learning and growth.

An association's board often changes each year as terms expire and new members are elected. This revolving door creates opportunities and challenges in terms of board competency. Maintaining a competent board requires recruiting strong leaders and engaging them in ongoing board development activities that create a learning culture and keep the board knowledgeable of effective governance and leadership practices.

“Maintaining a competent board requires recruiting strong leaders and engaging them in ongoing board development activities that create a learning culture and keep the board knowledgeable of effective governance and leadership practices.”

Planning for the association's future involves recruiting, coaching, mentoring, and securing leaders who demonstrate the passion and skills to become the board members of the future. Ensuring leadership succession planning is essential. Board members are always on the lookout for the rising stars who will one day be their successors.

8. Assure Executive Performance

Boards have various structures in place for performing the day-to-day operations of the association. Most boards have a chief staff officer; titles may vary from executive director to chief executive officer. For purposes of this book, the title 'staff executive' will be used. This may be a full or part-time position. Some boards hire a staff executive who hires and manages the association's headquarters office and staff. Other boards contract with an association management company that provides the staff executive along with a full range of other services such as conference management, marketing, advertising and exhibit management, information management, as well as education, art, editorial, and publishing services.

The board is responsible for selecting the staff executive or the association management company, working in partnership with them, supporting their efforts, and reviewing their performance. It must be assured that staff is serving the association's needs and implementing its policies.

9. Form and Maintain Linkages with Other Organizations

Initiating and supporting collaboration with other professional, community, consumer, and industry organizations is essential to keep current and share valuable resources and services. Linkages with other organizations can achieve greater outcomes than either organization can accomplish alone. In today's world, partnerships, coalitions, alliances, mergers, and other forms of collaboration are more the norm rather than the exception.

Associations today are faced with a wide array of organizations with which to collaborate. Sometimes, the decision to collaborate is not easy. Collaboration in many instances involves time and money. Too often boards decide to collaborate only to find out down the road that the resources to collaborate dwindle quickly or, when a new board takes over, the collaborative efforts may not be deemed a priority. Boards must ensure they are providing the programs and services needed and valued by their members, and determine if collaboration would be a viable way to expand their ability and capacity to do this. Collaboration can be extremely effective if done for the right reasons and with adequate resources to support it.

"Boards must ensure they are providing the programs and services needed and valued by their members, and determine if collaboration would be a viable way to expand their ability and capacity to do this. Collaboration can be extremely effective if done for the right reasons and with adequate resources to support it."

10. Assess Board and Organizational Performance

Every few years, if not annually, the board and executive staff should review how the board is meeting its responsibilities. This includes looking at board composition, board recruitment and selection process, related policies and role descriptions, the processes used to accomplish board work, board orientation and development process, board meeting process, successes and strengths, and how overall performance could be strengthened. The board responsibilities listed in this section can be used as criteria to review performance.

In addition to assessing board performance, the board is responsible for assessing the association as a whole. This type of evaluation would include such areas as the mission, vision, and strategic direction, strategic plan progress and outcomes, governance, organizational structure, staff structure and performance, volunteer units such as committees and task forces, programs and services, financial management and investments, fundraising, advocacy efforts, customer service, public relations and marketing, recruitment and retention, technology and information services, and collaborations. After assessing these areas, the board determines areas for improvement and ensures quality performance.

Board Member Competencies

The board, as a whole, is accountable for performing the above 10 responsibilities. Board members, individually, must also be competent in their executive roles. This section will discuss 11 board member competencies as indentified in Table 2-2.

Table 2-2 Board Member Competencies
1. Know, interpret, communicate, and support the association's mission, vision, values, and goals.
2. Oversee, promote, and evaluate the association's programs and services.
3. Use a consensus-building approach to make decisions that are in the best interest of the association.
4. Participate in strategic thinking and planning to direct the future of the association.
5. Effectively communicate with all internal and external stakeholders.
6. Work as a team with fellow board members and the management staff in accomplishing the goals of the association.
7. Oversee the allocation of financial resources to maintain fiscal accountability and viability.
8. Conduct all association business in a legal and ethical manner.
9. Actively contribute to productive and effective board and committee meetings.
10. Engage in activities to enhance the executive leadership role.
11. Oversee and actively participate in member recruitment and retention.

Source: Nowicki, 1998.

Competency 1: Know, interpret, communicate, and support the association's mission, vision, values, and goals.

Board members must know the association's mission, vision, values, and goals well enough to communicate and interpret them to others in ways that make them come alive. They live the mission and keep it foremost in their minds when performing any activity of the association. Board members give voice to the mission, vision, values, and strategic direction of the association. No one is better qualified to articulate them and build relationships around them with members, prospective members, and other stakeholders.

Board members encounter many opportunities to convey the mission and goals to members, prospective members, colleagues, and the public. It is helpful to prepare a 20-second statement (e.g., elevator speech) that will capture the essence of what the association is about, highlighting the mission and goals. For example:

ABC Professional Association is a nonprofit association of xxx (#) members who work in the xxx profession. ABC exists to promote excellence in xxx (i.e., the mission statement). Our goals are knowledge source, research, education, advocacy, and community.

"Board members must ask themselves what the members need and expect, then make decisions based on the members' best interests."

This statement covers the essential elements from which further elaboration may ensue. It is important to create this type of statement and practice the message so it can be easily articulated when the time is appropriate.

Competency 2: Oversee, promote, and evaluate the association's programs and services.

The programs and services are the activities of the association from which members receive value. Board members communicate with the membership to determine the extent to which the programs and services meet members' needs. They solicit feedback and suggestions for improvement and new services. It is the board member's responsibility to know all programs and services in enough detail to promote them to others.

Board members must continuously ask the following critical questions about the association's programs and services:

1. Are our programs and services meeting the members' needs? Are we proactive in developing them? Are they available before our members realize they need them?
2. Do our members perceive value in our programs and services? Keep in mind **Value = Cost + Quality**. In other words, are the programs and services adding value to their financial investment in the association? Are they getting their money's worth...and then some?

Competency 3: Use a consensus-building approach to make decisions that are in the best interest of the association.

Board members are committed to achieving consensus when making decisions. This involves all board members contributing their opinions and ideas, discussing situations and alternatives, and determining a solution and plan of action that the board can support. The key in consensus decision making is that all board members thoroughly discuss the situation and various alternative solutions. While every board member may not completely agree with the decision, everyone is willing to give it a try and they agree to support the decision – especially outside of the boardroom.

Board members must ask themselves what the members need and expect, then make decisions based on the members' best interests. Keeping in touch with members through direct contact or through various representatives in the association is critical to obtaining current member input and knowing how to represent their interests.

Making decisions based on the members' and association's best interests means looking at the big picture and focusing on "all" versus "some." New board members may find it difficult removing themselves from a former position in the association where they represented the interests of a particular group such as a chapter, committee, or special interest group. Upon becoming a board member, the individual must consider the interests of all members and the association as a whole, and not act as a representative from the former group or allegiance.

"Board members focus on the mission, how the association maintains its uniqueness and makes a difference that others don't or can't make, and where the association will be in the future."

Competency 4: Participate in strategic thinking and planning to direct the future of the association.

Board members take an active role in strategic thinking and planning. Their actions reflect their ability to consider the big picture, scan the environment, recognize trends and patterns, determine priorities, anticipate issues, take risks, and envision alternative solutions and paths. They focus on the mission, how the association maintains its uniqueness and makes a difference that others don't or can't make, and where the association will be in the future.

Board members support the strategic plan, including the goals and objectives that make the plan a living document. They communicate the plan to all individuals involved, support those who assist in carrying out the plan, and continuously evaluate and revise it as needed. Board members use the plan as a blueprint for success.

As new ideas surface, board members question how new activities fit into the strategic plan or suggest ways in which the plan should be modified to accommodate the new activities. Board members demonstrate flexibility in overseeing the plan because new opportunities and needs are not always predictable at the time the plan is developed.

Competency 5: Effectively communicate with all internal and external stakeholders.

"Board members have an obligation to work in unity and to concentrate on building relationships with each other."

Being a member of an effective board involves communication that is open, honest, and caring. Board members are expected to be role models and demonstrate appropriate behavior. They are responsible for clearly communicating the mission, providing direction for important work to be done, coaching and advising volunteers, and sometimes delivering unpopular information. Board members often communicate with stakeholders external to the association such as employers, legislators, and other associations. They are always "on stage" because their behavior is observed by others.

While verbal communication skills are essential, written communication is equally important. Many associations are state, national, or international in scope, and written communication is used extensively. Board members are expected to use the various written and electronic communication avenues to keep in contact with fellow board members, members-at-large, chapter representatives, committee chairpersons and members, staff, and external sources. Written communication says as much about our image as what we say verbally.

Competency 6: Work as a team with fellow board members and the management staff in accomplishing the goals of the association.

Board members need to work together as a team committed to providing quality programs and services to the members. Team work involves "work." It doesn't just happen. Board members have an obligation to work in unity and to concentrate on building relationships with each other. Their ability to create and maintain a team effort is critical to the success of their roles as board members and to the success of the association during their terms.

Equally important is the partnership that must be built and nurtured between the board and management staff. Together board members and staff combine their leadership and management expertise to accomplish the association's goals.

Competency 7: Oversee the allocation of financial resources to maintain fiscal accountability and viability.

Generating revenue through dues, programs, fundraising, investments, or other sources is necessary to have the funds to operate the association and to continuously develop new products and services. Board members assess member needs and bring creative ideas for revenue-generating sources. They also oversee the management of expenses, the budget process, and investment plan to ensure financial viability.

"The association expects board members to act in a fair and just manner and make decisions that are in the best interest of the owners."

Competency 8: Conduct all association business in a legal and ethical manner.

Board members set an example for the membership through their conduct. They must be aware of their legal responsibilities and act in a manner that does not put them or the association in legal jeopardy. Board members need to be aware of the association's conflict of interest policy and not become involved in activities that may be perceived as or become a direct conflict of interest.

Ethical conduct is also an important consideration in the role of board members. The association expects board members to act in a fair and just manner and make decisions that are in the best interest of the owners. As ethical dilemmas surface within the association, board members need to be skilled in identifying them and determining methods for resolution. Board members also need to be acutely aware of situations that require confidentiality.

Competency 9: Actively contribute to productive and effective board and committee meetings.

A majority of the association's work is accomplished through various types of meetings, both in person and electronically. Board members must be knowledgeable and skilled in participating in and leading meetings that are time efficient and productive. Their skills extend to other volunteer leaders such as committee chairs as the board members frequently coach new leaders in conducting effective meetings.

Competency 10: Engage in activities to enhance the executive leadership role.

Effective board members are committed to taking the responsibility of learning the roles and expectations for their positions.

They understand the concept of executive leadership and strive to lead through example and empowerment. Their leadership focuses on vision, mission, values, and goals. They empower others to accomplish the association's work without getting involved in operational details. Board members seek opportunities for learning, ask a lot of questions, and share their expertise so others can, in turn, learn from them.

"Effective board members are committed to their roles, seek opportunities for learning, ask a lot of questions, and share their expertise so others can, in turn, learn from them."

Competency 11: Oversee and actively participate in member recruitment and retention.

Recruitment and retention of members is everyone's responsibility, and board members are first in line to model the way. Without attracting new members and retaining current ones, associations would not exist. Setting direction for membership recruitment and retention plans, overseeing implementation, and evaluating outcomes are the board's responsibility. In addition, the board's actions and ability to make decisions that are member-focused and value-added contribute significantly to whether members join and stay.

Board Member Position Description

Each board member should receive a position or role description even before the consent to serve is made. A position description can help clarify what is involved in board leadership. It can be helpful in board orientation as a framework to discuss role responsibilities. It can also serve as a reference to help board members stay on track. The specific responsibilities listed in position descriptions can be used as criteria for ongoing performance evaluation.

By now, you should have received and reviewed your position description. Look at the position description once again and answer the following questions.

Position Description Review

1. Does the position description adequately reflect what you said you would do?
2. Are there any responsibilities you do not understand?
3. What parts of the role responsibilities are you looking forward to doing?
4. What parts of the role responsibilities are new or a concern for you?

5. What skills do you possess that will help you in fulfilling the position description?
6. What do you need to learn about your role?

Ethical and Legal Responsibilities

Given the many responsibilities and competencies of board members, acting in an ethical and legal manner while representing the association ranks among the most important duties of a board member. Often there is a fine line when trying to distinguish between ethical behavior and legal obligations. For example, the issue of confidentiality can pose both legal and ethical dilemmas. Therefore, the scope of this section will focus on behaviors and duties that will lead the board member to perform in both an ethical and legal manner.

"Influential boards speak with one voice, do not undermine each other, show respect for the chief volunteer and staff officers and their authority, and ethically deal with other volunteers and staff."

Ethical Standards and Culture

Board members are responsible for creating and sustaining an ethical culture within the association that ensures transparency and accountability. An association's culture is composed of informal rules which define how things really work. According to Navran (2006), culture is what people do independently of the written rules, but includes the rules we need to know to navigate the association successfully. Ethical culture is guided by ethical values or principles such as trust, honesty, respect, accountability, fairness, and integrity.

In sustaining an ethical culture, the board influences behaviors both at the board and organizational levels. While influence over the association's ethical culture may be less direct, the board models the way by using ethical values as the basis for board behaviors and decisions. Navran (2006) describes ways of ensuring an ethical culture at the board level as: demonstrating full responsibility and accountability, being truthful even if it means being blunt, and exercising fairness in the allocation of work by not overburdening the most competent and masking the limitations of those who are less competent or the inaction of those who are unaccountable.

Boards extend their influence to the association by communicating the association's ethical values or standards to other leaders and members, performing an ethics audit, and establishing an ethics committee. These boards walk the talk by speaking with one voice, not undermining each other, showing respect for the chief volunteer and staff officers and their authority, and ethically dealing with other volunteers and staff. Given the many scandals that have occurred in the corporate world, many visionary boards are now paying more attention to ethical standards and culture.

"Fiduciary is the legal obligation of boards to hold in trust the association and act in its best interests. As fiduciaries, board members must put their own personal and professional interests aside and act in the best interests of the association and its members."

Code of Conduct/Ethics

Some associations have a code of conduct or code of ethics that describes the standards for ethical behavior. Some board members are required to sign a code of ethics statement upon accepting their leadership positions within the association. These documents solidify the board member's commitment to serving the best interests of the association. An organizational culture in which values are embedded and taken seriously is an important precursor to ethical performance. This culture builds strong community within the association and is often referred to as the social fabric.

Legal Responsibilities and Considerations

The board and its members must operate within their limitations and hold themselves accountable at all times. Given the very litigious society in which we live today, board members can never be too careful in their decision making responsibilities. People, even members, will sue for a wide array of reasons. These reasons include such things as making decisions based on inadequate information, poor judgment, failure to attend board meetings, inefficient fiscal management resulting in losses, not obtaining appropriate legal or financial consultations, and failure to examine agreements before signing.

While board members can be held liable and sued for the above reasons, it is an uncommon occurrence. Board members should not allow the potential liabilities to detract them from participating and contributing their expertise to their associations. Rather, they should be aware of these liabilities and determine ways to minimize their risks.

Fiduciary Responsibilities

Mention the term fiduciary, and most people think of money or financial responsibility. However, it is more than that. Fiduciary is the legal obligation of boards to hold in trust the association and act in its best interests. As fiduciaries, board members must put their own personal and professional interests aside and act in the best interests of the association and its members.

Board members must meet certain standards of conduct in carrying out their fiduciary responsibilities. These standards are described as duty of care, duty of loyalty, and duty of obedience.

The duty of care or diligence. The duty of care describes the level of competence that is expected of a board member. The board member must perform in a manner that a reasonably prudent person would exercise in a similar position and under like circumstances. In complying with this duty, board members must act in good faith and actively participate in board decisions, ask questions and base decisions on knowledge, exercise independent judgment, and protect any confidential association information. Board members are responsible for the acts or the failures of their volunteers and staff.

The duty of loyalty. This duty requires board members to put the interests of the association over their own. Board members must be loyal to the association and never use information obtained as a member for personal advantage. The board member is permitted only to act in the interest of the association and avoid potential conflicts of interest. The duty of loyalty prohibits competition by a board member with the association itself.

Associations are held responsible for the illegal activities of their volunteers if the volunteers "appeared" to be acting on behalf of the association, even if the board did not approve the activities. It is necessary for associations to limit those individuals who have the authority to act or speak for the association.

The duty of obedience. This requires board members to be faithful and act in a manner consistent with the association's mission and purposes as expressed in the articles of incorporation, bylaws, and policies. The board member's behavior and focus must be guided in the direction of achieving the goals of the association. Board members participate in decision making and they are legally obligated to support and implement the decisions and not undermine them.

These duties require board members to act in a reasonable manner and in the best interest of the association. Board members are required to act honestly and in good faith, while avoiding negligence, fraud, and conflicts of interest. In the event that they breach these duties, they can be held liable for any damages to the association as a result of their breach (Jacobs, 2008).

Confidentiality

Maintaining confidentiality is an ethical and legal responsibility of a board member. Occasionally, board members have access to confidential information. The issue of confidentiality may be raised because it is in the best interest of the association to maintain confidentiality or because disclosure of information could injure individuals or the association.

Some information is specifically designated as confidential, such as documents or conversations that explicitly state "confidential." Discussions and minutes from executive sessions are designated as confidential. Confidentiality may extend to other instances not designated as "confidential," and it is up to the board member to determine when it would not be in the association's best interest to disclose the information to a third party. Board members need to keep confidentiality foremost in their minds and not share association information with third parties or with persons within the association who do not have a need to know. If ever in doubt about whether information should be kept confidential, chances are if you are questioning it, it is in the association's best interest not to disclose it.

"A conflict of interest should not be perceived as a negative strike against a person, but it is important to identify that a conflict or potential conflict of interest exists and manage it. Disclosure is the first step in preventing an actual conflict of interest that could pose serious legal and ethical problems for the association."

Conflict of Interest

A conflict of interest exists when a board member, staff, or other volunteer leader has a professional, business, personal, or other volunteer interest that is inconsistent with the interests of the association. It may result in a bias and subjectivity when participating in decision making for the association. A conflict of interest is ultimately what the association defines it to be. Often, individuals are unaware of the impact of their personal interests on their roles as volunteers and staff.

Conflicts of interest are common especially among groups of individuals who lead busy lives and are engaged in their careers and professions. Conflicts can be actual, potential, or perceived. A conflict of interest should not be perceived as a negative strike against a person, but it is important to identify that a conflict or potential conflict of interest exists and manage it. Disclosure is the first step in identifying a conflict. Disclosing the personal interest is all that may be necessary with potential conflicts. That way everyone is informed and can make their own decisions as to whether or not this conflict has an impact on decision making.

Most boards require all volunteers and staff to read and sign an annual conflict of interest disclosure statement of all relevant personal, professional, and business affiliations that might affect their judgment. It is important to make this an annual event since personal and business relationships often change and it serves as a reminder to board members of their duties related to conflicts. Disclosure is the first step in preventing an actual conflict of interest that could pose serious legal and ethical problems for the association. Disclosure of these interests is required to the extent and in the manner as requested by the association.

Recusal. Board members who have a conflict of interest with an agenda item, discussion, or decision should recuse or remove themselves from the decision-making process regarding the issue. Some boards may allow the persons to engage in the discussion, but not deliberation. The minutes should reflect the recusal of the board members in the decision. It may be necessary for board members to resign if the conflict interferes with their abilities to participate in decision making in a non-biased, objective manner. While it can happen, these types of resignations are the exception rather than the rule.

It may be challenging to confront situations dealing with actual or potential conflicts of interests. Board members may deny or minimize the impact of their personal interests on their objectivity or decision-making abilities. A good rule of thumb is if there is even a hint or a question as to whether a situation is a conflict of interest, consider it as at least a potential conflict, act accordingly, and err on the side of caution. Boards must be astute and follow their guidelines regarding conflicts of interest to fulfill their fiduciary responsibilities in the nonprofit realm.

"A good rule of thumb is if there is even a hint or a question as to whether a situation is a conflict of interest, consider it as at least a potential conflict, act accordingly, and err on the side of caution."

Antitrust

Boards can legally jeopardize the association by engaging in activities that may be deemed antitrust. The purpose of Federal antitrust laws and fair trade regulations is to promote open and fair competition in all commercial endeavors. Any actions taken by associations that would attempt to regulate or fix prices and inhibit competition may raise antitrust issues. Examples of actions taken by associations that may raise antitrust issues include: agreements to fix prices or fees or set floors or ceilings on prices; agreements among competitors to divide or allocate markets; agreements to boycott others; and agreements coerced by a provider of a dominant market position tying the purchase of a product or service to the purchase of another product.

Sarbanes-Oxley Act

The Sarbanes-Oxley Act, referred to as SOX, was passed in 2002 after the scandals and collapse of such companies as Enron and Tyco. The act was intended to promote greater accountability, disclosure, and transparency for public trust in publicly traded companies. While the act is specific to for-profit businesses, it has many implications for nonprofits as well. It essentially tightens the reigns on the disclosure and oversight of accounting practices, financial statements, audits, and internal controls related to reporting of financial information. The act increases the responsibility of corporate governance boards in providing oversight of financial reporting.

While the SOX Act refers to financial oversight, there are overriding ethical and legal implications that boards need to consider including transparency, accountability, disclosure, and conflicts of interest. Astute board members pay attention to legislation affecting businesses and question the potential implications for their nonprofit associations.

“Board membership should not be considered simply as an honorary position. A board member must be prepared to devote the time and attention necessary to fulfill the fiduciary responsibilities involved.”

Minimizing Risk and Liability

In most instances, legal liability results from acting in bad faith or without adherence to the duties of care, loyalty, and obedience. Therefore, the best protection from liability is prevention. Given the various responsibilities of board leadership, one should not consider board membership simply as an honorary position. A board member must be prepared to devote the time and attention necessary to fulfill the fiduciary responsibilities involved. This does not mean that a board member should fear liability and be paralyzed from performing the expected responsibilities. Rather, board members should be aware of potential liabilities and act in ways that a prudent person would act in a similar situation.

Understanding the board's responsibilities and performing as a competent board member are the best strategies to prevent legal liability. Other ways to minimize risk include abiding by the Volunteer Protection Act of 1997, obtaining insurance, and choosing indemnification.

Volunteer Protection Act of 1997

The federal Volunteer Protection Act of 1997 grants immunity from personal liability to those who volunteer for nonprofit associations. The Act preempts state laws to provide that volunteers would not be held liable for harm if: (a) they were acting within the scope of the volunteer activity, (b) the harm was not caused by willful or criminal misconduct, gross negligence, reckless misconduct, or a conscious indifference to the safety or rights of the claimant, (c) the harm was not caused by a volunteer operating a vehicle, and (d) they were properly licensed, if applicable. The law applies to any claim filed on or after the effective date, but not for claims filed prior to the date of enactment (Jacobs, 2007).

Director's and Officer's Liability Insurance

Director's and Officer's (D&O) liability insurance is a type of policy that protects board members, other volunteers, staff, and the association against wrongdoing that may arise from their governance and management roles. This insurance does not cover criminal activities. Individuals are rarely subject to D&O lawsuits except in cases when personal misconduct is alleged.

D&O policies and premiums are based on the actual and perceived risks of the association. Therefore, they will differ from association to association. Most D&O policies cover defense expenses, and some may cover settlements and judgments.

While incorporation and the Volunteer Protection Act of 1997 provide volunteer protection against liability, boards may question the need for D&O insurance. Unfortunately, there are few criteria to help in making this decision. Associations need to assess their activities and the probabilities of liability, the magnitude of potential loss, and the available financial resources to determine whether D&O insurance is worth the investment. Policies must be read carefully to determine exactly what is covered and how much. Sometimes what is covered and at what price can make the policy worthless, given the cost. It is helpful also to consult with legal counsel to assist in making this decision.

Indemnification

An alternative to D&O insurance is indemnification in which the association chooses to indemnify its board members by using its own financial resources to cover the cost of a lawsuit. This type of self-insurance is possible predominately for associations that have enough fiscal resources. Many associations do not have this luxury. Therefore, insurance may be the best safety net.

Other Insurances

Board members may be protected under other insurance policies such as general liability and errors and omissions. Associations may purchase other insurances such as errors and omissions (E&O), business owner's policy (BOP), publication liability, and employment practices liability insurance (EPLI) if the association has employees. D&O insurance is the baseline protection for board members, and the need for other insurances should be discussed with the senior staff and insurance professionals.

Avoiding Personal Liability

Tips for avoiding personal liability are included in Table 2-3 (next page).

Table 2-3
Tips for Avoiding Personal Liability

- Comply with the association's mission.
- Know the association's bylaws and policies, and keep informed of the association's operations.
- Participate in strategic thinking and planning to ensure a viable future direction.
- Trust others and inspire trust of others through truthful interactions, honoring commitments, and modeling integrity.
- Convey a personal value system and embrace the values of the association.
- Maintain objectivity, fairness, and personal integrity.
- Place the association's interests first in all dealings on the association's behalf.
- Represent the interests of all members and do not favor special groups inside or external to the association.
- Know the types and terms of insurance carried by the association.
- Attend all the association's meetings, read the association's official publications, and keep informed of what is going on.
- Be prepared to make knowledge-based decisions by having the facts, asking pertinent questions, and being actively involved in deliberations.
- Disclose any conflicts of interest. Decline to vote on issues in which there is a potential conflict of interest or possibility of personal gain.
- Support board decisions, especially outside of the boardroom.
- Be prepared for and attend all board meetings. Insist on meaningful and productive meetings.
- Hold all members required to submit a board report accountable for doing so.
- Request that meeting minutes reflect votes in opposition to actions.
- Carefully review all financial statements and audits, and ensure adequate financial resources.
- Ensure that legal and other reports such as tax forms are filed in a timely manner.
- Comply with antitrust laws by avoiding actions that may restrict competition.
- Comply with civil rights laws and avoid discrimination.
- Perform a risk analysis, determine risk tolerance, and implement an emergency or disaster preparedness plan.
- Request outside counsel from attorneys, accountants, and other professionals as the needs arise.
- Respect and maintain the confidentiality of information acquired in the role of a board member.
- Select competent volunteer leaders and staff, and review their performance.
- Assess the performance of the board and association.

Source: Adapted from Nowicki, 1998.

What Can Go Wrong with Boards

Board Behavior Challenges

While boards are composed of successful individuals who have demonstrated the knowledge, skills, and talent to succeed, these directors are also people. People, no matter how intelligent or successful, act as people act. Some board members are stunning role models while others exhibit personalities and behaviors that can undermine effective board performance. Nadler, Behan, and Nadler (2006) describe six types of board members that can present challenges to board effectiveness.

The CEO Wannabe. This board member wants to be in charge of the association, rather than just being a board member. In some cases the CEO Wannabe may have been frustrated at previous attempts to become a CEO and chooses to use this opportunity to prove herself. In other cases, a retired CEO may be unhappy with her current situation and cannot let go of the CEO role. These individuals constantly second-guess the CEO/staff executive or waste the board's time with continuous attempts at micromanaging. In other cases, the CEO Wannabe has a personal agenda to get the CEO/staff executive fired or wants the position because she can do a better job.

The Pit Bull. This board member is overly aggressive and combative. His questions and comments usually sound accusatory. Sometimes he becomes verbally abusive in and outside of the boardroom. Pit Bulls generate unnecessary tension and put others on the defensive. Most people want to avoid the Pit Bull altogether.

There are times when board members don't get their way and they resort to Pit Bull behavior. They become verbally aggressive, throw tantrums, pound their fists on the table, curse, or storm out of a meeting. While their behavior in the boardroom is inappropriate, it often doesn't stop there. The board is always on guard because you never know when this behavior will occur again.

The Superdirector. On some boards, there is one board member whose experience and intelligence is far superior to anyone else on the board. This board member has a large influence on the other board members and they often look to her for answers. Board members are hesitant to challenge the Superdirector and it may seem like it is essentially a one-person board. Although the person's credentials are outstanding, the situation creates a dysfunctional board with minimal engagement and even less diversity of opinion. In some instances, the Superdirector will rally the board against the staff executive, creating even further dysfunction or a departure of one or both individuals.

The Management Lapdog. The Lapdog bows down to management and supports everything management says. This board member often lets management off the hook and downplays any issues or problems. Lapdogs do not have much credibility with the other board members. They become marginalized and their opinions are often dismissed. Often, these individuals are unable to think critically or act independently. A real problem arises when the Lapdog mentality permeates the board. Board members fail to address the behavior and actually deny any problems exist, and count on management to take care of everything. Associations such as this can easily go into a tailspin and end up disbanding.

The Checked-Out Director. Just about every board has or has had a Checked-Out Director. This person arrives late to meetings or doesn't show up at all, is late for conference calls, doesn't read the board materials or meeting minutes, and remains fairly silent except for rare occurrences when he makes an off-the-wall comment. The Checked-Out Director spends board time on extraneous activities (text messaging, answering e-mails, surfing the Internet, answering phone calls in the back of the room). The behavior is discourteous and the director has little positive impact on the board's effectiveness, apart from the fact that he is filling a seat that could be used by someone who could have a significant impact on the association.

The Overwhelmed Director. Some board members are in over their heads in terms of competent board service. During substantive discussions, they become paralyzed. They have the "deer in the headlights" look on their face. Often, Overwhelmed Directors know they do not "fit" on the board and realize they are not respected by others on the board. They often contribute little for fear that they may be off the mark. In other cases, they say too much when trying to make their point and demonstrate their value. The more they talk, the more the other board members' eyes roll in frustration.

Addressing Behavior Challenges

Often the above types of behaviors are ignored. No one wants to rock the boat or confront the issues and their impact on the board. However, some boards are skilled in addressing these issues. Some wait until the terms are over, others confront the behavior and ask for a change to occur. If a positive change does not occur, the board member may be asked to resign. In other scenarios, the board member is asked to leave. It is never a pleasant situation to "fire a volunteer."

"Problem behaviors with board members should be addressed by the board chairperson. Likewise, staff problems should be addressed by the staff executive."

New board members need to be aware that these types of behaviors do happen in boardrooms. Their occurrence and the manner in which they are addressed are dependent on the board's culture, and often the style of the board chairperson. Problem behaviors with board members should be addressed by the board chairperson. Likewise, staff problems should be addressed by the staff executive. New board members should assess their own behaviors and performance and take action not to become problem directors. Mentors may be effective in confronting and influencing positive behaviors, especially if their mentees are exhibiting behavior challenges.

Unsuccessful Boards

Sometimes boards fail. Hardy (1990) identifies five reasons why this occurs. First, boards fail because the selection of board members is based on inadequate or inappropriate criteria. Some associations have a difficult time recruiting candidates for the board and will accept just about anyone who will say yes. Some have said yes without having a clear sense of what they were signing up for. Other board members fail to grasp that they are "in charge."

Some board members are selected based on personal friendships. Others are told that all they have to do is attend a few meetings – it does not take much time! On the contrary, board members should be selected because they have the abilities, skills, and competencies that the association needs to move forward.

A second reason boards fail is because of the inability or reluctance of board members to use their expertise while serving on the board. Board members may not be given responsibility, or if it is given, responsibilities are ill-defined. Other boards may not provide an orientation for their new members or the orientation may be ineffective. Too often board members feel underutilized.

Another reason why boards fail is because of large omissions – they simply leave things undone that they were responsible for performing. Some boards spend too much time getting involved in day-to-day operations instead of focusing on their critical responsibility of leading the association.

A fourth reason is because a strong staff may dominate all actions of the board. Boards must maintain their leadership functions and hold staff accountable for the operational aspects.

Fifth, boards fail because of ineffective team relationships among board members or between the board and staff. Effective associations rely on strong partnership relationships among board members and between the board and staff.

While boards can fail and experience these problems, staying alert to signs that begin to indicate a problem is a responsibility of all board members. Asking questions and keeping on top of things that "just don't seem right" will help to avoid problems or at least address issues before they have the chance to become serious. The following information will help the board member focus on those activities that will build an effective board and decrease the potential of devastating problems.

"When one or more new members join the board, the entire board changes because the dynamics change. Therefore, board orientation is most effective when all board members participate and contribute their experiences and tips for leading effectively."

Building an Effective Board

An effective board utilizes the collective wisdom and expertise of its carefully selected members. It believes each member is an asset to the association and brings unique knowledge, skills, and insight. Working together interdependently, board members create synergy. They blend their qualities to build more than any of them could build independently. Boards that understand their role and fulfill their responsibilities can make a significant difference in the association. Volunteers who feel valued as board members will grow personally and continue to play vital roles in supporting the mission of the association even after their terms on the board expire.

The effectiveness of a board is contingent on many things. It depends just as much on its results as the process it uses to achieve those results. The process involves interpersonal dynamics and a commitment from all board members to work towards building a unified team that works interdependently to achieve synergy.

An effective board also engages in initial and ongoing board development activities. Successful boards provide an orientation for their new members. When one or more new members join the board, the entire board changes because the dynamics change.

Therefore, board orientation is most effective when all board members participate and contribute their experiences and tips for leading effectively. A mentoring program, such as *Mentoring the Stars*, can be effective in taking an orientation program to the next level and beyond by helping new board members apply and synthesize new learnings to real situations.

Structured learning activities for continuous board development are also essential. Board development is a joint responsibility among the board chairperson, all board members, and the executive staff. An excellent resource for board development is *The Volunteer Leadership Issue* of *Associations Now*, published each January by the American Society of Association Executives (ASAE) and the Center for Association Leadership.

An excellent resource for board development is *The Volunteer Leadership Issue* of *Associations Now*, published each January by the American Society of Association Executives (ASAE) and the Center for Association Leadership.

Characteristics of Effective Board Members

Effective boards recruit individuals who have the abilities, characteristics, and skills to be effective board members. Effective board members posses the following characteristics:

- Enthusiasm
- Willingness to take risks
- Trustworthiness
- Integrity
- Accountability
- Interest in people
- Interest in volunteer service
- Confidence
- Forward thinking
- Systems and critical thinking skills
- Selflessness
- Self-awareness
- Persistence
- Willingness to commit time, energy, and resources to the work of the association
- Willingness to state own views on important issues
- Willingness to accept and support board decisions
- Goal orientation
- Dedication
- Positive attitude
- Willingness to share expertise
- Team players
- Vision

You probably identify with these characteristics — that is why you have been selected to be a board member!

Guidelines for Becoming an Effective Board Member

Table 2-4 identifies specific actions that will assist you in becoming a competent, credible, and effective board member.

Table 2-4
Guidelines for Becoming an Effective Board Member

- At the beginning of each year of board service, become familiar with the association's goals for the year and establish your own goals in terms of your learning needs, your most valuable contributions, and your anticipated outcomes.
- Come to board meetings well-prepared and well-informed to discuss agenda items. Keep issues on the table, not under it.
- Attend and actively participate in all board meetings, appropriate committee meetings, activities, programs, and special events. Visibility to the membership is important.
- Be familiar with all of the association's programs and services.
- Keep informed and know what is going on in the association and take every opportunity to ask questions.
- Actively listen and speak with brevity.
- Be prepared to lead, and model good board behavior.
- Assume other leadership roles when asked, but balance new activities with your ability to also maintain your primary board responsibilities.
- Always be enthusiastic and positive when representing the board/association. Negative comments should be reserved to private times with a trusted colleague.
- Accept the responsibilities of a board member, commit the time necessary to fulfill them, and be accountable. If you are unable to fulfill your role, take responsibility for informing the right people and respectfully resign your position. It is better to confront this situation head on than to become unaccountable and unreliable, and lose the respect that you have worked hard to achieve. You will feel better that you are doing the right thing for yourself and the association. Leaving on a positive note paves the way for a possible return at some point in the future.
- Take responsibility for your own learning. Do not wait for someone to provide explanations for things you do not understand.
- Accept conflict as an opportunity to grow and build positive relationships.

Table 2-4 (continued)
Guidelines for Becoming an Effective Board Member

- Always arrive on time for activities. If you know you will be late or must cancel, inform the appropriate person and find a substitute if able and appropriate.
- Have a clear understanding of your role and responsibilities. Expect continued guidance and direction; however, if you do not get it, ask!
- Act in good faith and deal fairly with everyone in the association.
- Work in partnership with other volunteer leaders and the staff.
- Know what needs to be kept confidential and act accordingly.
- Put the interests of the association before any personal or professional interests. Declare any potential or actual conflicts of interest.
- Listen to the members.
- Read publications and keep in touch with trends and best practices in your profession or industry. Share and apply your knowledge and perspectives to the strategic direction of the association.
- Encourage others with special abilities to take on projects and become future leaders of the association.
- Keep a sense of humor.
- Celebrate and reward successes.
- When your board service is complete, say thank you and good-bye. If you have been a competent board member, created value for the association, and a good succession plan is in place, it is time to step aside and allow new leaders to stand guard.

Source: Nowicki, 1998.

Board Evaluation

One of the board's overall responsibilities is to evaluate performance and outcomes. A component of this is evaluating the workforce, both volunteers and staff. Tecker (2007) states that before evaluating the performance of the staff executive, the board should first evaluate itself in terms of how well it has met its share of responsibilities.

Boards that evaluate themselves demonstrate a high level of accountability and a commitment to continuous improvement. Board evaluations have the ability to:

- Refresh board members about their responsibilities
- Encourage board members to reflect upon their responsibilities and learn how they can perform better
- Assist individual members in learning how they are contributing and how they may be delaying/derailing progress
- Increase self-awareness of the board's partnership relationship with other volunteers and staff
- Enhance effective decision making
- Increase the board members' level of satisfaction with board service
- Ensure effective governance that leads to a more successful association

> ***"The remaining chapters of this book have been designed to assist the new board member in achieving these competencies and becoming productive and successful."***

Summary

Boards have a great responsibility in establishing the direction and leading the association. To be successful, boards must have board members who have been carefully selected because of their demonstrated abilities and skills to accomplish the association's mission and goals. This chapter provided an introduction to the various roles and responsibilities of boards and the responsibilities and competencies of board members.

The remaining chapters of this book have been designed to assist the new board member in achieving these competencies and becoming productive and successful. Successful board members will not stop at anything less than leading a successful association.

Serving on a volunteer board can be one of the most memorable and professionally enriching experiences of a lifetime. If you are willing to invest your time and energy, consider what the association needs and what knowledge and talent you have to offer, and thoughtfully plan your course, you will reap greater rewards than what you could ever contribute.

Learning Assessment

Chapter 2: Board Roles and Responsibilities

Reflect on the knowledge you gained from this chapter by answering the following questions. Some of the questions suggest that you discuss the topic with your mentor. You may have already determined additional questions that you will discuss with your mentor.

1. You meet a colleague on the elevator in your work setting. He states, "tell me about your association." Here is your chance to give your 20-second elevator speech. What will you say?

2. A member asks you, "What do you do as a member of the board?" Based on the board roles and responsibilities and board member competencies discussed in this chapter, how would you respond to this member?

3. Discuss the responsibilities of both the board and board members (competencies) with your mentor. Ask the questions you may have identified as you read the chapter. Briefly describe what you learned about your role as a board member.

4. Discuss the board's culture with your mentor, specifically how problem board members and behaviors are handled by the board.

5. Describe your ethical and legal responsibilities as a board member.

6. What characteristics do you possess that will make you an effective board member?

7. What do you plan to do to enhance your effectiveness as a board member?

Comments? Other thoughts?

Chapter 3

Governance and Leadership

Key Points

- Characteristics of Effective Governance
- Leadership and Management
- Leadership Process
- Creating Synergy
- Systems Thinking
- Elements of Empowerment and Levels of Authority
- Avoiding Micromanagement
- Inspiring and Motivating Volunteers
- Board Liaison Role
- Situational Leadership
- Use of Charters or Communication Briefs
- Governance Through Mission, Vision, Values, and Culture
- Governance Documents
  • Strategic Plan • Articles of Incorporation • Bylaws • Organizational Chart • Policies • Position Descriptions
- Roles of Officers, Committees, and Staff

Tables

- Table 3-1 Differences Between Management and Leadership
- Table 3-2 Characteristics of Effective Leaders
- Table 3-3 Levels of Authority
- Table 3-4 Board Liaison Guidelines
- Table 3-5 Situational Leadership Behaviors
- Table 3-6 Charter or Communication Brief
- Table 3-7 Sample Bylaws

Mentoring Opportunity

- Learning Assessment

Download the Chapter 3 Tables and Learning Assessment online at www.ajj.com/mentoring — Use password MTS2E989

Governance is a process within an association that determines how the association will conduct its business. It encompasses the structures, processes, systems, and culture that provide the foundation for the association's work and outcomes. Governance provides decision-making mechanisms that focus and direct the association's effort. It is a process in which policy is determined, oversight is provided, and accountability to the mission and members is assured.

Characteristics of Effective Governance

The board of directors is responsible for governing the association. A governance model provides the framework to organize thoughts, activities, programs, structures, and relationships. In a volunteer association, governance involves leadership that relies on influence rather than power. An effective governance model is characterized by the following components (Carver, 2006; Tecker, Frankel, & Meyer, 2002):

- Is driven by a compelling mission
- Focuses on vision and values
- Builds a nimble infrastructure
- Develops an enjoyable organizational culture based on trust
- Creates value for members and stakeholders

- Maintains a balance between internal and external focuses
- Looks at the big picture and concentrates on the larger and important issues
- Strategically thinks into the future, not the past or present
- Facilitates both diversity and unity
- Embraces responsibility and accountability

- Values its relationship with constituents
- Solicits and uses stakeholder input
- Determines what information is needed and important
- Makes decisions based on knowledge and insight
- Maximizes the use of resources
- Uses board and volunteer time efficiently and effectively
- Fosters an effective board-staff partnership
- Builds a knowledge community and a learning organization

Associations need to determine which governance models and structures work best for them. It is important that they do not create so much infrastructure that the associations cannot turn on a dime when new opportunities or challenges arise. Today's competition is fierce, there are multiple competing priorities and demands on time, and constituents expect more. The successful associations of today and tomorrow will increasingly be driven by what will constitute value for their members. Boards must have a governance structure that facilitates innovation so that new value can be created for constituents without layers of bureaucracy that may slow down the process (De Cagna, 2007).

A board that can effectively govern an association according to the above components is one that demonstrates exemplary performance and one that is composed of individuals whose focus is to lead, not manage. Since leadership is the key element in effective governance, a large section of this chapter discusses leadership and the differences between leadership and management.

"A board that can effectively govern an association according to the characteristics of effective governance is one that demonstrates exemplary performance and is composed of individuals whose focus is to lead, not manage."

Leadership and Management

Board members are charged with using the above governance elements to lead the association into the future. Most individuals who assume board positions have had little experience in leading an association at the executive level. However, they have often had many experiences as managers. They may have had a management or supervisory position in their work setting. Often, they worked their way up through the ranks of the association through such positions as committee or task force chairs, project leaders, local chapter presidents, or similar opportunities.

A majority of the above positions call for good organizational and management skills. While it is important to have these skills, leadership at the executive level involves more than management skills. The primary role of the board is to lead, and many board members have not had the life experiences to prepare them for this executive role. Some board members do not know the differences between leadership and management. The following sections provide a brief summary of how leadership differs from management and how new board members can enhance their leadership skills.

Bennis and Nanus (2003) state that managers are people who do things right and leaders are those who do the right thing. The words 'leader' and 'manager' have two separate meanings. A manager is described as analytical, controlled, orderly, structured, and deliberate. A leader, on the other hand, is described as visionary, flexible, uncontrolled, and creative. Leaders are proactive – they don't wait for things to happen, they make things happen. Leaders are self-empowered and assist in the empowerment of others.

"Boards should spend 80% of their time on external issues important to the membership instead of internal issues that can be managed by others."

In his classic book on how leadership differs from management, Kotter (1990) describes the differences between these concepts. Management gets things done through specific policies and procedures, planning, budgeting, organizing, staffing, controlling, and problem solving. Leadership gets things done through establishing direction, aligning people, and motivating and inspiring others. Management focuses on today and maintaining the status quo in an efficient manner. Leadership thinks into the future and sets direction for how to get there. Differences between leadership and management are found in Table 3-1.

Table 3-1
Differences Between Management and Leadership

Management	Leadership
Thinks methodically	Thinks and plans strategically
Engages in routine decision making	Engages in critical decision making
Reduces uncertainties	Widens options/alternatives
Searches for problems	Scans for opportunities
Achieves goals	Sets and changes goals
Administers	Innovates
Focuses on systems and structure	Focuses on people
Relies on control	Inspires trust
Asks how and when	Asks what and why
Accepts and works within the status quo	Challenges the status quo
Is reactive	Is proactive
Works within the association's culture	Shapes the association's culture
Does things right	Does the right things

Source: Adapted from Nowicki, 1998.

Successful board members must be able to do both – manage and lead. Governing an association involves planning, budgeting, organizing, and problem solving (i.e. managing). In addition, and with a greater emphasis of importance, governance must meet the association's future commitments by establishing a vision, setting direction, and aligning followers to move in the right direction (i.e. leading). Remember, successful leaders must be able to do both. This is not the case with managers. Managers do not have to be skilled leaders to be successful managers. There is nothing wrong with being an excellent manager because we need excellent managers in our society. However, we need more than management at the executive board level.

Boards should spend 80% of their time on external issues important to the membership instead of internal issues that can be managed by others. While many boards do not yet allocate their time in this manner, they may increase their effectiveness and value by moving board agendas in this direction. Focusing on external issues, strategic direction, and outcomes rather than implementation issues will progressively bring boards closer to a leadership approach to governance (Tecker et al, 2002).

"Today's leaders push people into a new reality. They are concerned with the people, the process, and the outcome. They are equally concerned with keeping their eye on the vision, and living with the ambiguity that occurs on the journey toward reaching that vision."

Leadership Process

Over the past few decades there have been numerous books and articles written about leadership. From this literature we can learn to be a servant, limitless, transactional, transformational, situational, or a variety of other types of leaders. Each person will develop their own leadership style according to their beliefs, experiences, and comfort.

Today's leaders push people into a new reality. They are concerned with the people, the process, and the outcome. They are equally concerned with keeping their eye on the vision, and living with the ambiguity that occurs on the journey toward reaching that vision. Leadership has to do with tomorrow, with creating and managing change, and with doing the right thing. Kotter (1990) describes the three components of the leadership process as:

- Establishing direction
- Aligning people
- Motivating and inspiring

Establishing direction involves gathering information from a wide range of people, especially constituents. By analyzing this information, alternative directions are determined and tested. A vision for the future is created along with strategies for achieving it.

Aligning people involves communicating the direction to everyone who is affected, as often as possible and in as many ways as possible. Training is provided for those people who do not have the necessary knowledge and skills, or need enhancement of their skills. Leaders must be clear about the direction and those involved must understand, believe, and trust in that direction and be willing to work toward making it a reality. Leaders must communicate the vision and direction repeatedly and continuously reinforce its importance. The words and actions of the leaders must be consistent. In other words, they must walk the talk.

> ***"Leaders must be clear about the association's direction and those involved must understand, believe, and trust in that direction and be willing to work toward making it a reality."***

The third component involves *motivating and inspiring* people so they will have the energy to move in the right direction and overcome obstacles along the way. Motivation is not a control mechanism to get people to do what we want them to do, but rather a method of satisfying their most basic human needs for achievement, recognition, belonging, self-esteem, a sense of control over one's life, and living up to one's potential.

Motivating and inspiring includes articulating the vision in a manner that stresses the values that are important to the people. Individuals are involved in decision making and they are supported and coached in their efforts to achieve. They are publicly rewarded for their successes and they feel a sense of belonging to an association that cares about them. In a sense, the work itself becomes a strong motivating factor and an important learning opportunity.

Board members who practice these three components of leadership will be successful and lead successful associations. But, leadership involves a lot of time and energy. Leaders must be willing to commit to this. Leadership involves critical and visionary thinking, asking pertinent and numerous questions, and communicating lavishly with everyone involved in the association. Leadership also involves a commitment to lifelong learning. The characteristics of an effective leader are described in Table 3-2 (next page).

Table 3-2
Characteristics of Effective Leaders

- Have guiding vision
- Love their work
- Believe in other people
- Have trust and integrity
- Are service oriented
- Are curious and daring
- Are continuously learning
- Are candid and mature
- Focus on possibilities, don't dwell on limitations
- Make the abstract understandable
- Are synergistic
- Have high energy levels and radiate positive energy
- Lead balanced lives
- Are innovative and willing to challenge the status quo
- Pleased to have the opportunity to lead
- View luck as the combination of preparation and opportunity

Source: Bennis & Nanus, 2003; Covey, 1990.

Leaders are optimistic and focus on solutions rather than problems. They do not have all of the answers, but they do two important things – they ask critical questions and they listen to the responses. They search for win-win outcomes and are not interested in adversarial relationships.

Creating Synergy

Synergy is an important leadership characteristic. It occurs when the leader and follower partner and help each other rise to higher levels of achievement than either one of them could achieve alone. Leaders engage with others in such a way that together, leaders and followers raise one another to higher levels of motivation and functioning. They are partners and help one another. These leaders have the vision and they develop clear plans or strategies that followers can implement. They are there to support and coach their followers, and provide the resources that will assist their followers in being successful.

"Synergy occurs when the leader and follower partner and help each other rise to higher levels of achievement than either one of them could achieve alone."

In his book, *Leadership Jazz,* DePree (1992) compares leadership to orchestrating a jazz band. A jazz band leader sets the stage for the concert. This involves choosing the music, finding the right musicians, practicing, and performing in public. The effect of the performance is contingent upon several things – the environment, the musicians, and the need for everyone to perform as individuals and as a group.

The jazz band leader brings together a group of musicians and draws out their best. Like the leader of an association, the jazz band leader combines the unpredictability of the future with the gifts of individuals. The leader defines the style, picks the tune, sets the tempo, and starts the music. It is up to the band members to take it from there and give it their best. The members are expected to play solo and also play together. The leader tries to integrate the various sounds without diminishing the uniqueness of each individual. Together, they create synergy and play music, a beautiful sound that none of them could produce individually.

"Like the leader of an association, the jazz band leader combines the unpredictability of the future with the gifts of individuals. The leader defines the style, picks the tune, sets the tempo, and starts the music. It is up to the band members to take it from there and give it their best."

Sometimes we think of leadership as a high-level activity that involves only complex processes. We forget about some of the simple, common sense things that make us human. In one of my doctoral courses, a professor shared some thoughts about transformational leadership that he learned from a colleague. To become a leader, one must:

- Say please and thank you.
- Learn people's names and use them.
- Put honoring diversity and what it means on every agenda.
- Help people become even better than they thought they could be.
- Check out your assumptions.
- Focus on people, not structures.
- Build trust by trusting and build support by supporting.
- Forget control. Think of shaping.
- Live your values.
- Model the way.

(Bef Forbes, Seattle University, personal communication, 1992)

Systems Thinking

Senge (1990), in his book *The Fifth Discipline,* describes the fifth discipline as systems thinking. Systems thinking or looking at the big picture is critical to successful leadership. Board members must be able to look at the whole picture and realize that a change in a piece of the puzzle will affect the total picture. With systems thinking we learn to see wholes. It is a framework for seeing interrelationships rather than things, for seeing patterns of change rather than static snapshots.

Systems thinking is important today because our world is full of so much complexity. We often feel overwhelmed with the complexity and feel helpless. Senge (1990) states that systems thinking is the antidote for this sense of helplessness. It helps us to see the structures and patterns that underlie complex situations. It helps us to put things into perspective and determine relevance and importance.

"Systems thinking or looking at the big picture is critical to successful leadership. Board members must be able to look at the whole picture and realize that a change in a piece of the puzzle will affect the total picture."

Boards are faced with both complex and minute situations. Systems thinking helps to sort out what is important and what is not. Boards can easily be swayed to focus on the minutia because sometimes the minutia is presented by others as being critically important. The board needs to sort through all of the issues and ideas brought forth and, through a systems thinking approach, determine those that are truly important and truly board work. Boards should take time to ask the questions: "How does this fit into the whole picture?" "How does this fit with the mission and strategic plan?" "Is this important and is it the right thing to do?" "What would our members say or want?" Boards must always keep focused on the bigger picture.

Elements of Empowerment and Levels of Authority

Effective associations that focus on leading into the future call for empowerment and collaboration of individuals and associations. Board members are faced not only with leading the association as a whole, but also leading a group of volunteers who will help the board do its work. Effective boards create environments in which the volunteers feel empowered to take on responsibilities. Empowered volunteers are committed to their positions, feel responsible for working together with other volunteers, and help the board do its work and lead the association.

Empowerment is a concept that is central to working together effectively with others and delegating tasks. Empowerment involves four key elements:

Ability + Responsibility + Authority + Accountability

> ***"The four elements of empowerment are ability, responsibility, authority, and accountability. All four elements must be present for true empowerment to occur."***

All four elements must be present for true empowerment to occur.

The first element is *ability*. People cannot be empowered to do something they do not know how to do. They first need to have the ability – knowledge and/or skills. The second element is *responsibility*. This means individuals are given an assignment and they accept it. It is clear to everyone involved what the job is, who will do what, when it should be completed, and the intended outcome with a description of what success will look like.

Once an assignment is given and accepted, the individuals responsible for carrying it out must have the *authority* to do so. It is important to be clear about the extent of their authority and to clearly define the boundaries or parameters. Giving authority is not as simple as "Here is the assignment, do it." There are levels of authority that will help boards in further clarifying the direction given for assignments or projects (see Table 3-3).

Table 3-3
Levels of Authority

Level One:	Collect Information
Level Two:	Collect Information + Recommend
Level Three:	Collect Information + Recommend with Feedback + Act
Level Four:	Collect Information + Plan What Needs to be Done + Do It

Source: Nowicki, 1998.

Level One Authority means we can collect information only and report it. Level Two means we can collect information and make a recommendation about what should be done with that information. With Level Three Authority, we can collect information, make a recommendation, get feedback on the recommendation and clarify what should be done, then act on the recommendation. Level Four means we have the authority to just do the task.

The persons who give us Level Four Authority know we are able to do the task and they trust us. We don't need approval to do the work within our scope of the task. There are few times in which we will be given Level Four Authority.

The fourth element of empowerment is *accountability.* This means the individuals who have accepted the assignment do what they say they will do and are responsible for the results, reporting, and follow-up.

> ***"Effective boards give roots to their followers by providing direction, specific information, and the boundaries within which to work. After providing the right information and assessing their abilities, boards give their followers the freedom to get the job done."***

Too often this is the scenario – The board gives an assignment to a committee without much direction or any boundaries. The committee accepts the assignment, but does not ask for clarification. The committee works on the assignment and reports its recommendations to the board. The board rejects the committee's recommendations or makes major changes to them; essentially redoing the work. The board feels the committee did not understand the assignment, and therefore did not produce the desired outcome. The committee feels it wasted its time and the board should have just done the work itself.

What is wrong with this scenario? Plenty! The board did not do its job in giving clear direction or assessing whether the committee understood its assignment, AND, the committee accepted the responsibility for the assignment without clearly understanding it.

The board created an environment of disempowerment. First of all, it did not give clear direction to the committee. Yet, when the committee completed its assignment, the board essentially stated the committee's work did not meet its expectations. Secondly, to make matters worse, the board took the assignment away and did it themselves, totally taking the power away from the committee. Do you think the committee felt good about its work? What did this situation do for the relationship between the committee and the board? Will the committee want to take on any future assignments?

Unfortunately, situations such as this one happen more often than we would like to admit. Board members do not have malicious intentions when they "disempower." Often they do not realize the power they hold and how their behaviors and actions impact others.

Effective boards delegate tasks effectively by creating environments of empowerment. They use the four elements of empowerment consistently and give specific direction about the level of authority they are granting. Effective boards give roots to their followers by providing direction, specific information, and the boundaries within which to work. They also give their followers wings. After providing the right information and assessing their abilities, boards give their followers the freedom to get the job done. They coach and inspire them through the process, make sure they have the needed resources, and reward them in the end.

"Board members are responsible for overseeing and evaluating the volunteers and staff, but not repeating their work and micromanaging the association. The board needs to be free from the operational matters because it is usually a part-time body and barely has enough time to do its own strategic work."

Avoiding Micromanagement

While a component of the board's role is management, some board members become too involved in the day-to-day operations of the association. The work, or management, of most associations is predominately done by a workforce (i.e., volunteers, other than the board, and paid staff). Board members are responsible for overseeing and evaluating the volunteers and staff, but not repeating their work and micromanaging the association. The board needs to be free from the operational matters because it is usually a part-time body and barely has enough time to do its own strategic work.

Boards that make decisions that are within the workforce's domain trivialize their own jobs and disempower and interfere with the function of those who were assigned the work. Some boards try to do the work of committees or, worse yet, re-do the work of their volunteers. Other boards try to make staff decisions through various means such as making a motion to hire someone or awarding a contract to a certain vendor. Some require staff to change the budget and accounting reporting so it is similar to the type of reporting found at the board members' places of employment, only to change it again when new members join the board. Other boards allow staff to manage their half-million dollar budgets, but don't allow staff to make a decision about whether to order 1,000 or 2,000 brochures because the larger quantity is $300 more than the other.

Boards that interfere with the workforce's functions may mean well, but their intentions are often perceived by the workforce as a lack of trust. Micromanagement hampers the vital relationship that must occur between the board and its workforce. Effective boards concentrate on strategic leadership and allow everyone to do the jobs they were hired or appointed to do. They create trusting and synergistic relationships – the types of relationships needed to move the association into the future.

Inspiring and Motivating Volunteers

Leading through vision and empowerment requires the ability of board members to recruit and coach volunteers who are willing to help the board accomplish the work of the association. Sometimes this is easier said than done. Often board members will have a difficult time "motivating" others to become involved. They will state, "How can we motivate them?" or "How can we keep them motivated?" Some will say you cannot motivate others, only yourself. In reality, leaders can inspire motivation, but they cannot impose it.

"Effective boards concentrate on strategic leadership and allow everyone to do the jobs they were hired or appointed to do. They create trusting and synergistic relationships – the types of relationships needed to move the association into the future."

Board members are faced with recruiting volunteers to become and continue to be involved in select projects, committees, or chapter work. Sometimes it seems there just are not enough people to do the work that needs to be done. Board members will send out a call for volunteers and only a few people respond or no one responds. They think no one is willing. However, this is often not the case. Over 50% of the association's members will volunteer for activities if they are asked. These potential volunteers constitute an untapped resource that few realize exists.

The reasons why some members do not volunteer to become actively involved are, perhaps, because no one has personally asked them, they may not think they have much to contribute, or they may think they are not part of the in-crowd of people who seem to have their names linked with every association activity. Boards must reach out and engage these members. It is called the "power of the ask."

Boards that decide there is no one in the association who is interested in volunteering for a project will often find that is true. Boards that believe there is a lot of untapped potential in their membership, on the other hand, will find more than enough volunteers to accomplish the work. Boards do not create motivation; they discover it by talking and listening to their members. They look for a diversity of qualities in their members, and they try to match projects with those individuals who demonstrate the qualities and abilities to accomplish those tasks.

Effective boards actively seek out and recruit individuals to fill needed positions. They are proactive and do not just wait for someone to turn up on the doorstep. Potential volunteers are often honored when approached to work on an important project for the association. A win-win situation materializes.

"Recruitment and retention of volunteers is vitally important. The key in today's world is to offer opportunities with short-term tasks rather than those that require a longer time commitment."

Finding the right person for a project/job is half the battle in "motivating" others. Volunteers are motivated most by the work itself. The work needs to be something they are interested in doing, it needs to be meaningful and challenging, they must feel they have the skills to do the job, and today's volunteers prefer work that is short in duration. In working with volunteers, board members will be most successful when they realize that volunteers want to:

- Be involved in the decision-making process that affects their work
- Understand the expectations for the job
- Feel capable of handling the tasks offered
- Have ownership of their volunteer job
- Control their project from beginning to end
- Feel a sense of community and teamwork among other volunteers
- Have an opportunity for growth and advancement
- See that their presence and their work are making a difference
- Feel a sense of accomplishment
- Have fun
- Enjoy their work
- Receive private and public recognition
- Know that they and their work are valued
- Have their personal needs met

In today's fast-paced world, there are multiple demands competing for our time. This applies to volunteers also, as volunteer time seems to be decreasing by the day. This is alarming for associations that are primarily volunteer driven. Therefore, recruitment and retention of volunteers is vitally important. The key in today's world is to offer opportunities with short-term tasks rather than those that require a longer time commitment. Many boards are abandoning most standing committees and creating shorter term task forces that are relevant to current issues and needs.

When working with volunteers, it is important to coach them throughout their work, ask how they are doing, encourage them to accomplish their work, make sure they have the resources needed to do the job, and praise them lavishly for their accomplishments. Make it a practice to recognize achievement, especially in front of others. Certificates and plaques of appreciation presented to volunteers in front of their peers can be an effective way of recognizing achievement and creating a motivating environment.

The board is responsible for setting direction and inspiring others to become involved. Keeping these thoughts on motivation in mind will help the board in recruiting interested and qualified volunteers to help in accomplishing the association's mission and goals. Satisfied volunteers will remain committed and encourage others to become involved.

Board Liaison Role

Board members will be provided many opportunities to inspire and motivate other volunteer leaders. Most board members will serve as liaisons or line officers from the board to committees, task forces, or other individuals or groups within the association. While this role is very important to the successful implementation of the association's work, it often goes unrecognized and undervalued.

"The board liaison's role is communicator, advisor, coach, and cheerleader. They ensure that the group is clear about its purpose and expected outcomes, and they connect the group with resources needed to do the job."

The primary function of a board liaison is to be a two-way communication vehicle to and from the board. Board liaisons must be in touch with their group leaders periodically to communicate what is going on in the association, how it affects the committee/group, and to give direction, guidance, and support to the group. Listening to the concerns and issues posed by these groups can provide valuable information and insight back to the board. The liaisons must also understand the group and the group's work well enough to communicate the work to the board.

Board liaisons conduct progress checks with their groups and offer any assistance to accomplish their work. In most associations, they do not get involved in the group's work because they are not a member of the group. Rather, their role is communicator, advisor, coach, and cheerleader. They ensure that the group is clear about its purpose and expected outcomes, and they connect the group with resources needed to do the job.

Board liaisons must take the initiative in communicating with their group(s). Too often board members will state, "I haven't heard a word from the group." Board liaisons serve as coaches who inspire and motivate their groups. It is difficult to do this if the liaison is not communicating with them. Prior to board meetings, the liaison should communicate with the group leader to elicit a progress check and to determine if there is anything that should be discussed at the board meeting related to the group. If the group submitted an agenda item, the board liaison should know the agenda item/topic in sufficient detail to be able to address questions or concerns at the board meeting. After board meetings, the liaison should contact the group leader to discuss issues or topics of concern to the group. This is especially important if the group submitted an agenda item or proposal that required board input or approval. A sample of board liaison guidelines is included in Table 3-4 (next page).

Table 3-4
Academy of Medical-Surgical Nurses (AMSN)
Board Liaison Guidelines

Purpose of the Board Liaison - Provides a channel for volunteer unit communication with the Board of Directors

Timeline/Activities	Responsibilities
Initial Contact Usually after appointment of chair or assumption of board of director role)	**Communication** • Communicate with the volunteer unit chair to discuss the board liaison role • Join the volunteer unit's listserv [the liaison only fulfills a communications role]. **Action Planning** • Obtain the current action plan and discuss the chairperson's ideas for implementing the plan over the next year.
Monthly • Communication • Action Planning	• Maintain at least monthly communication (e.g., e-mail, listserv, phone call, etc.) to assure that there is volunteer unit work occurring. • Monitor the volunteer unit's adherence to its action plan and provide guidance as needed. • Work with the volunteer unit to recommend changes to the volunteer unit's action plan to insure that it remains up to date and of value.
Volunteer Unit Meeting/Conference Call	• Participate in volunteer unit activities in an advisory capacity. • The board liaison works with the chairperson to help her/him be successful in the role. This may include discussing the agenda and process prior to a volunteer unit meeting/call or suggesting how best to conduct the meeting/call.
Board Meetings • Prior to Board Meetings	Agenda Items • Advise volunteer units about when it is appropriate to present an agenda item, usually interim and final reports or specific recommendations, for Board consideration. • Review all proposed agenda items for the Board and obtain appropriate background information from volunteer units prior to the Board meeting. Volunteer unit chairs should send all agenda items to the liaison at least six weeks before the scheduled Board meeting to allow ample time for review by the president, board liaison and executive director before the meeting.

Table 3-4 (continued)
Academy of Medical-Surgical Nurses (AMSN)
Board Liaison Guidelines

Timeline/Activities	Responsibilities
Board Meetings continued	Board Reports • Prior to submission of the volunteer unit's board report, the volunteer unit chair will forward the board report to the board liaison. The liaison will review the report and offer any suggestions or comments.
• During Board Meetings	• Present volunteer unit agenda items at Board meetings and lead the discussion.
• After Board Meetings	• Report back to the volunteer unit promptly, generally within one week, via telephone or e-mail regarding the discussion and any action taken by the Board related to volunteer unit agenda items. The board liaison also sends a follow-up letter/e-mail to the volunteer unit chair. • Communicates with the chair about any pertinent information that was discussed at the meeting.
Convention/Annual Meeting	• Attend volunteer unit meetings, if possible, during the annual convention. Ask to be on the agenda of the incoming volunteer unit's first meeting to introduce yourself and explain your function. • Current and new board liaisons should communicate with each other about who is attending what volunteer unit meetings at the annual meeting. Although the current board liaison is responsible, sometimes it makes sense for the new board liaison to attend that meeting also in order to be aware of issues that will be addressed by the volunteer unit in the future. • Remember to pass along any files or information that the new board liaison needs.
Ongoing	• Advise and assist volunteer units that need to communicate with the Board. • The board liaison should actively reach out to help the volunteer unit to be productive, keeping in mind that the liaison serves as an advisor and coach, and is not intended to be a part of the volunteer unit or to participate in the volunteer unit's work. • Ask the volunteer unit chair to send you copies of important correspondence, budget proposals, and reports. • Encourage the volunteer unit chair to keep proper records and to forward appropriate documents to the succeeding chair. • Be alert to potential problems, e.g., volunteer unit inactivity in execution of its goals or specific assignments from the Board, expenditures, etc. Notify the president as needed. • Be sensitive to potential duplication of effort between volunteer units and attempt to eliminate or minimize duplication by suggesting communication and/or coordination among relevant groups within the Association. If such communication occurs, the board liaison(s) to the other groups should be notified.

Source: Used with permission from the Academy of Medical-Surgical Nurses, 2009.

Situational Leadership

As board members and liaisons, many opportunities will arise to work with other volunteers to accomplish the work of the association. Often, the board member will work directly with chairpersons to coach them in leading their own groups. Since volunteers make significant contributions to an association, boards need to ensure that the work is important and meaningful, provides enjoyment, and enhances the volunteer's growth and professional development. As leaders set direction, they must assure that those who are carrying out the direction understand the charge, have the knowledge and ability to carry it out, and perform effectively. This can be one of the most challenging roles for a board member.

The Situational Leadership model by Hersey, Blanchard, and Johnson (2001) is a very effective process for board members to use when delegating tasks and projects to others such as committee and task force chairpersons. Situational Leadership is an interaction between the leader and the follower. It is based on the amount of guidance, direction, and support given by the leader in response to the competence and commitment followers exhibit when faced with performing a task. The model has two sections, the leader's behavior and the follower's development level.

> ***"Situational leadership is based on the amount of guidance, direction, and support given by the leader in response to the competence and commitment followers exhibit when faced with performing a task."***

A simplified way of using the model is described in Table 3-5. Let us assume that the follower is a committee chairperson and you are the leader as the board liaison. Using the Follower Behavior column on the left, determine your chairperson's level of development to perform the task (D1-D4). Based on your assessment of the chairperson, look at the corresponding column on the right (S1-S4) to determine how you should support the chairperson in accomplishing the task. If the chairperson's behavior is D2, your leader behavior would be S2.

Table 3-5
Situational Leadership Behaviors

The leader's behavior is determined by assessing the follower's competence and commitment. For example, if the follower's competence and commitment are determined to be D2, the corresponding leader behavior would be S2.

Follower Behavior	Leader Behavior
D1: Lacks skills, but is committed to doing the task.	**S1: Directing**
The follower lacks the specific skills required for the job, but is enthusiastic and committed to do it. The follower might say: I am willing to give it a chance, but I really do not know what I am doing. I am scared I will mess it up. I am not even sure what questions to ask. I have never done it before. Tell me what to do and I will give it my best. Can we go back to the basics?	The leader gives clear, specific directions, provides structure on what, when, how, and where to do the task, shows pictures, and suggests actions to be taken to accomplish the task. The leader focuses on the task with less emphasis on the relationship.
D1: Low Competence and High Commitment	**S1: High Directive and Low Supportive**

Follower Behavior	Leader Behavior
D2: Has some skills, but is hesitant about doing the task.	**S2: Coaching**
The follower may have some relevant skills but isn't willing to commit to the task without guidance. The follower might say: It is a good idea. I am not sure how I can do it. Can you help? Where can I get more information? Do you have the time to show me? Where are the policies and procedures for this task? I would be more convinced about doing this task if you could explain why it is important.	The leader defines the roles and tasks, but seeks ideas and suggestions from the follower. Direction is still needed because of the follower's inexperience. The leader provides support and praise to build the follower's self-esteem and encourages involvement in decision making to enhance the follower's commitment.
D2: Low to Some Competence and Low Commitment	**S2: High Directive and High Supportive**

Table 3-5 (continued)
Situational Leadership Behaviors

Follower Behavior	Leader Behavior
D3: Has the skills, but is not sure about getting involved.	**S3: Supporting**
The follower is experienced and capable, but may lack the desire or confidence to go it alone. The follower might say: I have done it so many times, do I have to do it again? I do not think it will work, so what is the use of trying? What is in it for me? I will do it if I can work with my colleagues on this project. I am not going to make a suggestion, because they will ask me to do the work.	The leader passes day to day decisions to the follower such as how tasks are allocated and the processes for doing the task. The leader facilitates and takes part in decisions, but the control is with the follower. The follower doesn't need much direction, but needs support to bolster their confidence and motivation.
D3: Moderate to High Competence and Variable Commitment	**S3: Low Directive and High Supportive**
Follower Behavior	**Leader Behavior**
D4: Has the skills and is interested in doing the task.	**S4: Delegating**
The follower is experienced with the task and comfortable with their ability to do it well. The follower might say: I will be glad to assume this responsibility. I have had success doing it before. I have identified a problem and I have a few ideas on how to solve it. I will see to it that the project meets the deadline. I would like to train the rest of my team on.... Just tell me what you want done and leave me alone to do it.	The leader is involved with decisions and problem solving, but the follower takes the lead and is accountable for getting the work done. The leader obtains progress reports, but leaves the follower alone to get the job done. The follower decides how and when to involve the leader, and requires little support from the leader.
D4: High Competence and High Commitment	**S4: Low Directive and Low Supportive**

Source: Adapted from Hersey, Blanchard, & Johnson, 2001; Nowicki, 1998.

Development Level of the Follower

In Situational Leadership, leaders assess the development level of followers to perform a task. The development level depends on the follower's previous experience with the task, their competence to perform it, and their desire or commitment. The statements below are three important considerations of the follower's development level.

- The development level should be considered only in relation to the specific task to be performed. Development levels may vary depending on the task. A person may be a mature and competent professional, but not have the skills to perform the specific task at hand.
- The development level involves job maturity and psychological maturity. These refer to the follower's technical knowledge and skill to do the task along with feelings of self-confidence and desire or willingness.
- The follower's development level may change as the task is being performed, indicating movement to the next quadrant of the model. As the follower progresses in the task, the leader's behavior may move progressively toward the S4 quadrant of the curve. If the follower regresses in performing the task, the leader's behavior may move back to a prior quadrant of the model.

For example, a board member may be assigned to work with a new task force chairperson to develop a comprehensive plan to assess the learning needs of members. The board member would need to assess the chairperson's development level by asking questions such as the following:

- Has the chairperson led a task force before?
- What are the chairperson's knowledge and skills related to the task?
- Is the chairperson experienced in developing action plans with timelines?
- To what degree is the chairperson interested in and willing to lead the task force?

Once the leader determines the chairperson's development level, the appropriate leader behavior is determined to support the chairperson in leading the task force.

Leader Behaviors

Leadership is composed of directive and supportive behaviors. Instead of acting the same way in every situation, leaders assess the development level of the follower and adapt their behavior to suit the follower's ability and willingness. Directive behavior refers to the extent to which the leader provides direction by telling followers what to do, how to do it, when to do it, and where to do it. It sets goals for them and defines their roles.

Supportive behavior refers to the extent to which the leader enters into two-way communication with the follower. The leader may provide support, encouragement, and positive strokes. Leadership behavior varies according to the task that must be accomplished and the follower's development level.

The following scenarios describe how to use Situational Leadership in accomplishing tasks.

> ***"Leadership is composed of directive and supportive behaviors. Instead of acting the same way in every situation, leaders assess the development level of the follower and adapt their behavior to suit the follower's ability and willingness."***

Scenario 1
D1 Follower Behavior – Low Competence & High Commitment
S1 Leader Behavior – High Directive & Low Supportive

A former board member (volunteer) is approached to chair a task force to begin a Foundation that would provide research grants and scholarships. This volunteer has made significant contributions to the scholarship fund in the past, is passionate about professional development, and has effective leadership skills. The volunteer states, "I would be happy to do anything for the association, but I do not know much about fundraising." This volunteer is at the D1 development level in terms of facilitating fundraising (low on fundraising skills, but willing to do the job) and needs the S1 leadership behavior of directing (high directive, low supportive).

The leader needs to provide specific direction on what needs to be done, suggest possible ways to do the work, provide resources including fundraising training, and provide supervision as the work gets started. Once the volunteer obtains more knowledge of fundraising, has the resources to do the job, and determines how to structure the task force, the leader needs to provide less motivation or support.

Scenario 2
D2 Follower Behavior – Low to Some Competence & Low Commitment
S2 Leader Behavior – High Directive & High Supportive

The board sends out a call for members interested in working on a member retention task force. Several members indicate their interest in volunteering for this task force, but no one is willing to chair it. One member (volunteer) has some previous experience in working on member retention initiatives from her work with another association. The board liaison approaches the volunteer to chair the task force. The volunteer states "I've never chaired a task force before and I'm not sure I could be successful doing it...Maybe I could give it a try if someone could help me." This volunteer is at the D2 development level (some competence, low commitment).

The volunteer agrees to chair the task force and is paired up with a staff member from the association marketing department who is also experienced in working with task forces. The board liaison also agrees to coach and direct the volunteer. Between the staff member and board liaison, the S2 leader behavior is initiated where clear direction is given, the volunteer is involved in decision making about the task force, and the leaders recognize accomplishments along the way and praise the volunteer to enhance self-confidence (high direction and high support).

Scenario 3
D3 Follower Behavior – Moderate to High Competence & Variable Commitment
S3 Leader Behavior – Low Directive & High Supportive

A board needs to fill the newsletter editor position. The board decides to approach a volunteer leader who has been very successful in the association, knows the association well, has excellent writing and proofreading skills, and has demonstrated the ability to coach and inspire others. This volunteer is approached about the position and states, "Oh, I could never do anything like that." In this situation, the volunteer is able to do the job, from the board's perspective, but the volunteer is insecure (high competence, low commitment). After some encouragement and reinforcement that she can do the job, the volunteer accepts the position. The leader shares ideas, connects with resources, and participates in making decisions, but the editor takes charge of the task. The leader's primary role is to bolster confidence and praise the editor along the way as tasks are being accomplished.

> *"Leaders need to monitor the progress of their followers. They need to help the followers as movement occurs from one stage to the next."*

Scenario 4
D4 Follower Behavior – High Competence & High Commitment
S4 Leader Behavior – Low Directive & Low Supportive

The second edition of a publication needs to be developed. The board decides to approach the first edition editor to manage the project and he accepts. The editor is able, willing, and confident to manage this project since he had the experience of editing the first edition (high competence, high commitment). The leader behavior needs to focus on delegating the task, providing overall direction, and allowing the editor to make decisions and manage the project (low direction and low support).

Situational Leadership Involves Matching and Monitoring

The key in Situational Leadership is to match the leadership behavior with the follower's development level. The leader helps followers grow in maturity as far as they are able and willing to go. Regardless of an individual's development level, change may occur. The person may slip back in ability or motivation. Signs of this may include decreased communication, no progress reports, and delayed or halted work. The leader may need to reassess the development level and provide the appropriate support and direction. To provide the appropriate leader behavior for a given situation, leaders must be competent in all four of the leadership behavior categories (S1-S4).

Leaders need to monitor the progress of their followers. They need to help the follower as movement occurs from one stage to the next. The leadership behavior should be geared to the follower's current development level with the goal of helping the follower to develop and require progressively less direction and gain more self-control and confidence. Sometimes leaders move too quickly through the various stages, such as prematurely advancing from coaching behavior (S2) to supporting behavior (S3). They mistakenly expect followers to use their new skills immediately without the benefits of coaching and supporting.

In other cases, the leader may not be willing to give up control or direction as the follower begins to grow. Leaders need to reduce their directive behavior in these instances and increase their supportive behavior. The follower no longer needs to be told what to do, but rather encouraged to continue on the right path.

When a follower's performance is at a low level, it is important not to delegate too rapidly. The slightest progress should be reinforced. As the person matures, the leader pulls back and includes the follower in determining what should be done. This leadership behavior helps to build confidence and can have an impact on the follower's success or failure.

"Initially, preparing a written charter helps the board come to clarity and consensus on the charge given to the group. The charter is then discussed with the group and can be modified based on the group's input. It provides direction to the group and serves as the foundation for the group's action plan."

Use of Charters or Communication Briefs

An important communication tool that will help the board and board liaisons work effectively with other volunteer leaders is a charter or communication brief. A charter or communication brief is simply a means of written communication for initiating and completing a charge or task. Table 3-6 contains the components of a charter along with a brief explanation for each component (next page).

Table 3-6
Charter or Communication Brief

Charter:	Charter name (or topic)
Strategic Plan Goal #__:	Goal number and goal statement
Strategic Plan Objective #__:	Objective number and objective statement
Responsible Group:	The group that has been asked to meet the charge
Charge to Responsible Group:	The specific task requested of this group
History:	Background information that prompted the board to develop the charter
Outcome/Deliverable:	Statement of what is expected as an outcome of the group's work
Accountable to:	Identify the board liaison or other designee
Staff Liaison:	The national office staff person who will assist the group
Parameters:	Any specific directions or boundaries provided to the group (e.g., include the level of authority, budgetary factors, methods of communication, suggestions for research/data to be obtained, etc.)
Resources:	Key people who can be helpful; tangible resources such as strategic plan, policies, publications, finances
Target Date for Completion:	There may be more than one target date if there are multiple steps in the charter.
Reporting Times:	Frequency of progress reports to the board liaison/board

The charter provides clear direction to the group. It is interesting to watch the dynamics of how an idea is generated by or given to the board, how a charge to a group to do something about the idea is conceived, how the charge is interpreted by the board member communicating the charge to the implementation group, how the group's chair and members interpret the charge, how the work gets done, how the outcomes are communicated to the board, and how the board evaluates the outcomes according to the charge. Is there any point at which miscommunication might happen? Absolutely. This is why a written charge to any group is important.

Initially, preparing a written charter helps the board come to clarity and consensus on the charge given to the group. The charter is then discussed with the group and can be modified based on the group's input. It provides direction to the group and serves as the foundation for the group's action plan. Sometimes projects drag on to the point where committee members do not remember the charge they were given. The charter serves as a reminder of what is expected. It can also serve as the basis for evaluating the outcomes of the task.

"The mission is the fuel that propels us to produce worthwhile results."

Governance Through Mission, Vision, Values, and Culture

Effective leadership is a key element of governance. Other essential elements include: (a) mission, vision, and values that guide all actions and activities, (b) a culture within which the association lives and functions, and (c) structures that provide the operating rules and human resources to accomplish the association's work. It is critical for board members to understand these elements to govern the association effectively.

Mission

The association's mission describes why the association exists or its purpose. The mission provides the foundation for all decision making. The most important work of a board is to create and re-create the reason for which the association exists. A mission statement is more than a collection of words that is developed once and then forgotten. Reaffirming the mission is a continuous board responsibility. The mission serves as a guide to organizational planning, decision making, programs and services, and setting priorities among competing demands for scarce resources. Obtain a copy of your association's mission, if you are not already familiar with it.

The reason associations exist is to produce worthwhile results. The results must meet a human need and satisfy the association's constituents. What constitutes need and value, and their level of satisfaction must be continuously assessed. A mission will not only describe why the association exists, but will imply how the world will be different as a result of the association's work.

Everyone, including the board, staff, members, and other volunteers must have the same answer to the question, "Why does our association exist?" Everyone should be able to state the association's mission in one or two sentences. If not, perhaps the mission has not yet been crystallized. The board may have some work to do.

Vision

A vision is a picture of the association in the future. It is the essence of what the association should become. A vision should be specific enough to provide guidance to members, but vague enough to encourage creativity and initiative, and to remain relevant in a variety of conditions. An association's vision must serve the interests of its members and be real enough that progress toward reaching the vision can be achieved.

President John F. Kennedy, in his inaugural speech, articulated a clear vision when he said "We will have a man on the moon by the end of the decade." You could picture a person walking on the moon. The vision was simple and clear. It was inspiring and challenging. A plan and strategies were determined, and much teamwork got us there. The vision became a reality.

A vision is a destination. It provides us with a place for where we want to be in the distant future. Once we reach the destination, we build a new vision to drive the future. In many cases, we may never reach the destination, but the vision will provide us with the motivation to continue stretching to reach it.

> ***"The vision is a destination that we want to reach in the future. The values are the association's beliefs and principles that help us make sound decisions. Culture provides the norms for how we will work."***

Values

Core values are the association's beliefs and principles that guide its planning and operations. They provide an ethical framework from which behaviors and actions are judged. Values may include such things as trust, honesty, integrity, open communication, accountability, teamwork, compassion, and caring, to name a few. They serve as controls that informally allow or forbid our behaviors. The board and senior staff must constantly live the values and teach them to others. They must walk the talk.

Values help us to make better decisions and to improve the performance of our mission. Shared values are one of the essential elements of a strong association.

Culture

Every association has its own culture. Culture defines the norms of behavior within the association. There are certain ways of acting that are acceptable within a given culture and other ways that are unacceptable. Behaviors that may be acceptable in one culture may be totally unacceptable in another. Culture determines how decisions are made, problems are solved, and conflicts are handled. In general, culture determines how an association will go about conducting its business. It is important for board members to know the current state of the association's culture so business can be conducted in a way that is acceptable, expected, and politically correct. Kirk (2007) states that the association's culture directly reflects and is influenced by the board's culture. Therefore, board members play a critical role in shaping, reshaping, and providing oversight of the association's culture.

> *"A strategic plan is the roadmap for the association's goals and the strategies for accomplishing them."*

Governance Documents

Strategic Plan

The mission, vision, values, culture, and strategic plan are interrelated. The mission is the fuel that propels us to produce worthwhile results. The vision is a destination that we want to reach in the future. The values are the association's beliefs and principles that help us make sound decisions. Culture provides the norms for how we will work. A strategic plan is the roadmap for all of these goals and the strategies for accomplishing them. All of the elements guide the board's strategic thinking and planning. An effective strategic plan is a dynamic document which everyone uses to provide direction, evaluate outcomes, and move the association toward the vision. Strategic thinking and planning will be covered in greater detail in Chapter 6 – Strategic Thinking and Planning.

There are several structures within an association that provide the rules, boundaries, communication patterns, and human resources to help the board run the association. These structures include the articles of incorporation, bylaws, organizational chart, policies and procedures, and role or position descriptions for officers, committees, and staff.

Articles of Incorporation

The articles of incorporation, or corporate charter, are initiated when the association first incorporates and becomes a legal entity. The articles are a legal document that set forth the name, purpose of the association, and any other information required to incorporate in a particular state. Incorporation is advisable if the association intends to hold property, inherit a legacy, make legally binding contracts, hire employees, and be in a position to sue or be sued. One of the advantages of incorporation is that it provides a level of protection from personal liability for officers and members who act as representatives of the association.

The articles of incorporation supersede all other rules of the association, none of which can be in conflict with the articles. Nothing in the articles can be suspended unless the articles provide for it. For these reasons, the articles should contain only the essential elements required by the state of incorporation. Other rules governing the association should be placed in the bylaws or other lower-ranking rules. Board members rarely refer to the articles of incorporation as a practical, working document. The bylaws, organizational chart, and policies are used much more frequently and with greater meaning.

Bylaws

Bylaws contain the rules governing the structure and behavior of the association. They are often required by law if a nonprofit group wishes to obtain tax exempt status.

Bylaws should be simple, brief, and flexible. They should not contain rigid restrictions or specifics, such as the amount of dues, since these will lead to continual amending when changes are made. Bylaws are adopted by the members and go into effect immediately upon adoption. Once the bylaws are adopted initially, the association may begin its business.

Once adopted, bylaws cannot be suspended. The board does not have the authority to change the bylaws. They may be changed according to the rules for amendment that have been established. In most instances, members must be notified of the proposed amendment(s) within a given time period, then a vote of a specified majority is required as stated in the bylaws. Bylaws constitute a legal document. Therefore, any substantive changes should be reviewed by legal counsel.

Most bylaws look very similar and are usually written as articles (Table 3-7). Board members should have a copy of the bylaws when attending board meetings since they often provide the structure the board needs to make decisions. For example, if a member of the board resigns, the board may need to refer to the bylaws to determine how that vacancy must be filled. At various times boards will redefine the categories of membership or redesign the executive board or committee structure. Since all of these changes might indicate a change in the bylaws, these changes or amendments must be brought to the membership for approval.

Table 3-7
Sample Bylaws

Article I: Name and Purpose

Article II: Membership
This section defines the membership and any related categories of membership.

Article III: Meetings
The types of meetings to be held by the association will be listed here. Any specifics regarding number of meetings, notification of meetings, quorums, and voting are identified in this section.

Article IV: Board Members and Officers
Board members and officers are identified along with their method of election, term of office, and brief description of responsibilities. The procedure to fill a vacancy is also listed here.

Article V: Committees
The types of committees or task forces and a brief description of their duties are listed.

Article VI: Bylaws Amendments
This section describes the procedure for amending the bylaws. It states who must be notified, how, and by when.

Organizational Chart

Another component of the governance structure is the organizational chart. An organizational chart displays a diagram of the structure of an association. It identifies the key players and who reports to whom. It helps to identify the levels of authority in the association and explains the chain of command. Organizational charts will look different for each association. In most instances they will identify the positions of the membership, board of directors, officers, committees, staff, and other constituencies such as chapters. Many organizational charts also identify the relationship with other related boards such as journal editorial boards, certification boards, and foundations.

Policies and Procedures

Policies and procedures also assist the board in governing the association's activities. The board establishes policies and procedures as pre-determined rules that can be amended by the board. These rules are more specific than the rules in the bylaws, but the bylaws must take precedence over policies. Policies and procedures assist the board in its operations and they are based on the needs of the association.

Policies serve as references for decision making. They describe values and perspectives of the governing body. Policies should be written, explicit, current, centrally available, and brief. Policies should be developed proactively to address broad issues. It is helpful to note that sometimes policies are developed out of a problem situation that occurs for which there is no written information to guide in problem solving or decision making.

Since policies govern the association, they must remain current. Most associations have a "policy" to review their policies at specific intervals. Policies need to remain living documents; therefore policy books should not grow too large. Policies or policy changes can be initiated anywhere. It is not important to restrict the sources from which the board receives its impetus to establish or change its policies. However, it is important to distinguish that the responsibility for policy making rests with the board.

"Often, board members are accustomed to large policy books that are necessary in their employment settings. Associations, unless they are regulated by another body, do not need to have a policy for everything. Each association determines the need for policies related to its operations."

Often, board members are accustomed to large policy books that are necessary in their employment settings. Associations, unless they are regulated by another body, do not need to have a policy for everything. Each association determines the need for policies related to its operations.

Position Descriptions

The next component of governance is the position or role description. A position description is a document that is written for each role or position in the association. It identifies the job title, qualifications, term of service, person to whom responsible, and the job responsibilities. It provides direction for the person who assumes the position. A position description can be helpful when recruiting new board members by clarifying what is involved in board membership. It can also serve as a foundation for discussion during board orientation and as a continuous reference to assist in keeping the board or committee member on track. The criteria contained in position descriptions can be used for evaluating those individuals who hold positions within the association.

Roles of Officers, Committees, and Staff

The board divides its work among other mechanisms to make sure it is accomplished. These mechanisms include officers, committees, task forces, and staff. The structure that the board establishes is best kept to a minimum and as simple as possible. The more hierarchy that is created, the more steps and individuals are involved, and the more time is expended in accomplishing the real work. The less hierarchy established, the clearer the rules and the process.

Officers

Officers exist to help the board do its job; they are not powers unto themselves. The president or chairperson acts as the chief volunteer leader who coordinates and leads group effort. Other officers may include a treasurer who is responsible for financial accountability of the association's funds. A secretary is responsible for recording the business conducted by the association. Other officers may include a president-elect, vice president, or immediate past president.

Committees and Task Forces

Some associations have an executive team or committee that conducts business in between board meetings on behalf of the board. Any decisions that must be made by the board must come to the board for approval. A position description for the executive team will help to describe its function and decision making authority. It is helpful for the executive team to communicate its work to the entire board so the board is apprised of the association's activities. This communication is best delivered in a written executive summary and not by a verbal report read during a board meeting.

Committees and task forces, or ad hoc committees, represent the major method of organizing the volunteer work of the association and getting it done. Standing committees are permanent committees established in the association's bylaws. They serve a function for the ongoing governance of the association. Task forces are special committees that have a limited charge and exist only until the charge is completed. It is best to have only the number of committees needed to accomplish the association's work. There are no rules about the types or numbers of committees a board must have.

Today's associations are downsizing the number of standing committees and forming task forces only when needed. Task forces can be quickly formed, accomplish a given task, and disband when the work is completed. They can often be an efficient and cost-effective way to accomplish the association's work.

"Committees and task forces represent the major method of organizing the volunteer work of the association and getting it done. Standing committees serve a function for the ongoing governance of the association. Task forces are special committees that have a limited charge and exist only until the charge is completed."

Committees delve into more detail than the board as a whole. Committees study, debate, formulate, and determine a course of action or recommendation that they make to the board. The board reviews the committees' work and accepts, modifies, or rejects the recommendations. Often if the board has given clear direction and a board liaison has helped coach the committee chair, the committee's work and recommendations are accepted.

Committees must be large enough to get the work done with a fair sharing of responsibility, but small enough to allow for ample involvement. Usually a group of three to nine members is the best size for group process. Committees with an odd number of members are usually preferable. A member of the executive board is usually assigned as a liaison to each committee for the purpose of directing, reporting, and supporting. The president most often serves as a non-voting, ex-officio member of all committees.

A committee's work will be most effective when its members know the purpose of the committee, are committed to this purpose, have received the necessary direction and authority for the committee's work, and work well together as a team. Committee appointments should be made with careful attention to the mix of skills, perspectives, and personalities. Task forces should be composed of individuals who have expertise in the topic related to their purpose.

If committees or task forces do not seem to be the solution for an issue or task, the board may consider an advisory group or sounding board. An advisory group can be used for short-term projects where specific industry or profession-related knowledge or expertise is needed. A sounding board is an even more informal group that might meet only one time to provide insight or feedback on new ideas/projects the association is thinking of implementing.

Committees or other informal groups serve various purposes. In addition to helping the board accomplish its goals, committees increase the members' participation in the association. This increases their sense of ownership and provides opportunities for leadership development. Engaging members in the direction and work of the association is an effective method of member retention. Through committee participation, leadership skills can be identified and nurtured. Succession planning begins with the identification and mentoring of emerging leaders.

"Staff is often an asset to the association because it carries the history of the association. Staff is the stable component of the equation as volunteers come and go. They provide valuable insight into decision making and how best to operationalize the association's goals."

Staff

A majority of the association's day-to-day work is accomplished by paid staff. These individuals bring expertise in association management to the table and their efforts complement the work of the volunteer leaders whose expertise lies in the knowledge of their profession or industry. Together, the volunteer leaders and staff create a partnership to ensure that strategic work is accomplished along with the daily operations. Maintaining this partnership is critical to the association's success.

Staff is often an asset to the association because it carries the history of the association. Staff is the stable component of the equation as volunteers come and go. Staff members know how to efficiently and cost effectively get things done. They provide valuable insight into decision making and how best to operationalize the association's goals. Senior staff participate in strategic planning and board work, and communicate the strategic direction to the rest of the staff.

It is important for new board members to get to know the senior staff, primarily the staff executive, and the person(s) directly next in line. In addition to performing the operations of the association, the senior staff can greatly contribute to the board member's orientation and ongoing development. Staff serves as a resource, advisor, guide, coach, and most important, a partner. Since staff has "been there and done that," these individuals know what needs to happen next in the annual cycle of an association's work. Staff advises board members of the duties that need to be fulfilled and helps to steer them in the right direction. Since most board members have full-time jobs in their profession or industry, they often do not know all of the activities that happen with the association. They greatly appreciate the coaching from staff to keep them on task with their responsibilities.

Summary

A governance model provides the framework for the board to organize its thoughts, activities, programs, structures, and relationships. An effective governance structure is composed of individuals who lead the association through vision, mission, and values. Since leadership is the key element in effective governance, this chapter explored several leadership concepts to help new board members in broadening their thinking about leadership and their own leadership styles.

Effective board members achieve the association's mission by setting direction and empowering other volunteers to accomplish specific tasks and projects. They realize the importance of followership to their success as leaders. Successful leaders work with their followers and together they create a synergistic relationship in which they raise one another to higher levels of functioning than either could achieve alone.

Learning Assessment

Chapter 3: Governance and Leadership

Reflect on the knowledge you gained from this chapter by answering the following questions. Some of the questions suggest that you discuss the topic with your mentor. You may have already determined additional questions that you will discuss with your mentor.

1. Describe what you learned in this chapter about the differences between leadership and management.

2. Identify the characteristics that you possess that make/will make you an effective leader.

3. What do you plan to do to enhance your leadership skills?

4. Read your association's articles of incorporation and bylaws, and review the organization chart. What questions do you have about them? Discuss your questions with your mentor. If you have no questions, briefly describe what you learned about these documents from this chapter.

5. You have been asked to form a new committee to administer the awards program for your organization. You will serve as the board liaison to this committee. How will you recruit members to serve on this committee? What qualifications will you look for in the committee members? What kind of direction and ongoing support will you give the chair of the committee? How will you use the situational leadership model to work with the volunteers on this committee?

6. Discuss your response to #5 with your mentor. Obtain suggestions about other ways to inspire volunteers to assist the board in accomplishing its work.

7. What is the single most important thing you learned from reading this chapter?

Chapter 4

Decision Making

Key Points

- Simple and Complex Decisions
- Critical and Creative Thinking
- Systems Thinking
- Consensus Decision Making
- Knowledge-Based Decision Making
- Decision Making on Issues of Strategic Importance
- Simple Decision Making Process
- Self-Discipline During Decision Making
- Decision Making Techniques
- Tension and Anxiety in Decision Making
- Challenges in Decision Making

Tables and Figures

Mentoring Opportunity

- Learning Assessment

Download the Chapter 4 Tables, Figure, and Learning Assessment online at www.ajj.com/mentoring — Use password MTS2E989

Decision making is perhaps the most critically important skill in which board members must be competent, especially since it is one of the most frequently occurring activities they perform in their roles. Board members find themselves making such types of decisions as determining whether or not to initiate a new program or service; reviewing and approving budgets; collaborating with other associations; disciplining a fellow leader; resolving an ethical dilemma; interpreting a policy; and assisting a committee with a problem. While some decisions may be made on an individual basis, other decisions are greater in scope and must be made as a group by the entire board.

Individual decision making in some ways is easier because there are fewer people, ideas, and alternatives to consider. Group decision making on the other hand involves more time and work, but often, in the long run, the value of the diversity of opinions, ideas, and thoughts is well worth the time and effort. Most boards today arrive at decisions through a consensus approach which is discussed later in the chapter.

Group decision making poses many opportunities for the board to work together collaboratively for the best interest of the association. It is important for board members to realize that when making a board decision for the association, they must represent the association as a whole. While an individual's life experiences bring value to decision making, board members do not make decisions based on how things are done in their own work setting, chapter, or region.

Being a board member means representing the whole, not segmented parts. Sometimes this is difficult and often challenging, especially for board members who worked their way up to the board level because they were successful helping to make decisions for their local or regional groups. You will often hear, "Well this is how we do/did it at..." It is helpful for board members to keep each other on track by pointing out situations where other board members are segmenting their thinking to a particular few.

Simple and Complex Decisions

Decision making is a process of bridging a gap between the state of what is and what ought to be. Board members individually and collectively are faced with numerous opportunities to make decisions. Some decisions are simple, easily made, and do not consume much time. Examples may be whether or not to attend a meeting hosted by a collaborating association or whether to sign on to a legislative initiative that the association has approved in previous years. A complex decision making process is not needed in these instances. However, other decisions are more complex, have far-reaching consequences, and require a higher degree of risk. For example, the decisions to redefine membership categories or institute a new and costly, but much requested, program require much more thought and discussion prior to reaching a decision.

In many instances, it would be easy to jump right from the problem to the solution. Time would be saved and we could move on to something else. However, with decisions involving complex issues, the quality of the decision would not be good and we probably would not solve the problems, just give them a quick fix. Unfortunately, that is what we do a lot of the time when we think we are solving complex problems. While this may be acceptable in crisis situations, it does not work well when long-term solutions are needed. Decision making based on knowledge and insight is needed to solve these types of problems effectively.

> ***"Both critical and creative thinking are important to effective decision making. Critical thinking involves tying together pieces of information, relating one to another, and examining the consequences of potential solutions. Creative thinking stimulates us to stretch our imaginations and boundaries, color outside the lines, and arrive at alternative solutions."***

Critical and Creative Thinking

Effective decision making involves both critical, or analytic, and creative thinking. Critical thinking is an analytic process in which we use a systematic method to derive a clear definition of the problem, viable alternatives, and a workable solution. Critical thinking involves tying together pieces of information, relating one to another, and examining the consequences of potential solutions.

Creative thinking, on the other hand, is a more free-flowing form of processing information. It stimulates us to stretch our imaginations and boundaries, color outside the lines, and arrive at alternative solutions that may be quite different from those obtained through the critical thinking process. Creative thinking involves the use of intuition and a sense of "my gut tells me this is right." Some criticize the intuitive aspect of thinking, others rely on it heavily.

Both critical and creative thinking are important to effective decision making. All of us are capable of doing both, although we are probably more skilled at one than the other. In fact, creative thinking is subject-specific. In other words, a person may be a very creative thinker about one subject, but the creative thinking may not be transferable to another subject. The key is to create a climate for creative thinking and determine who within the group has the ability to engage in creative thinking about the topic at hand.

"A systems thinking approach reminds us that the whole can exceed the sum of its parts. Systems thinking is a framework for seeing interrelationships rather than things, for seeing patterns of change rather than static snapshots."

Boards need to break down problems and situations into component parts so they have the time and intellectual capacity to solve them. Simplifying problems into manageable parts helps board members weed out the important and significant aspects of problems. Often this is a difficult task because we feel if we have not used every bit of information to solve a problem, we have not done our job. In reality, we sometimes make data collection and problem solving so complex, we become exhausted before we get to the creative stage of determining alternative solutions.

It can be very helpful for new board members to listen to other more experienced board members as they make decisions. Asking the board members questions about how they arrived at their decision and what their thought processes were can be very helpful for the novice board member. While none of us will solve problems in the same way, we can learn tips from others that will strengthen our abilities.

Systems Thinking

A form of critical thinking, systems thinking, is vital in making decisions that impact a large organization. Senge (1990), in his book *The Fifth Discipline,* describes systems thinking as the discipline that integrates all other disciplines within an organization. A systems thinking approach reminds us that the whole can exceed the sum of its parts. Systems thinking is a framework for seeing interrelationships rather than things, for seeing patterns of change rather than static snapshots.

Systems thinking is important today because our world is complex. We often become overwhelmed with the complexity and feel helpless - "There's nothing I can do about it, so why try?" Senge (1990) states that systems thinking is the antidote for this sense of helplessness that we feel as we enter the age of interdependence. Systems thinking helps us see the structures that are underlying complex situations. It simplifies life by helping us see the deeper patterns lying behind the events and details. Seeing the whole and how the pieces fit together to create the whole is the beginning of restructuring how we think. Systems thinking helps us sort out what is important and what is not. It identifies variables to focus on and those with which to pay less attention.

When making decisions or solving problems for an association, it is important for board members to keep the big picture in focus. By looking at the whole, board members can better understand where the pieces fit. When some pieces fall out of place, the board is able to determine from where those pieces fell, and how their falling will impact the rest of the association. Systems thinking is similar to a puzzle. While each piece is important to the whole puzzle, each piece does not have the same degree of value as when all the pieces are placed together to form a picture. When we have all the puzzle pieces in their right places, we are able to see the puzzle as a whole. When a piece is missing, it is obvious. The puzzle does not look or function in the same way.

It is the board's responsibility to be the keeper of the bigger picture. Systems thinking is a way to keep that big picture foremost in the minds of its members. Some questions that can be asked when using a systems thinking approach to decision making are found in Table 4-1.

Table 4-1
Making Decisions Through A Systems Thinking Approach

Questions to ask...

- Who owns this decision or problem?
- How does this decision or problem fit within the bigger picture? How does it fit with the association's vision and mission?
- Who will this decision affect?
- Who is involved in making this decision?
- Who isn't involved in making this decision that should be?
- What are the legal, ethical, and financial implications of this decision?

Source: Nowicki, 1998.

Consensus Decision Making

Decisions made by a group should be given careful consideration before conclusions are reached. In many associations, voting has gone by the wayside. Instead, decisions are being reached by consensus. Unfortunately, while people know the word, not everyone understands what consensus means.

> *"In consensus decision making, the group contributes opinions and ideas, discusses situations and alternatives, and determines a solution and plan of action that everyone can support. While all participants may not agree totally with the decision, or they may not think it is the ideal solution, everyone is willing to give it a try and they agree to support it."*

Consensus decision making involves everyone contributing their opinions and ideas, discussing situations and alternatives, and determining a solution and plan of action that everyone can support. If someone is unable to accept the decision, further discussion needs to occur. That person should state other alternatives and jointly the group arrives at a decision that is acceptable to everyone.

Consensus is a process that creates win/win situations. The solutions that are arrived at do not compromise any strong convictions or values of those involved. Consensus is not compromise. No one should have to give up something to gain something in return. While all participants may not agree totally with the decision, or they may not think it is the ideal solution, everyone is willing to give it a try and they agree to support it. This means when participants leave the meeting, they do not sabotage the decision.

If consensus cannot be reached, at least the group has given it their best effort. The issue may need to be tabled until another time when more information or other alternatives are available. The experience of consensus building can be a powerful way for individuals to learn how to work thoroughly through situations and explore alternatives. It is much different from voting. With voting, usually some win and some lose. With consensus, no one must lose in order for someone else to win. The interaction is collaborative. When individuals experience success with consensus building, they feel good about the process because they know they have been heard, their ideas have been given a chance, all options are considered, and the rationale(s) behind the decision is understood.

Knowledge-Based Decision Making

Tecker's Knowledge-Based Decision Making (KBDM) model is a valid method for making decisions, especially those of strategic importance (Tecker et al, 2002). Tecker states that when knowledge-based decision making is used for significant decisions, the following four bases must be addressed:

- Sensitivity to stakeholders' views that provide knowledge and insight about the issue
- Foresight about the profession or industry
- Insight into the capacity and strategic position of the association, providing both internal and external perspectives
- Awareness of ethical issues related to the possible choices of decisions

In creating knowledge, random data are taken from various sources and translated into a meaningful context through study, investigation, observation, and experience. The data are organized into information, the information is analyzed and then transformed into knowledge. Knowledge becomes the basis for decision making. Decisions made in this way shift the focus away from personal opinion and power (political decision making) toward good data and collective wisdom (rational decision making) (Tecker et al, 2002).

Decisions must be based on data and knowledge. The book, *Seven Measures of Success,* published by the American Society of Association Executives (2006), describes the measures by which associations are rated as remarkable. One of the measures that sets remarkable associations apart is data-driven strategies. This measure refers to associations that continuously track member needs and issues, as well as issues from the external world, and collectively analyze the data to reach a shared understanding of, "What do we know?" and "What are we going to do about it?" These associations incorporate their knowledge into strategic and operational planning. Remarkable associations nurture a culture in which there is a continuous loop of data and information coming into and being disbursed by the association.

Boards gather and obtain a wealth of information and knowledge that is greater than that possessed by members and stakeholders. This is why boards make decisions based on member input and also the other three knowledge bases of the KBDM model. When all of the information obtained from the four knowledge bases is discussed and synthesized, a decision based on knowledge and informed intuition is possible.

KBDM is based on obtaining knowledge and insight from stakeholders before making the decision. Of equal importance is

"The Knowledge-Based Decision Making model is based on obtaining knowledge and insight from stakeholders before making the decision. Of equal importance is communicating back to them the decisions that were made along with the basis of those decisions in terms of judgment, logic, and rationale."

communicating back to them the decisions that were made along with the basis of those decisions in terms of judgment, logic, and rationale. This two-way communication between the board and stakeholders creates synergy between the real world as perceived by the stakeholders and the view of their world as perceived by the association's leaders. Members and stakeholders feel part of the decisions and know why they were made.

> *"Addressing issues of strategic importance takes time to gather data and information on the issue, and to create an opportunity for dialogue and decision making. Some boards will allot a concentrated block of time on their board agendas to discuss these types of strategic issues."*

Decision Making on Issues of Strategic Importance

The board may determine strategic issues that need to be addressed through the annual evaluation of the strategic plan, by doing an organization assessment, or in dealing with major issues that may have surfaced. Issues of strategic importance may include:

- How to restructure the board
- What to do with chapters and other components
- Expanding membership categories
- Redefining the core business
- How to deal with an intense competitor

The KBDM model suggests the following process to guide the board in making these decisions (Tecker et al, 2002). Addressing issues of strategic importance takes time to gather data and information on the issue, and to create an opportunity for dialogue and decision making. Some boards will allot a concentrated block of time on their board agendas to discuss these types of strategic issues. The following nine-step process will provide the framework for conducting this type of dialogue and decision making.

Step 1: Identify the Mega Question

The board determines an issue of strategic importance that the association and its membership will be facing in the upcoming year(s). The issue is stated in the form of a question that does not have a yes or no answer. The question may begin with phrases like,

"How can we....?"

"How could we...?"

"What should our role be in...?"

The mega question may be drafted by staff or the board, but the board needs to come to consensus on what the question is and how clearly it is stated.

Example: A board has determined that the individuals elected to the board do not have the qualifications to effectively lead the association. A mega question could be, "How can we recruit qualified individuals to serve on the board?" Another question might be, "How can we move from a constituency-based board to a competency-based board?"

Step 2: Prepare Background Information

Staff, a committee, or another group that is knowledgeable about the issue prepares background information framed around the following four knowledge-based questions. Ideally, the information is prepared in the form of a background paper that is distributed to the board prior to discussion of the question. This gives board members time to analyze the information, reflect, and prepare for dialogue about the question. If the issue is urgent in nature and there is not time to prepare background information in advance, the board will use the four knowledge-based questions as a basis for its dialogue.

"The four knowledge-based questions explore member/stakeholder needs and preferences, current realities and evolving dynamics, internal capacity and external strategic position, and ethical implications."

The background paper provides preliminary data, in the form of bullets responding to each of the following knowledge-based questions.

1. What do we know about our members' and stakeholders' wants, needs, and preferences related to this issue? (Data collection to answer this question may involve interviews, surveys, database information, previous survey results, etc.)
2. What do we know about the current realities and evolving dynamics of our members' marketplace, industry, or profession related to this issue? (Consider the issues of today, trends, and assumptions about the future.)
3. What do we know about the capacity and strategic position of our association related to this issue? (Capacity is internal to the association. It involves resources such as finances, core competencies, human resources, intellectual assets, structures, and processes. Strategic position involves the external world and its impact on this decision.)
4. What are the ethical implications of our choices in making this decision? (Consider the association's core values and how they may be impacted by the potential decisions. Values may include fairness, transparency, and doing the right thing for members.)

Step 3: Conduct Dialogue on Informing the Issue

In this step, the board uses the information in the background paper as a starting point to answer the following questions about what they know.

1. What points are particularly significant?
2. On which points are there questions or disagreement?
3. What else do we know that is not in the background information? What is missing?
4. What do we wish we knew but do not?

> *"When determining possible choices, keep in mind that one choice of decision may be to keep the status quo and do nothing."*

Step 4: Conduct Dialogue on Identifying Choices

This step involves looking at the previous information as a whole and determining possible choices of action or strategy. The dialogue focuses on the question, "What could we do with regard to this issue?" Possible choices are determined. Keep in mind that one choice of decision may be to keep the status quo and do nothing.

Step 5: Conduct Dialogue on Evaluation of Choices

Using the choices in Step 4, the advantages and disadvantages of each of the choices are determined. The process in Step 5 centers on dialogue, not deliberation. In other words, the purpose of dialogue is to understand the issues rather than develop an opinion or be persuaded by others to conform to theirs. It is inappropriate at this point for individuals to advocate for their choices – they will have plenty of time to do that in the next steps.

Step 6: Determine Areas of Consensus or Further Information Needed to Reach a Decision in the Future

Through dialogue in previous steps, a consensus may have begun to emerge about the choice(s) that appear(s) to be most appropriate. Some choices may be outright rejected, others may overlap and be combined. The board determines if there are choices on which the group can agree. If not, there needs to be a determination of what additional information is necessary to make the decision.

Step 7: Identify Actions, Intent, and Accountability

For the preferred choice(s) of the decision, the board determines the implications of the decision for the board, staff, and other volunteer work groups. The board discusses who will do what and who will be accountable. At this point, a written declaration of the choice or choices should be drafted and agreed upon by those present. This is not a final decision, but it articulates the outcome of the group at this point.

"Boards must determine the method by which they will make decisions and solve problems, and use it consistently."

Step 8: Make the Decision

Some boards will deliberate on the choice or choices and through consensus determine the decision. Other boards will go through parliamentary process to make their decision.

Step 9: Determine Next Steps for Communication and Implementation of the Decision

This step is dependent on the actual decision and its implications. It may involve a simple communication with members and stakeholders or a new task force may be developed to implement the strategies of this decision. Care must be taken in communicating this decision, its process, and its rationale to the members and other stakeholders.

Simple Decision Making Process

When the board makes simple decisions, the degree of knowledge obtained is often less than with major issues of strategic importance. For simple decisions, the following is a process for making a knowledge-based decision (see Figure 4-1).

1. Determine the issue or problem to be solved.
    - Articulate the issue well enough so everyone understands it.
    - Collect data about the signs, symptoms, and central issues involved.
    - Determine the facts and feelings that may be associated with the issue.
    - Refrain from the natural inclination of jumping directly to the decision or solution at this point.
2. Gather data and analyze the background of the issue. In the case of a problem, analyze the cause(s).
    - Collect further data about the implications or causes of the issue.

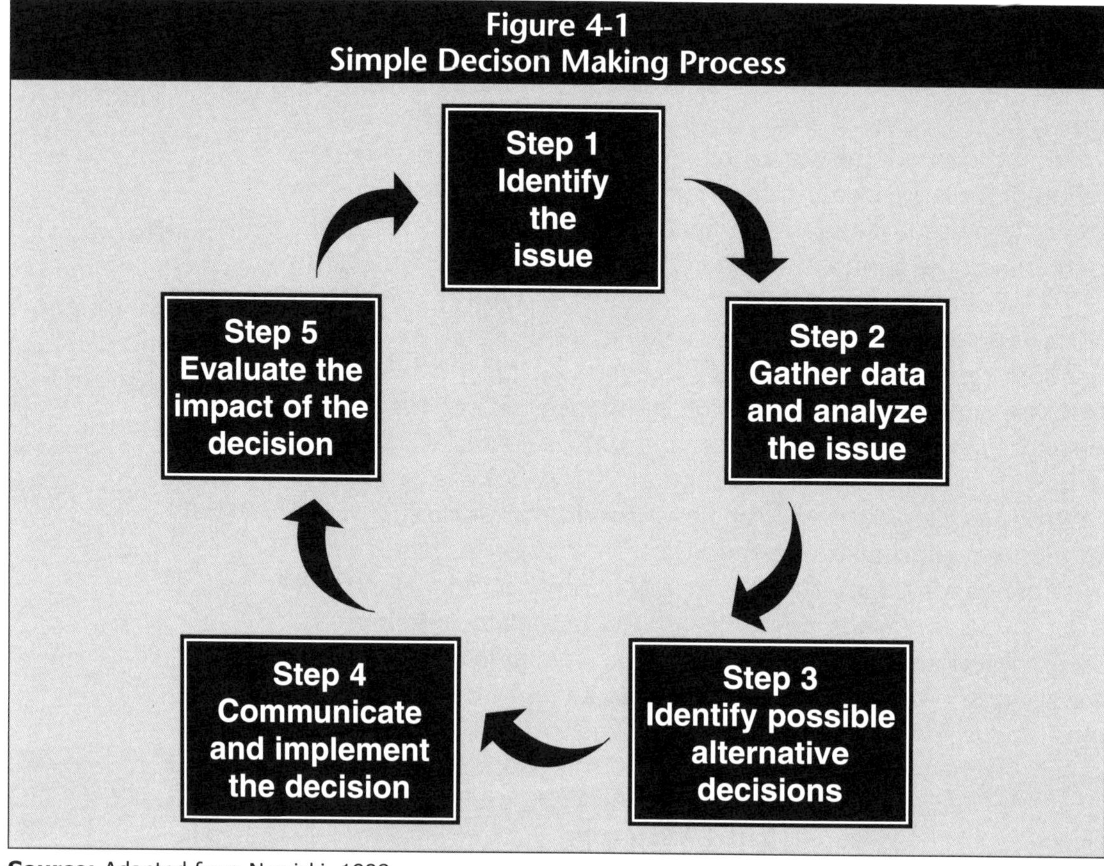

Source: Adapted from Nowicki, 1998.

- Consider the four knowledge-based questions (insight into members' views, current realities and evolving dynamics of the members' world, internal capacity and external strategic position, and ethical issues related to the decision).
- Also consider the following questions:
  - ➢ Who will be impacted by this decision, and how?
  - ➢ What resources would it take to implement this decision?
  - ➢ What are the financial implications of the decision?
  - ➢ Do we need the opinion of any outside resources (e.g., attorney, accountant, etc.)?
  - ➢ Do we have all the information we need before making the decision?
  - ➢ Does the decision require full board approval?

3. Identify possible alternative decisions or solutions, and make the final decision.
   - Brainstorm possible decisions.
   - Determine the advantages and disadvantages of each possible decision.
   - Make the decision.
4. Communicate and implement the decision or solution.
   - Communicate the decision, including the way it was made and the rationale.
   - Appoint a task force, if necessary, to develop an action plan that addresses the implementation.
   - If the decision may cause negative reactions, discuss proactive ways to address them.
   - Determine contingency plans in case the intended decision does not work.
5. Evaluate the impact of the decision or solution.
   - Solicit feedback from those involved in the decision or for whom the decision has had an impact.
   - Evaluate the outcome by answering the following questions:
     - ➢ Did we make the right decision?
     - ➢ How do we know that?
     - ➢ What do those who were involved in making the decision think about the outcome?
     - ➢ What do others who were affected by the decision think about the outcome?
     - ➢ What is being done/needs to be done to stabilize the impact of the decision?
     - ➢ Are there any signs that the decision needs to be reconsidered?
     - ➢ What have we learned through this decision making experience?
     - ➢ What might we do differently next time?

Boards must determine the method by which they will make decisions and solve problems, and use it consistently. The above steps provide a systematic or analytic way to make a decision or solve a problem. The amount of time spent in each step of the process will vary from situation to situation. In some instances, steps of the process may have already been dealt with or researched. In these instances, certain steps of the process may simply be reviewed, with not much depth invested in them. Some of the steps are engrained in the common decision making processes of the board and staff, so progression through the steps may occur quickly. The lesson to be learned here is not to omit any of the steps.

> *“Each board member is responsible for the decisions that the board makes and for the quality of the process in which those decisions are made.”*

Self-Discipline During Decision Making

Each board member is responsible for the decisions that the board makes and for the quality of the process in which those decisions are made. Board members are responsible for their own behavior and are required to make decisions based on the best interests of the members and the association. Their behavior will contribute to the function or dysfunction of decision making. Below are some tips for effective decision making behavior.

- LISTEN. Listen to others' points of view. Listen to understand, not to determine how you will counteract others' points. Actively listen to hear what is being said rather than thinking about what you will say next.
- Consume only your share of the air space. State your views and opinions succinctly. Answer questions when asked. Don't interrupt when another person is talking.
- During dialogue, remember that the purpose is to understand, not to debate and advocate for your point of view.
- Own your idea. If you say "I/we know...," make sure you have the data and facts to back it up. If you say "I believe...," be prepared to state why you believe or what previous experience makes you believe this way. If you say "I feel...," be prepared to say why and upon what values you are basing your statement.
- Be civil, even if others do not agree with your position, and even if they are not behaving appropriately.
- During deliberation, offer your opinion and your rationale for it.
- Try to contribute to a win/win outcome for everyone.
- Support all board decisions, even if they were made by consensus and you did not wholeheartedly agree with them.
- Keep board business in the boardroom. Refrain from discussing who said what and why once you leave the room.

Decision Making Techniques

Decision making in an efficient and constructive manner will increase the board's overall effectiveness. Various techniques may be used at various times to facilitate decision making. A description of two of the more commonly used techniques, brainstorming and nominal group technique, are found in Tables 4-2 and 4-3.

Table 4-2
Techniques for Decision Making – Brainstorming

Description
Brainstorming is a technique used to generate a large number of creative ideas or creative alternatives in a non-threatening atmosphere. Brainstorming helps to uncover facts and ideas in situations where complexity or other restraints would ordinarily inhibit free discussion. It encourages participants to build upon each other's ideas.

Ground Rules
For brainstorming to be effective, these ground rules should be used:
- Accept everyone's ideas. Do not judge or criticize.
- Do not edit any ideas.
- Generate as many ideas as possible.
- Build on the ideas of others.
- Offer wild, off the wall ideas. Creativity is the key.

Steps
1. Plan for the brainstorming session.
2. Determine the brainstorming method to use.
   a. Freewheeling - Ideas are shared at random. Each idea is recorded when given.
   b. Round Robin - Everyone takes a turn and states one idea. Each idea is recorded. Anyone can pass when it is their turn. The process is continued until there are no more ideas offered.
3. Announce the purpose of the session and write it down for the group to see.
4. State the ground rules.
5. Generate ideas.
6. Record all ideas for everyone to view as they are offered.
7. Wrap Up - Recognize and reward achievement.
8. The next step will be determined by the purpose of the session. Usually there is some form of filtering or prioritizing the ideas to a select few.

Advantages
- Generates a large quantity of ideas.
- Requires the active involvement of all participants.

Source: Nowicki, 1998.

Table 4-3
Techniques for Decision Making – Nominal Group Technique

Description

Nominal Group Technique (NGT) is a method of using face-to-face interaction to generate ideas and reach consensus. It involves a high degree of participant interaction while reducing the potential for group dominance by a few vocal individuals. NGT combines the aspects of silent individual expression with the benefit of group processing of ideas and decisions. The technique builds consensus among participants and can be used for a variety of reasons such as decision making and goal setting.

Steps

1. Plan for the session.
2. Clearly define the purpose of the session and the problem to be solved or decision to be made.
3. Briefly explain the Nominal Group Technique.
4. Ask each participant to silently and individually brainstorm and write down their ideas. Give specific parameters such as a fixed time limit or a number of ideas to develop.
5. In round robin fashion, participants offer one idea from their list. Record all ideas for everyone to view as they are offered. Continue until all ideas are given. Encourage participants to piggyback on each other's ideas and offer them on their next turn.
6. Clarify each item on the list by asking if there are any questions about what the idea means. Ideas are clarified, not changed or debated.
7. Assign a letter to each idea listed. Ask each participant to write down the letters corresponding to the letters listed on the easel chart (ie. A, B, C, etc).
8. Ask each participant to vote silently for the idea that best solves the problem or addresses the issue and assign a "1" to that idea. Assign a "2" to the second best idea. Continue in this manner until all ideas are assigned a number rating.
   a. As an alternative, if there are a large number of ideas to rank (>12), the participants may be asked to rate only a certain number of items by using the half plus one rule. This rule indicates that only half the ideas plus one need to be ranked by the group. For example, if there were 40 ideas generated, only the top 21 would be ranked.
9. Ask each participant for their rankings for each of the letters. For example, A=4, B=9, etc. Record these ratings for each participant on the easel chart.
10. Add up the scores for each letter. The item with the lowest total represents the decision at this point.
11. List the ideas in decreasing order on the easel chart. Discuss and clarify each of the top items, then discuss the vote. The purpose of this step is to validate that the top idea voted upon was indeed the best solution. If there is a wide discrepancy in votes, after discussion, a second vote may be taken.
12. Determine with the group where to go from here (most likely an action plan would be developed).

Advantages

- Provides an effective method to deal with controversial and sensitive issues.
- Ensures equal involvement by all participants.

Source: Nowicki, 1998.

Tension and Anxiety in Decision Making

Our life is full of opportunities to make decisions. For every decision, there are two potential sources of tension and conflict. First, whenever a decision involves a choice between alternatives, there is a win-lose factor that must be considered. For example, to lose weight, one must give up some desired foods, and to buy a new car means giving up the money we have saved over the last few years. Working together in a group presents additional sources of tension and conflict when trying to make decisions. Individuals who are new to a group may take their time in observing decision making in action before they choose to become involved. They may be thinking, What do I need to do to be accepted here? They tell me to be open and offer my opinion, but should I risk having it rejected?

A second source of natural tension and anxiety occurs after the decision is made. This stems from having to live with the decision, supporting and justifying it, and communicating it to others. It is natural to feel tension and anxiety associated with decision making. The key in dealing effectively with the emotional side of decision making lies in using the sources of tension as constructively as possible. Tension and anxiety can prompt us to have the interest and energy to be persistent in solving our problems. They can also do the opposite. Tension and anxiety can surface during group decision making and cause heated debate and disagreement instead of collaborative dialogue. The process is sidetracked into dealing with emotional issues instead of the intellectual issue at hand.

> *"Tension and anxiety can surface during group decision making and cause heated debate and disagreement instead of collaborative dialogue. The key in dealing effectively with the emotional side of decision making lies in using the sources of tension as constructively as possible."*

It is important for effective group dynamics, and ultimately group decision making, to realize the probable sources and reasons for tension and anxiety that occur with the decision making process. Knowing that these feelings occur and are natural can help board members put emotions in perspective and not allow them to interfere with successful decision making. Until a decision is made, expect some tension and anxiety and consider it natural.

Once decisions are made, even if the board knows the decision is the right one for the association, board members may experience some tension in anticipation of the potential reaction from members or a segment of them. Board members need to feel and demonstrate confidence that the decision was made in a fair and analytic manner. They need to resist the temptation of becoming defensive when the decision is questioned by others. Sometimes, no matter how right the decision, there will be some individuals who are unhappy with it and will make their dissatisfaction known in various ways. It helps to keep in mind that a decision will bring change and with change comes resistance.

There are times also when the amount of tension and anxiety during decision making reaches a level that exceeds "natural" and becomes very uncomfortable for everyone involved. *SCENARIO:* A board is discussing its investment policy and whether it needs to be revised. In the course of the discussion, one member becomes very vocal and relentlessly challenges the current investment strategy and the investment advisor. As the discussion ensues, he becomes increasingly vocal and irate, escalating the tension of the decision making process. His friend and fellow board member then joins in and adds fuel to the fire. What should be done in situations such as this? Read on...

Sometimes the decision making process breaks down over personal issues that are not easily raised to the surface, but which leave a residual tension on the group and the process. The tension builds. In many cases, the issues causing the conflict are personal and emotional while the process for making the decision was intended to be intellectual. The intellectual component is blocked by the tension that is created. If the tension is caused by emotions, they must be addressed.

In the above situation, the tension felt by the board was blocking effective, intellectual decision making. *SCENARIO CONTINUES:* One member stops the discussion, states she is feeling uncomfortable with the tension, and asks other board members what they are experiencing. A majority agree the atmosphere is very tense and needs to be addressed. Consequently, after some discussion, the relentless board member states he had some very serious problems recently with his investments and his investment advisor, and did not want the board to experience the same type of situation. After working through his emotions and their impact on the group, the board is able to bring the discussion back to an intellectual level and effectively make its decision. Unfortunately, while the board member had the board's best interests at heart, his emotions overruled his objectivity.

Challenges in Decision Making

As with anything, challenges and problems can occur with the decision making process. The following situations can occur on the path to successful problem solving and decision making (Chang & Kelly, 1993).

"Decision making will be ineffective if the right people are not involved in the process. The most important people to include in the process are those who have the power to make decisions, those who will carry out the decisions, and those who will be affected by them."

#1 Tackling Issues That May Be Too General, Too Large, or Not Well-Defined

Trying to tackle issues that are too broad in scope or not well-defined tends to add frustration to the decision making process because those involved are not able to experience much success in any stage of the process. This leads to less motivation and less interest in the issue at hand and the decision making process in general.

#2 Using the Band-Aid Approach

Jumping directly from the issue or problem to the solution without the analysis stages leads to a quick fix which is equivalent to putting a band-aid on an open wound that needs stitches. It may cover the wound and absorb the bleeding, but it does not help the wound heal. The band-aid approach to decision making puts a temporary and quick fix on the problem. The issue may go away for a short while, but it is sure to resurface again. It happens when an individual or group is impatient and is more focused on getting to a resolution than getting to the right decision.

#3 Failing to Involve The Right People

Decision making will be ineffective if the right people are not involved in the process. The most important people to include in the process are those who have the power to make decisions, those who will carry out the decisions, and those who will be affected by them. Those individuals closest to the work or issues are those who best know the issues and what needs to be done to resolve them. Failure to involve these individuals is a sure way to sabotage even the best of decision making processes and solutions.

#4 Tackling Issues That Are Beyond Our Scope of Control

Sometimes we take on issues that are not ours to solve. Either we are not directly involved in the issue, have not included the right people, or do not have the authority or control to make or influence any decisions about the issue. At times we try to solve someone else's problems that they do not want to be solved. Our efforts in these situations are futile and a waste of time. Unfortunately, we may not realize this until our well-thought-out solutions do not work or we are told to mind our own business.

#5 Applying a "Pet" Solution Rather Than a Creative One

In this case, someone, either the group leader or a very vocal person, has a pet solution to the problem that may have worked once or twice in the past. The group goes along with the solution only to find out that it does not work. The good and creative ideas that could have been generated from the group are minimized or ignored. You will hear the saying, "Well it has always worked in the past."

#6 Failing to Develop Good Reasons for Choosing a Solution

Sometimes faulty criteria are used to judge or choose the right decision, or the rationale for making the decision may not be clearly stated or discussed. When people are not really interested in the issue or decision, or they do not fully understand the alternatives, they may agree on a decision just for the sake of coming to closure.

#7 Failing to Plan Adequate Implementation and Evaluation Strategies

This occurs when the process stops short of the implementation and evaluation steps. Some individuals are so happy and relieved to have a decision that they forget about how the decision will be carried out and how its results will be measured. This happens frequently when groups run out of energy or have limited time and resources to solve issues.

#8 Engaging in Analysis Paralysis

This problem occurs when decision makers spin their wheels trying to analyze the issue and its causes. They spend so much time in the analysis process that they do not have enough time or energy to progress through the rest of the process and make the decision.

Summary

Decision making or problem solving is performed by the board more frequently than any other type of activity. As leaders set direction for the association, inspire and motivate volunteers and members, approve budgets, determine the need for new programs and services, and participate effectively in meetings, they must be competent in making decisions and solving problems effectively. Given the fast pace of today's world and the competing demands on our time, decisions must be made more quickly than ever before. Boards do not have the luxury of spending days solving a problem. However, they must make decisions effectively and in the best interest of their members. They are responsible for making sure the decisions are carried out and holding themselves accountable for the outcomes of those decisions.

Decision making involves gathering data and information, discussing and analyzing it, then transforming it into knowledge. The Knowledge-Based Decision Making process is an effective way of gathering data and ultimately making decisions that are in the best interest of the members and the association.

Since boards work together to make decisions, there is the added dimension of group process and group dynamics that can both help and hinder the process. New board members can best prepare themselves for their role in decision making by first examining their own decision making and problem solving styles and abilities. Talking with other board members, the board chairperson, and the staff executive about their perceptions of the board's decision making style will help in understanding how the board operates. Attending board meetings as an observer prior to taking office is perhaps one of the best learning opportunities to see the board in action from an objective point of view.

> ***"Attending board meetings as an observer prior to taking office is perhaps one of the best learning opportunities to see board decision making in action from an objective point of view."***

Learning Assessment

Chapter 4: Decision Making

Reflect on the knowledge you gained from this chapter by answering the following questions. Some of the questions suggest that you discuss the topic with your mentor. You may have already determined additional questions that you will discuss with your mentor.

1. Talk with your mentor, fellow board members, the board chairperson, and/or the staff executive about their perceptions of the way the board makes decisions and solves problems. Then determine how the board's decision making process fits with what you learned in this chapter.

2. Describe your assessment of your decision making skills. How will they fit into the way the board makes decisions?

3. How will the information in this chapter help you enhance your decision making skills?

4. Describe your understanding of consensus decision making.

5. Think of an issue of strategic importance to your association. Using the Knowledge-Based Decision Making process, answer the following questions:
   - What do we know about our members' and stakeholders' wants, needs, and preferences related to this issue?

   - What do we know about the current realities and evolving dynamics of our members' marketplace, industry, or profession related to this issue?

   - What do we know about the capacity and strategic position of our association related to this issue?

   - What are the ethical implications of our choices in making this decision?

Chapter 5

Teamwork and the Board-Staff Partnership

Key Points

Section 1: Team Concepts

- ★ Definitions of Team, Teamwork, and Team Development/Team Building
- ★ Advantages of Working Together in a Team
- ★ Basic Elements of a Team
- ★ Five Stages of Team Development
- ★ Roles of Team Leader and Team Members
- ★ Potential Problems with Teams
  - Groupthink • Subgroups
- ★ Steps for Building a Team
  - Developing Team Expectations

Section 2: The Leadership Team

- ★ Board and Staff Partnership
- ★ Leadership Team Member Roles
- ★ Board Chairperson and Staff Executive Partnership

Tables

- ★ Table 5-1 Expectations of Team Members and Team Leaders
- ★ Table 5-2 Guiding Principles for an Effective Board and Staff Relationship
- ★ Table 5-3 Responsibilities of the Board Chairperson
- ★ Table 5-4 Responsibilities of the Staff Executive

Tool Kit

- ★ Tool 5-1 How Do You Rate as a Team Member?
- ★ Tool 5-2 Team Progress Check

Mentoring Opportunity

- ★ Learning Assessment

Download the Chapter 5 Tables, Tool Kit, and Learning Assessment online at www.ajj.com/mentoring — Use password MTS2E989

"Teams that quickly determine their purpose, set their direction and goals, and focus on building relationships with team members will produce results that are more timely and effective than those groups that are not skilled in team development."

Life involves working together with others in groups or teams. Associations create many opportunities for team work from the executive board to standing committees to task forces to networking or special interest groups. Since association work involves working together with others to accomplish tasks and goals, it is to our advantage to learn how to work together successfully with others as a team. Whether we are joining an existing team or creating a new one, knowing the essentials of team development and team work is important.

Section 1

This chapter is divided into two sections - both are equally important to the development of a new board member. The first section focuses on generic team concepts. This information is important for a new board member since team work is critical to the success of an executive team and an association. In addition, while serving as an executive leader, most board members serve as liaisons or line officers to committees and are sometimes asked to form and lead a task force or special interest group. This section is written generically and can be applied to any setting where team work is appropriate. New board members are challenged to apply this information to their roles in their associations.

Whether the board member is coaching an existing team or forming and developing a new team, team building skills are essential. Teams that get off to a good start by quickly determining their purpose, setting their direction and goals, and focusing on building relationships with team members will produce results that are more timely and effective than groups that are not skilled in team development. In our world today, timeliness is critical. We cannot spend years or sometimes even months solving a problem or working on a project. Needs that are identified by association members today need to be addressed quickly, otherwise members will find other avenues to have their needs met. What then happens to the credibility and value of the association?

Section 2

The second section of this chapter will discuss the roles of the leadership team, both board members and staff, and the partnership that must develop to ensure a successfully led association. An effective board member is skilled in working as a team member and in coaching and developing other new or existing teams. While it is important for a board member to develop a team-focused relationship with fellow board members and other committees or groups within the association, it is equally, if not more important, to develop a strong partnership between the board and staff. Perhaps the most critical relationship within an association is the board and staff partnership.

Section 1: Team Concepts

Definition of Terms

For the purpose of this chapter, several team-related terms will be defined. A *team* is defined as a unit consisting of two or more individuals who have a common purpose or goal. Some may argue this definition refers to a group, not necessarily a team. In many respects this may be true; however, for consistency and ease of reading, the term *team* will be used throughout the chapter.

Teamwork is defined as the actual activities and responsibilities assumed by the team. *Team development* or *team building* consists of all the processes and activities in which the team is involved that help in building the relationships among team members and help the team do its work most effectively.

Too often we think of "team building" as structured activities that must be facilitated by an outside consultant. While these activities may be very helpful, there is a lot more to team building. Many teams do not have the time or resources for outside facilitators. Working together effectively and using the expertise of each team member will help build a team. Successes experienced with effective team communication and problem solving processes can be very powerful team building activities. As teams work together, experience successes, learn from their mistakes, and celebrate their accomplishments, they build their teams.

Relationships that are built among team members are vital to the team's success and to the ability to accomplish work in an effective and harmonious way. Teams can plan simple activities that will help the members get to know each other better as individuals. The relationships they build are often as important as the work itself.

Advantages of Working Together in a Team

"One essential element in an effective team is the interdependency of team members on one another. Each member relies on the other and together everyone helps to meet the goals."

A team exists to meet a purpose or goal. Working together as a team helps to accomplish much more than any of us could do alone. A team provides opportunities to express ourselves and to get feedback and ideas from others. Team members influence each other and learn together. The opportunities a team offers are endless.

Every team is unique and develops its own personality or culture that is unlike any other team. Team members each bring different thoughts, experiences, and expertise that help to achieve team goals. One essential element in an effective team is the interdependency of team members on one another. What this means is that all members must do their part in making the team work. Each member relies on the other and together everyone helps to meet the goals. In an effective team, everyone takes responsibility for the team's work and its results. This is especially true with executive boards.

Teams cannot work in isolation, they need to be aware of the external environment so that their work is relevant (Ancona and Bresman, 2007). For example, teams within an association must know what the members are saying and what they need, and the team's focus is to enhance the value received by members. Teams that are externally focused create ways to make the association successful. They know what other teams, such as committees, are doing in the association so that there is coordination and collaboration, not duplication of effort. All team members must fulfill the responsibilities of their specific role on the team, while at the same time work interdependently with others to lead the efforts of the association.

Since this first section of the Team Work chapter will help new board members with team work skills for their roles as board members, coaches of existing committees or teams, and developers of new task forces or teams, it is written generically. The new board member is encouraged to use and apply this information when functioning in one of the roles or situations mentioned above or while leading or participating in team work outside of the association.

Basic Elements of a Team

To function well and to be successful, a team must have the following basic elements:

- Meaningful purpose
- Commitment to a common approach to the team's work
- Complementary and overlapping skills
- Role competence
- Shared values
- Clear expectations of team members
- Specific performance goals
- Mutual accountability
- Open and honest communication

"Team members will bond together through their similarities, but it is through their differences that they will learn from each other."

The basic elements of a team do not just happen. It takes thought and a commitment to work together. Working together involves acceptance and respect for individual differences. In many instances, the strength of the team actually comes from these differences. Team members will bond together through their similarities, but it is through their differences that they will learn from each other.

Five Stages of Team Development

Teams will go through several stages of development. Newly formed teams will have communication patterns that are different from a more mature team. It takes time and energy to make a team work. Five stages of team development will be presented in this section. It is important to understand the characteristics of each stage so teams will be able to identify their stage of development and recognize progression or regression to other stages. The stages include:

- Forming
- Storming
- Norming
- Performing
- Ending

Forming

Communication during the forming stage is uncertain, polite, and guarded. Trust is the major issue facing the team at this stage. Team members are just learning about each other and testing the waters. They need to have confidence that they will not be embarrassed in front of the team when presenting their thoughts and ideas. It takes time and favorable experiences within the team to develop trust. Members look for common threads among each other. These commonalities help to begin establishing a bond.

A priority during the forming stage is to get everyone involved and interested in achieving the team's goals. Greater involvement can be achieved if team members are clear about the team's purpose and goals, and they can see some personal gain in being involved in the team. During this stage, the leader takes a more active role in facilitating the team's work. The leader serves as a role model by setting an atmosphere for trust to build. Leadership begins to be shared by all team members as a basic level of trust builds among the team.

> ***"Once initial trust is established, there is some conflict in the storming stage as members attempt to find a place for themselves in the group and begin to function within the established norms."***

Storming

Once initial trust is established, there is some conflict as members attempt to find a place for themselves in the group and begin to function within the established norms. This stage is uncomfortable compared with the previous stage. There is conflict about the goals and the best way to reach them. As the team struggles with issues related to who will do what and how, some heated debate may occur. While this stage is uncomfortable, it is essential to the development of how the team will work to accomplish the task.

In the storming stage, members are testing whether the ground rules or expectations really work. They want to know whether it is acceptable to express their opinions and have their ideas acknowledged. This is not an easy stage for anyone, especially the leader. The leader tries to keep the team together and focused by maintaining open lines of communication. Helping members look beyond their personal concerns toward working collaboratively with the team members is essential in moving to the next stage.

Norming

In this stage, conflicts are resolved and group cohesion starts to develop. Members are accepting of each other. Becoming a valued member of the team is very important to all team members. The team is able to concentrate on issues as they relate to the accomplishment of its goals. Members understand the rules of the game and how to interact with each other. Trust continues to develop during this stage. Members begin to confide in each other and appear more genuinely friendly.

Performing

During the performing stage, team members agree on the roles each person plays on the team. Personal needs and the needs of the association are brought together. This makes the team's tasks much more interesting and members feel energized. Communication reflects cooperation rather than competition. Members feel more open in discussing their thoughts, feelings, and ideas. They ask for and give feedback freely. Group cohesion and morale are at their highest peak.

"In the performing stage, group cohesion and morale are highest, and the team completes its goals."

Leadership within the team is shared. The team is no longer solely dependent on the identified leader, although the leader maintains an active role in providing the structure for the work to get done. The team completes its goals during this stage.

Ending

This is the final stage of team life in which the team focuses on summarizing its accomplishments and completing any unfinished business. This stage is characterized by feelings of excitement and sadness. Members are excited about their accomplishments, but sad about leaving the team. It is important at this phase for the leader to remind team members that the cohesion and sense of accomplishment felt by the group are the direct result of active steps the team took to make things happen.

During this phase, the team looks at the significant things that happened, both positive and negative. Thanking each other for the significant contributions each person made is important. Any plans for follow-up are identified. Working through any unfinished business or less than positive feelings among members at this stage can make the difference in whether a person is willing to become involved in future team work. Effective team endings are just as important as effective team beginnings.

All teams will experience each of these stages. It is a development process similar to growing up. We cannot just skip from being an infant to being a school-age child. The toddler stage serves as a bridge from one stage to the next. The same is true with team development. When an existing team experiences a loss or change in its members, the team may revert back to a previous stage because even the addition of one new person will change the composition of the team. However, since the team has had experience at a more advanced stage of development, once the new member is acclimated, the team will be able to move fairly quickly through the stages and once again resume the level that it once achieved. This movement, though, is dependent on the number of new members joining the team, how they are oriented and enculturated into the team, how well their expertise blends into the team, and the quality of the relationships that are established.

"Most boards experience transition every year as new board members are elected and join the leadership team. It is important that new board members are not only assisted in learning their new role, but are also welcomed and oriented to the board's culture."

Most boards experience transition every year as new board members are elected and join the leadership team. It is important that new board members are not only assisted in learning their new role, but are also welcomed and oriented to the board's culture. One or a few new board members will change the board's culture. While "new blood" is good because it brings new ideas and opportunities, some existing board members may feel saddened or frustrated because a new culture means change and the board may have become very comfortable with the way it was. New board members should be aware of this transition period and realize that it is temporary until the board is once again able to achieve a sense of stability.

Roles of Team Leader and Team Members

In any given team, there are essentially two types of roles – team leader and team member. In an association, the team leader would be the board or committee/task force chairperson and the team members would be the board or committee/task force members. This section will briefly discuss the responsibilities of each role.

Team Leader

The leader of the team performs most of the functions that other team members do, but has additional responsibilities as well. The leader provides direction and guidance to the team so it can accomplish its goals. The leader is concerned with both the relationships among team members and getting the tasks accomplished. As the team matures, several members within the team share the leadership role at various times depending on the situation and the expertise of the team members. Shared leadership is welcomed within the team as long as it is collaborative and not competitive. Competition with the identified team leader can actually sabotage team work.

The team leader is the formal communicator within and outside of the team, often serving as the team's spokesperson. The leader helps the team know what is going on and keeps it on track. The leader also drives the work of the team by facilitating group decision making, preparing agendas for team meetings, conducting team meetings, keeping the ball rolling in the right direction, and assisting the team in the assessment of its progress.

"The team leader provides direction and guidance so the team can accomplish its goals. The leader is concerned with both the relationships among team members and getting the tasks accomplished."

The team leader role can be compared to the role of an orchestra conductor. The conductor and the orchestra are responsible for a good performance. The conductor's role is to make sure that all of the musicians are on the right sheet of music, and the right note, at the right time. Together the orchestra plays in harmony. The conductor doesn't play the instruments for the musicians, but coordinates group effort and expects every musician to be accountable for their part of the performance.

Team Members

Team members are responsible for their behavior and they share the responsibility for accomplishing team goals. They accept responsibility for the success or failure of the team's work. To function effectively, all team members need to cooperate with each other and assist the leader in conducting efficient and productive meetings.

Team members are brought together because they have expertise to share. The purpose of grouping these individuals together is to generate new ideas or perform work that would not be possible from one individual alone. Therefore, team members are expected to contribute their thoughts, ideas, and expertise to the team. Differences of opinion should be welcomed, respected, and encouraged. There will be times when team members are given an assignment and expected to report back to the team. Careful preparation of this report for presentation to the team is expected of the team member.

Effective teams focus on balancing the team's task with maintaining healthy working relationships among its members. Accomplishing the task and maintaining the relationship cannot happen without effective team communication. In an effective team, there is trust, open and honest communication, respect for differences, and a sense of cohesion. All members of the team are responsible for communicating effectively. When new members join the team, the best way to gain trust is to demonstrate competence by accepting responsibility, delivering results, and keeping commitments. Test your team member skills by answering the questions in Tool 1 in the Tool Kit at the end of this chapter.

"Time, energy, and money can be wasted on faulty decisions that are made through the process of groupthink. This form of decision making discourages critical evaluation of ideas and alternative solutions to problems."

Potential Problems With Teams

Teams are not perfect, nor are they the answer to everything. While there are many more advantages to working in teams than disadvantages, at times problems occur in team work. While communication problems may lead the list in problems with teams, those issues will be covered in the Effective Meetings chapter. This section will focus on two other potential problems - groupthink and subgroups.

Groupthink

While cohesiveness is necessary for effective group functioning, teams can become too cohesive. Cohesiveness can be carried to an extreme in which team members feel pressured to conform to ideas and decisions with which they may not agree. Members may feel that loyalty to the team and approval of other team members are more important than expressing an opinion that is different from the team, or they may think they are off target and are unwilling to express their thoughts. This is called "groupthink."

Following is an example of a typical groupthink situation that occurs at board meetings. A board member presents a proposal from the Education Committee to develop an independent learning module on a particular topic. The proposal is well written and the board member is very articulate in presenting it. Most board members are not very interested in the topic of this module and do not think the members would be very interested either. However, only one person speaks against the proposal. The other board members do not think it is acceptable to speak against it since the member who proposed it did a lot of work in helping the committee prepare it and was very enthusiastic about the project. The proposal is approved. Afterwards, the board member who spoke against the proposal asked a few of her colleagues for their rationale for approving the proposal. Her colleagues stated that they really did not understand the purpose or value of the proposal, but since everyone else seemed to go along with it, they did also.

The above situation continues...The module is completed and promoted to the membership. At the end of one year, only five members out of 2000 were interested in purchasing the module. As the board members talk about the project, they realize that no one, except the person who proposed it, was really in favor of it. The board was not surprised that the module did not meet the members' needs. No one thought it was a good idea right from the beginning! But the board thought that everyone was in favor of it and no one wanted to rock the boat. Time, energy, and money can be wasted on faulty decisions that are made through the process of groupthink.

With groupthink, the team tries to maintain harmony above all else. This form of decision making discourages critical evaluation of ideas and alternative solutions to problems. Everyone goes along with a decision because they are afraid of the possible consequences of speaking up. Preventing groupthink begins with an awareness that it can happen and be destructive to the team.

A culture of inquiry within a team should include a healthy debate where diverse views and perspectives are encouraged. The team learns that nobody is as smart as everybody, and the collective wisdom of all members of the team is more powerful than the voice of one (Hockman, 2008). The team should agree to always work through problems by critically analyzing them. A team member taking on the role of devil's advocate may also prevent the team from getting stuck in groupthink. Keep in mind, the devil's advocate should be a different person for each situation.

Subgroups

If the team does not meet the needs of some members, these members may feel anxious, frustrated, or rejected. They may split off from the team and form a small subgroup. Most teams will experience this to some degree. The split may become helpful or harmful to the team. If the subgroup becomes secretive, its members bond tightly to the subgroup and connections with the team loosen. These bonds have a powerful negative effect on the productivity of the team as a whole.

When a subgroup begins to disrupt the team, the situation needs to be placed quickly on the agenda and discussed. Feelings and thoughts need to be aired. If the team engages in open and honest confrontation, it can resolve the problem. Trust can be enhanced and team members can gain new skills in dealing effectively with confrontation. The opposite can happen also. The situation could be ignored, swept under the carpet, and alienation from the team brews. This sabotages the team's efforts and leads to its destruction.

Boards are prone to subgroups just like any other team. Sometimes subgroups form among a few board members because these individuals find they have a lot in common and think along the same lines. While this is positive, they may carry it a bit too far. They may constantly be together at the association's functions, sit next to each other in board meetings, plan activities and not invite others, talk on the phone often between board meetings, and seem to get on each other's bandwagons when their issues are raised at board meetings. These board members lose out on the value of what working as a team means – all members working and "playing" together. The board as a whole also loses out on the valuable contributions the subgroup could be making with the board.

"With the team concept, team members have the opportunity to learn how to get along better with people by focusing on what is really important – accomplishing the team's purpose. Working together to accomplish the team's purpose is the common goal of all members."

Since time is a precious commodity today, there is not enough time for splintering among board members. It wastes time and energy that could be used more productively. The membership expects board members to work together as a unified team to accomplish the goals of the association. As trustees, board members need to evaluate their behaviors and act in the best interests of the members.

One important point to remember is that teams are composed of people and people behave in different ways. Some teams may have members who simply do not want to be team players or perhaps they do not know how. Others have members who do not get along with each other. With the team concept, team members have the opportunity to learn how to get along better with people by focusing on what is really important – accomplishing the team's purpose. Working together to accomplish the team's purpose is the common goal of all members. Team members may not like each other, but they can learn to at least get along because the association's members are depending on them.

Steps for Building a Team

A team may get started in a variety of ways. This section will discuss how to build a team from beginning to end. Some of the actions may not be appropriate for all teams. This section will be especially valuable for a board member who is forming a new group or task force, or who is coaching a new committee or task force. It is also valuable for a chairperson who is forming a new committee or task force.

Preparation

Someone, usually the leader of a group, begins to prepare for the development of a team. The overall purpose of the team is used as a guide for the type of team members to select, the group size, where, when, and how to meet initially, recruiting members, and preparing members for the team experience. If members of the team can be selected, it is best to select individuals who have the capability to help the team meet its goals. Members should have enough in common to feel comfortable with each other, and also be different enough from each other so there is a variety of ideas and viewpoints. The key to member selection is getting the right people on the bus who can accomplish the team's purpose.

To be effective, a team should include enough members to carry out its tasks and to support the personal relationships needed to achieve the team purpose. A group size of five or six is ideal, but may increase to nine and still maintain a workable size. Larger-sized groups may compromise productivity.

> ***"This section will be especially valuable for a board member who is forming a new group, committee, or task force. When selecting team members, keep in mind that members should have enough in common to feel comfortable with each other, and also be different enough from each other so there is a variety of ideas and viewpoints."***

First Meeting

An agenda is prepared, if appropriate for the first meeting. The leader contacts team members and tells them about the group, its purpose, why they were selected for the team, and what their role will be. It also gives the person a chance to decline the invitation if unable or not interested in the team. It is helpful to find out a good meeting day and time for each person. The length of meetings should be scheduled to meet the needs of the team and to accomplish its purpose. Once team members are selected, the meeting date, time, and place are selected. The leader informs the members of the meeting and tells them how to prepare for it. A final agenda is developed and given to each team member.

The first team meeting usually focuses on getting acquainted with team members and the purpose and goals of the team. Team members introduce themselves to each other and talk about their positions and their specific reasons for joining the team. The leader may identify the various roles individual members may play within the team.

Since the team shares a common purpose as its reason for existing, it is important that all team members discuss and are clear about the purpose. The purpose will guide the remainder of the team's work. From the purpose, the team can begin developing its goals and specific action steps to meet the goals. Together, the team plans its work.

"Since the team shares a common purpose as its reason for existing, it is important that all team members discuss and are clear about the purpose."

Developing Team Expectations

With a purpose and some direction of where it is going, the team then focuses on how it will maintain an effective relationship among its members. Ground rules, or expectations, for group behavior are determined. Developing expectation statements can be a powerful way to build strong work relationships among team members. It also provides a framework for acceptable and unacceptable behaviors. Unclear expectations can break down communication and trust.

Expectation statements include behaviors that are:

- Observable – we can see them happening.
- Achievable and stated in a positive way.
- Reviewed frequently to be certain they are still current and being followed.
- Important, meaningful, and real to the team members – these behaviors must be lived.

It takes time, thought, and effort for the team to collectively develop expectations. Expectations may avoid misunderstandings and problems down the road. Once expectations are developed, the group needs to look them over carefully and agree to behave accordingly. The team should discuss what it will do if a member or a few members do not adhere to these expectations. Most teams decide on a way to confront individuals who do not "follow the rules."

Your association may have board member expectations, guiding principles, or work agreements for successful board work and relationships.

Examples of expectation statements for team members and the team leader are found in Table 5-1.

Table 5-1
Expectations of Team Members and Team Leaders

Expectations of Team Members
We expect team members to...
1. Be honest in interactions; say what they mean and mean what they say. 2. Be on time for meetings, come prepared, pay attention, and participate in discussions. 3. Voice concerns if they disagree with a decision or approach and be willing to participate in finding an alternative. 4. Be committed and share in the responsibilities of the work of the team. 5. Be willing to try new ideas, make mistakes, and learn from the experience. 6. Be visible, approachable, and member-concerned. 7. Be willing to give and receive constructive feedback. 8. Acknowledge and honor individual differences.
Expectations of Team Leaders
We expect the team leader to...
1. Keep informed and knowledgeable of issues and activities within and outside the team to provide team cohesiveness. 2. Respect confidences of team members. 3. Meet the expectations of a team member. 4. Treat all team members in a fair, objective, and unbiased manner. 5. Organize team meetings and provide direction to assure that goals are accomplished.

Source: Nowicki, 1998.

Subsequent Team Meetings

The team will continue to conduct its business until its goals are accomplished. It needs to stay focused on two things – the task at hand and the relationships among its members. Both are necessary to be productive and accomplish the goals. The team also needs to keep in mind that it will go through the stages of team development. It is a good idea at various times to put "progress check" on the agenda for a meeting. During this progress check, members can discuss how well they are progressing with the task, whether they are on track, if goals are being met or if they need to be revised, and how relationships among team members are going. Tool 2 in the Tool Kit at the end of this chapter contains questions that will assist in conducting a progress check.

Disbanding the Team

When the team's goals are accomplished, it may terminate its existence or it may determine new goals and continue. The team must make sure its accomplishments along with follow-up recommendations are reported to the appropriate people. The team may be asked or volunteer to take the project further, or it may decide to disband. Other teams may be long term in duration and develop new goals to accomplish their purposes. Terminating a team is as important as initiating it. Remember to celebrate accomplishments!

> *"The leadership team is composed of the elected volunteer leaders and the executive staff. Together these individuals form a partnership that leads the association's efforts."*

Section 2: The Leadership Team

The team development information in the first section of this chapter can be helpful as the new board member becomes a productive and effective member of the association's leadership team. The leadership team is composed of the elected volunteer leaders and the executive staff. Together these individuals form a partnership that leads the association's efforts. This section will discuss the critical importance of the board and staff relationship and define the roles of those individuals who are primarily responsible for leading and building the team partnership.

Board and Staff Partnership

Carver (2006) states that there is no relationship in the association more important than the partnership between the board and its executive staff. This relationship, if well conceived and nurtured, can set the stage for effective leadership – both governance and management. The opposite is also true. Boards and staff that do not have a strong partnership place the association and its goals in jeopardy. The association simply will not grow and achieve its true potential if the board and staff are not working together harmoniously.

The foundation for a strong board and staff partnership is trust. Each party must make a genuine and sincere effort to understand each other and each other's roles. Understanding leads to confidence and confidence in turn leads to trust. Trust must be based on the understanding that each party will act in the best interest of the association, not to fulfill self-interests. When the level of trust between staff and volunteers is low, the entire association is affected as the tension is sensed by its members. Boards and staff have an obligation to work together as partners to truly act in the best interest of the association.

The board and staff partnership is a very finely balanced relationship. The balance is maintained when both partners understand and accept their separate roles and the importance of working together interdependently. There is mutual respect that is real and genuine, not forced and controlled. Both partners realize and appreciate the different gifts that each person brings to the relationship and they trust in each other's competence. The partners are committed, caring, and willing to contribute to the limits of their ability. Each has a different role to perform but when brought together the results are far greater than each could have achieved separately.

"Boards and staff have an obligation to work together as partners to truly act in the best interest of the association. Each partner must be committed and want the relationship to succeed, and be willing to invest the time, effort, and energy needed to make it work."

An effective relationship is collegial, not hierarchical. Each partner respects the power and role of the other. Collegiality is much easier to achieve when both partners get along well with each other, although it can and must exist in any event. Even in the best of circumstances, the board and staff will experience periods of frustration and strain with each other. A certain degree of tension is expected and even may be helpful, if there is a foundation of trust and mutual concern, an appreciation for the ambiguity of both positions of leadership, and a genuine concern for serving the best interest of the association.

There are no magic prescriptions for ensuring a healthy board and staff relationship. A successful partnership is hard work. Each partner must be committed and want the relationship to succeed, and be willing to invest the time, effort, and energy needed to make it work. A successful partnership needs constant attention and nurturing to sustain it.

As the board and staff work together, each interaction has the potential to build and strengthen the relationship. Both share in the responsibility of successfully completing their work together. Each partner acts as a coach, cheerleader, and mentor for the other, and synergy is created. This takes place in a caring atmosphere where risk is encouraged, mistakes are expected, and the partners learn together from their successes and their mistakes.

Each partner feels safe from ridicule or failure because both are committed to each other's success.

Boards and staff who are truly committed to building and continuously developing their partnership can best serve their associations by following the guiding principles of effective relationships (found in Table 5-2).

Table 5-2
Guiding Principles for an Effective Board and Staff Relationship

- The relationship must be characterized by mutual trust, openness, and transparency.
  ...trust that each partner will act in the best interest of the association.
  ...openness and sharing, not withholding of information, concerns, feelings, expertise, and points of view.
  ...transparency demonstrated by operations that are conducted in an open manner that others, including the members, can observe and evaluate.
- The relationship should be based on mutual recognition and respect for the unique contributions that each member brings to the team.
- Both partners must be committed to the idea that working together leads to a synergistic relationship which is more effective and productive than either party could achieve working alone.
- The board is the responsible legal party of the association. It selects and employs/contracts with the staff executive/management firm.
- The board and staff each have their own roles and responsibilities. Sometimes there is overlap when the relationship is strong and individuals are working together to get the job done. The board and staff need to respect each other's roles and trust in each other's competence.
- The board chairperson is the chief elected officer of all policy groups (board and committees).
- The staff executive is the chief staff officer responsible for all aspects of managing other staff that serve the association.

Source: Hardy, 1990.

Leadership Team Member Roles

An effective partnership involves everyone working together as a leadership team and being accountable for individual responsibilities as well. One of the most important activities in building a partnership is the understanding of how each member of the team fits into the total picture of the association. Each member has an important contribution to make to the total success of the team, and knowledge of members' roles is essential. Chapter 2 discussed in detail the role of the board and board members. Therefore, this section will not discuss board member roles. It will focus on another critical partnership that must exist between the board chairperson and the staff executive, and the individual role responsibilities of each position.

"The board chairperson and staff executive work to advance not only the association, but the profession it represents as well."

Board Chairperson and Staff Executive Partnership

The relationship between the board chairperson, often referred to as the president of the association, and the staff executive, often carrying the title of executive director or chief executive officer, is critical to board performance. While the board chairperson is the steward of the association's mission and direction, the staff executive is at the helm daily to steer the association and its staff in that direction. Together, these partners work to advance not only the association, but the profession it represents as well – assuming that the two partners work together effectively. A strong working relationship can be created if both partners are willing to invest the necessary time and effort.

The board chairperson and staff executive must balance their distinct roles and share power and authority. These individuals emerge as the principal leaders who accept the responsibility of making sure both the work of the board and staff gets accomplished. They communicate frequently and jointly make the necessary decisions to run the association in between board meetings.

The relationship between the board chairperson and staff executive begins as soon as the board chairperson receives the election results or the appointment. While these two individuals have most likely worked together in the past, the relationship changes once the board chairperson assumes the top leadership position. The relationship becomes much closer and more intense given the greater responsibility the board chairperson is assuming.

Getting to know each other's work styles and expectations is important to begin this vital partnership. The chairperson might visit the headquarters office, if that has not yet happened, to meet other staff and observe how the day-to-day operations of the association are managed. Occasional social interactions to build the human interest side of the relationship are also important.

> ***"The relationship established between the board chairperson and staff executive sets the tone for achieving goals and has an immense influence on the effectiveness of the association."***

The relationship established between the board chairperson and staff executive sets the tone for achieving goals and has an immense influence on the effectiveness of the association. If the board chairperson energizes the board and establishes a strong partnership relationship with the staff executive, things happen and the association moves forward. The relationship needs to be understood and respected by other board members and staff. Sometimes board members and staff do not understand this relationship and feel resentment toward the amount of time these individuals spend together. They may feel also that too much information is shared between the board chairperson and staff executive. Both partners need to discuss the importance and context of their relationship with the board and staff, especially with new board members so misunderstandings are not created and then brewed.

Working together most effectively involves the board chairperson and staff executive assuming accountability for fulfilling their individual responsibilities. It is important also for board members to understand the individual role responsibilities of these individuals so they know what to expect in the performance of these roles.

Role of the Board Chairperson

The board chairperson position is one of prestige and recognition. It is also one of power and authority, as the individual is responsible for leading and guiding the efforts of the board. The association's board chairperson must be visible, involved, and approachable. This person must attend social functions and association meetings and interact with the members. To encourage full participation from the board and members, the board chairperson must listen well and be unbiased and neutral in approaching people and situations. The board chairperson must also possess effective leadership skills. Other responsibilities of the board chairperson are listed in Table 5-3.

Table 5-3
Responsibilities of the Board Chairperson

Responsibilities of the Board Chairperson
1. Leads the board in creating and achieving the strategic direction of the association.
2. Presides at all meetings of members and the board of directors. Coordinates an agenda with meeting attendees and the staff executive.
3. In concert with the staff executive, keeps the board informed on the issues affecting the association and pertinent operations.
4. Works collaboratively with the staff executive to oversee that policies and programs are planned, formulated, presented to the board, executed following board approval, and appropriate follow-up is planned.
5. Understands, supports, and defends policies and programs adopted by the membership and the association's leaders.
6. Promotes interest and active member involvement in the association's business through various written communication avenues and presentations.
7. In collaboration with the staff executive, acts as the spokesperson for the association to the press, public, legislative bodies, and other associations.
8. Presents an annual report to the membership on the state of the association.
9. Oversees the work and activities of the board, committees, and task forces.
10. Works with the staff executive in developing the leadership skills and potential of the board. Mentors the next board chairperson.
11. Serves as a leadership role model to the board and members. Cultivates effective leadership that paves the way for interested and competent successors.
12. Offers continuing praise and appreciation to those who work to accomplish the association's mission.
13. Makes the position appear within the reach of others so that potential leaders are able to see it as a job that can be done.

Source: Nowicki, 1998.

Role of the Staff Executive

One of the most important roles of a board is the selection of its staff executive; in some cases, the association management company selects this person. Therefore, while the selection may be important, the establishment of an effective relationship is even more important. A first step in establishing this relationship is understanding the role of the staff executive and how it relates to the functioning of the association.

The staff executive, otherwise known as the executive director or chief executive officer, is the person responsible for managing the operations of the association. The operations include managing other staff and any external outsourcing that may be done.

"The staff executive is a vital member of the leadership team and is responsible for managing the operations of the association. This person reports to the board and often advises the board on policy options."

The staff executive is a vital member of the leadership team. This person reports to the board and often advises the board on policy options. However, it is the board's ultimate responsibility to determine policy. The board's responsibility with the staff executive is to establish a trusting, partnership relationship, support the staff executive's initiatives, evaluate the staff executive, and hold the staff executive accountable. The staff executive should provide the board with enough information to keep the board informed, but not to encourage the board to become overly involved in day-to-day operations or micromanagement. Boards should have enough confidence in their staff executives' leadership to allow them to carry out the responsibilities for which they were hired or contracted to do.

The staff executive is the board's bridge to the rest of the staff. This position allows the board to focus on the strategic direction of the association and not become involved in the intricate details of management. Sometimes the staff executive's role becomes blurred, and board members think this person is in charge of the association. While the staff executive holds a high-level position and is "in charge" of the association's management, he or she reports to the board which is the ultimate decision maker.

Overall, the staff executive's role will be very similar from association to association. The specific functions or responsibilities may vary depending on each association's structure and resources. Some associations are large enough to have their own offices and staff. There are various departments within the headquarters office and the staff executive is administratively responsible for each of these departments. Other associations choose to contract with an association management company that provides a variety of services such as administration, conference management, association and corporate marketing services, education services, Internet and information services, and art and printing services, to name a few. The staff executive in this type of arrangement will serve in a team leader role, coordinating the effort of several services.

Other responsibilities of the staff executive are summarized in Table 5-4 (next page).

Table 5-4 Responsibilities of the Staff Executive	
Advisement	• Acts as a professional advisor to the board in leading and managing the association. • Recommends appropriate programs and policies for consideration and implements them as designated by the board. • Accurately informs the board on the status of the association, programs, services, and external influences. Brings meaningful information and data-based evidence to the board on significant issues. • Provides timely information when unacceptable situations occur, along with strategies for dealing with them. • Assists in the identification of member needs and recommends programs and services. • Makes recommendations for solving problems or resolving issues faced by the board. • Supports the board chairperson in achieving a positive and productive experience in the position.
Strategic Planning	• Works collaboratively with the board in establishing strategic direction and developing strategic plans. • Assists the board in accomplishing the goals set forth in the strategic plan. • Maintains consistency in implementing the strategic plan as board turnover occurs. • Participates in the review and evaluation of the plan.
Personnel	• Recruits, interviews, hires, supervises, develops, evaluates, and disciplines staff. • Determines staff salaries, promotions, benefits, and pensions.
Fiscal Management	• Develops, monitors, and reports on the operating and other special budgets according to the association's policy. • Facilitates the payment of all invoices and the accurate accounting of all transactions. • Recommends ways to increase revenues and decrease expenses. • Facilitates financial growth through an appropriate investment plan. • Works with an association-selected accounting firm for periodic audits or financial reviews.
Record Keeping	• Establishes and maintains a system for keeping the association's records. • Retrieves records when requested by members or regulatory agencies.

Table 5-4 (continued) Responsibilities of the Staff Executive	
Legal	• Obtains legal counsel for the association as needed. • Facilitates the development and maintenance of contracts and agreements.
Communications	• Obtains and maintains the technology and systems for electronic and written forms of communication. • Keeps apprised of advances in technology that will enhance the association's ability to communicate and offer programs and services in an efficient and cost-effective manner. • Oversees the mail distribution for the association. • Oversees the publications of the association, both print and electronic communication materials.
Meetings	• Works with the board chairperson to plan and implement effective board meetings. • Oversees coordination of and attends all association and board meetings. • Prepares meaningful and understandable reports as appropriate.
Membership Services	• Oversees the development and implementation of the programs and services offered to members. • Develops and implements marketing plans for specific products and services (i.e. education programs, books, videos, etc.).
Recruitment and Retention	• Develops and implements marketing plans for the ongoing recruitment and retention of members. • Monitors recruitment and retention efforts and related data. Provides a summary of activities and data to the board.
Performance Management	• Develops and oversees a performance management strategy to ensure quality customer service and delivery of value-added programs and services. • Maintains accountability for quality performance outcomes.
Supplies	• Purchases, obtains bids, authorizes, stores, distributes, and maintains inventories of supplies.
Facilities/Equipment	• Obtains and maintains adequate facilities to conduct the association's operations. • Supervises rentals, purchases, sales, maintenance, and refurbishing of facilities and equipment.

Source: Adapted from Nowicki, 1998.

Summary

The concept of team work is inherent in the effective functioning of an association. This chapter provided information for new board members to enhance their understanding and skills in being a team member, in addition to coaching an existing team and starting up a new one. Team development skills are vital in associations and in our personal lives as well. Life is abundant with opportunities to work with others to accomplish a task or goal.

This chapter also discussed the critical partnership relationship that must develop and be nurtured between the board and staff. Boards and staff that develop a strong partnership will lead their associations successfully into the future. Through a synergistic relationship, board and staff support each other, respect each other's competence, and work together as partners to help each other rise to a higher level of functioning. They learn from each other and achieve more together than either could achieve independently. The key is knowing one's responsibilities and being accountable for them.

CHAPTER 5 TOOL KIT

Teamwork and the Board-Staff Partnership

The following tool kit contains resources that have been mentioned throughout this chapter.

- ★ Tool 5-1 How Do You Rate as a Team Member?
- ★ Tool 5-2 Team Progress Check

Download this Tool Kit online at www.ajj.com/mentoring — Use password MTS2E989

Tool 5-1
How Do You Rate As A Team Member?

Assess your team member skills by answering the following questions. Check Yes or No in the column at the right. For open-ended questions, write your response following the question.

For any No responses, determine ways in which you can improve your skills.

Questions	Yes	No
1. Do you understand, support, and feel ownership of the team's goals?		
2. Are you willing to put the team's goals ahead of your own?		
3. Do you listen to everyone on the team?		
4. Do you listen to hear and understand the other person's point of view?		
5. Do you communicate openly and honestly with your team members?		
6. Do you begin to establish trust by trusting, and support by supporting?		
7. Do you respect and value the differences of your team members?		
8. Do you know what your team members expect from you?		
9. What do you expect from your team members?		
10. Do your team members know your expectations of them?		
11. Do you take the time to get to know your team members?		
12. Do you participate in team decision making and support the decisions of the team?		
13. In problem solving, are you part of the solution, not the problem?		
14. Do you value and use the expertise and strengths of your team members?		
15. Do you contribute your expertise and help your team members learn?		

Source: Adapted from Harper, A., & Harper, B., 1992.

Tool 5-2
Team Progress Check

Answer the following questions by checking Yes or No in the column at the right. For open-ended questions, write your response after the question.

Questions	Yes	No
1. Are we using our purpose to focus and guide our work?		
2. Are we accomplishing our goals through the steps of our action plan(s)?		
2.1. What is helping us to stay on target?		
2.2. What is causing us to stray off target?		
3. What stage of team development are we in? (Circle the stage) Forming Storming Norming Performing Ending		
3.1. How are we doing in this stage?		
3.2. Did we have any trouble getting to this stage?		
4. Are we having problems with communication?		
4.1. If yes, describe the problems with communication.		
5. Are we solving our problems and making decisions?		
6. Have we experienced groupthink?		
7. Do we have subgroups?		
7.1. If yes, how are they affecting us?		

Tool 5-2 (continued)
Team Progress Check

Questions	Yes	No
8. Are our team meetings efficient and productive?		
8.1. Are our meetings convenient for everyone?		
8.2. Are we having any problems with meetings?		
8.3. If yes, describe the problems with meetings.		
9. Is everyone participating in the team's work?		
10. Is the team leader accountable for his/her responsibilities?		
11. Are team members accountable for their responsibilities?		
12. Are we meeting our team expectations?		
13. Overall, how well is our team doing?		
14. What are our strengths?		
15. What do we need to improve?		
16. How are we celebrating our progress to this point?		

Learning Assessment

Chapter 5: Teamwork and the Board-Staff Partnership

Reflect on the knowledge you gained from this chapter by responding to the following statements and questions. Some of the statements suggest topics for you to discuss with your mentor. This chapter may also have prompted other thoughts and questions to discuss with your mentor.

1. Answer the questions in Tool 1 (in the Tool Kit), "How do you rate as a team member?" What are your strengths and areas for improvement as a team member?

   Strengths — Areas for Improvement

2. Complete the Team Progress Check (Tool 2 in the Tool Kit). Based on your response, describe your team's (i.e. the board's) strengths and areas for improvement.

   Strengths — Areas for Improvement

3. After answering question 2, discuss your responses and thoughts with your mentor. Discuss any recommendations you may have for team development.

4. This question is best answered after you have attended at least one board meeting. What type of relationship exists between the board and staff? What are the positive and negative aspects you observed about this relationship? Also, discuss your observations and thoughts with your mentor.

5. Set up a time to talk with the staff executive. This is a good opportunity to build a partnership relationship and for the executive to get to know you a little better. Discuss the executive's role in your association. Also discuss the executive's expectations of board members.

6. As you talk with your mentor, discuss how you might share the information from this assessment with the board.

Chapter 6

Strategic Thinking and Planning

Key Points

- Strategic Thinking
- Strategic Planning
- Board's Role in Strategic Planning
- Strategic Planning Framework (Mission, Vision, and Values)
- Eight Steps of the Strategic Planning Process
  • Plan the Process • Survey and Collect Data • Analyze Data • Build Consensus • Formulate Strategic Priorities, Goals, and Objectives • Develop Strategies and Tactics • Implement Strategies • Evaluate Progress and Effectiveness
- Strategic Management
- Problems Experienced with Strategic Planning

Tables

- Table 6-1 Questions Answered with Strategic Planning
- Table 6-2 Board Member's Role in Strategic Planning
- Table 6-3 Questions for Determining Strategic Priorities
- Table 6-4 Suggestions for Implementing the Strategic Plan
- Table 6-5 Questions for Evaluating the Strategic Planning Process
- Table 6-6 Annual Strategic Plan Evaluation

Mentoring Opportunity

- Learning Assessment

Download the Chapter 6 Tables and Learning Assessment online at www.ajj.com/mentoring — Use password MTS2E989

"Strategic planning, a vital component of an association's work, is a process of building a vision and determining the means for reaching it. To keep ahead, remain competitive, and grow, we must be proactive and plan for our future."

At one point or another all of us have been involved in some type of planning, whether it was planning an education program, planning to restructure our work setting/processes, or planning a wedding. What all of these activities have in common is that they involve making plans for something that is yet to come. Not knowing what the future will bring creates opportunities for us to envision a program or event the way we would like it to be and develop plans to make our vision a reality. This is strategic planning – a process of building a vision and determining the means of for reaching it.

Strategic planning is a vital component of the association's work. In today's dynamic, complex, and sometimes chaotic environment, strategic planning is a necessity. To keep ahead, remain competitive, and grow, we must be proactive and plan for our future. Associations that fail to plan ahead are likely to miss opportunities to expand and grow. Falling out of touch with the changing needs and demands of our members and the environment in which they function is a sure way to passively create the demise of our associations. In fact, if the association is not changing as fast as its members' world, then the board is not doing its job.

Board members are responsible for the leadership of the association, and this includes establishing direction. One important direction-setting process is strategic planning. To contribute effectively to the development and ongoing evaluation of the strategic plan, board members must understand the strategic planning process, how to use the plan to keep it a viable and working document, how to communicate it to all constituents, and how to regularly evaluate it. Strategic planning cannot be taught; the process must be experienced and lived in the form of strategic thinking on an ongoing basis.

Strategic Thinking

Strategic thinking is a precursor to strategic planning. Strategic thinking is the way in which people in an association think about and create the future. It is a proactive process that focuses on how to create a better future by developing a vision for the intended results and enhancing the value proposition for members and stakeholders. Strategic thinking is very flexible and fluid; it happens on a day-to-day basis. For boards, the result is that every time the board and staff get together, they do so for the purpose of strategic thinking (Tecker, et al, 2002).

Strategic thinking involves using intuition and insight. Leaders spend their time as strategic thinkers, not planners. Strategic thinkers start with what could be, as opposed to what is. Strategic thinking focuses on finding and developing unique opportunities to create value by enabling creative dialogue throughout the association, especially among those who can affect or will be affected by the association's direction.

> ***"Strategic thinking involves using intuition and insight. It focuses on finding and developing unique opportunities to create value by enabling creative dialogue throughout the association."***

As a democratic process, strategic thinking allows everyone an opportunity to champion their ideas and exert influence based on the quality of their views or ideas rather than their place in the hierarchy. Brilliant ideas can surface from anywhere and the strategic thinking board is just waiting for them to surface. This board is open minded and willing to listen. Board members spend their time together expanding a new idea instead of discussing the details of a plan. They progressively become the architects rather than the general contractors or the tradesmen (Chait, Ryan, & Taylor, 2005).

Strategic thinking is not easily compartmentalized because anyone can generate new ideas anywhere, without the confines of a line of authority. This has implications for the role of the board and its relationship with the workforce, both volunteers and staff. The board's role shifts from monitor to partner. The committee structure is also based on strategic priorities rather than the traditional organizational chart. More task forces are formed to work on the priorities, then they disband.

Board agendas look different. The board and staff think strategically together to discover strategic priorities. They use comparative data that are linked to strategic priorities and often use the data to rethink strategy. There is less time spent on reporting and "how to" details and larger concentrated blocks of time are carved out to engage in dialogue about the future or issues of strategic importance.

Strategic thinking skills develop over time with repeated use. Boards that think strategically do not have to come up with the answers, only the intelligent questions. They know and trust that there are plenty of other volunteers and members who can provide the answers to those questions. All they need to do is ask.

As board and staff become more strategic in their functioning, their thinking elevates to a higher level and strategic thinking begins to integrate into the association. They focus on the ends or the outcomes rather than the means for getting there. Chait et al. (2005) state that leaders are no longer in the details; they are in the clouds. Details are delegated to the workforce. Strategic thinking boards also focus on the external environment, how the association can impact it, and how the environment might impact the association.

> ***"Strategic thinking is creative thinking that challenges conventional wisdom and the status quo. It creates change and others in the association may need to unlearn previous ways of thinking and performing."***

Strategic thinking provides input into the strategic planning process. Effective strategic thinking will discover potential opportunities for creating new value, so when the strategic planning process begins, these opportunities become part of it. Strategic thinking is creative thinking that challenges conventional wisdom and the status quo. It creates change and others in the association may need to unlearn previous ways of thinking and performing. Strategic thinking also incorporates systems thinking in which relationships among the various parts of the association are identified.

Although strategic thinking is a precursor to strategic planning, it does not imply that all boards engage in strategic thinking prior to participating in the strategic planning process. Strategic thinking is a process that develops over time, often when the individuals involved have reached a level of understanding of how to create a vision, develop a strategic plan to reach toward that vision, and mobilize the workforce to accomplish the strategic goals. Through the experience of strategic planning and direction setting, the board and staff learn to think differently. Strategic thinking is an evolving process that eventually permeates throughout the association.

Strategic Planning

Strategic thinking paves the way for a more formal process of strategic planning. A strategic plan conveys where the association is going, its destination, and the means for getting it there – the road map. Development of the plan takes a lot of time and energy and involves a large number of individuals who have a stake in the success of the association. The actual strategic planning document will differ from association to association. No two plans look alike and the length of the document is not an indication of its worth. Shorter plans are more likely to be read and used than are plans that go into enormous detail. Some plans are so lengthy that you get exhausted before you have had the chance to finish reading them, let alone before beginning to implement them.

Effective strategic plans are simple, user-friendly, clear in intent and direction, and are inspiring and motivating to those who are charged with creating and implementing them. While the strategic plan is the ultimate outcome of the strategic planning process, we cannot lose sight of the importance of the process of planning for and developing it. Strategic planning takes time, effort, and an enormous amount of critical and creative thinking.

"Effective strategic plans are simple, user-friendly, clear in intent and direction, and are inspiring and motivating to those who are charged with creating and implementing them."

Strategic planning is critical for all businesses, but especially for associations that experience a frequent changing of the guard. Boards whose leaders change each year can change the association's focus every year to every few years because of the new faces and ideas. While new blood is good, an association needs some stability in its direction. A strategic plan provides this stability and helps the boards, especially new board members, in getting and staying on track.

Why Strategic Planning?

Strategic planning can help an association set its course and maintain it even in the midst of uncertainty. When properly conducted, strategic planning can be very effective and powerful. Strategic planning answers questions such as those found in Table 6-1.

Strategic planning will affect all aspects of the association including members, volunteers, staff, supporters, programs and services, recruitment and retention efforts, technologic and communication systems, finances, and public relations. Given the impact of this process, effective planning depends on the collection and analysis of accurate information from both within and external to the association. Some aspects of the plan will have an immediate effect, while others will be longer term in nature.

Obtain a copy of your association's strategic plan and refer to it as you read this chapter.

Table 6-1
Questions Answered with Strategic Planning

- What is the association's mission? Why does it exist? What are the compelling reasons for the association's continuing existence?
- Who cares if we exist? What would happen if we no longer existed? Who would meet our members' needs?
- What vision does the association hold for its future?
- What are the association's values?
- What does the history of the association tell us about our identity?
- Who are the association's stakeholders? Who does the association serve?
- What are the needs of our members/customers?
- What programs and services does the association provide for its members? How effective are they? What programs and services should it provide in the future?
- Who benefits from these programs and services? How might these individuals change in the future? How will these changes impact the association? How could the association respond to these changes?
- What are the opportunities and threats posed by influences external to the association?
- What are the association's strengths and limitations? What is its capacity?
- Given the environment surrounding the association and the association's strengths, where should it concentrate its efforts to carry out its vision for the future?
- What are the association's strategic priorities for the given time period?
- What are the association's objectives and strategies that will accomplish the vision and strategic priorities?
- What performance measures will be used to track progress in meeting the strategic priorities and goals?
- What efforts will be made to revise these priorities as changes occur and new opportunities arise?
- How will the strategic plan be communicated to all constituents?
- What resources will be needed and how will they be mobilized? How will the volunteer and staff workforces be aligned to accomplish the goals?
- How will we integrate the strategic plan with our budget and ongoing operations?
- How will the association evaluate its strategic planning efforts?
- How will the association conduct periodic evaluations of the plan and its outcomes? How will the plan be updated?
- What will success look like and how will we celebrate it?

Source: Adapted from Park, 1990.

Board's Role in Strategic Planning

Strategic planning is conducted in myriad ways throughout various associations. In some associations the board is primarily involved in the strategic planning process. In others, a committee or task force is charged with the responsibility of formulating the plan and presenting it to the board. Whatever the process, the board needs to understand the critical nature of its role in guiding the strategic direction of the association and in ensuring alignment of all constituents with that direction. It is imperative that board members and the executive staff understand thoroughly all components of the strategic plan, communicate its direction at every opportunity, support the plan, and be committed to it. Without board and staff commitment, the plan will die on the shelf or in someone's file cabinet. Refer to Table 6-2 for a summary of the board member's role in strategic planning.

Table 6-2 Board Member's Role in Strategic Planning
1. Know what the plan means, all components of it.
2. Support the plan, including the goals and objectives that make the plan a living document.
3. Communicate the plan to others.
4. Support those who assist in carrying out the plan.
5. Monitor and evaluate progress.
6. Participate in revising the plan as needed.
7. Participate in developing a new plan, when appropriate.
8. Scan the environment to determine what is changing in the members' world and beyond.
9. As new ideas surface, question how they fit into the plan or suggest ways for how the plan could be modified.

Strategic Planning Framework

The framework for strategic planning includes the association's mission, vision, and values. Through these structures, the association determines its direction, its purpose, and its foundation. Strategic planning begins with the vision, mission, and values. Associations that do not have these components defined will need to develop them during the planning process or prior to it. For those associations with these elements, the strategic planning process will begin with a recommitment to them or a revision of the statements if conditions have changed since their development.

> ***"The mission is the fuel, the vision represents the destination, values help to guide our behavior, and the strategic plan is the road map to achieving the vision."***

Mission

The mission is the purpose or driving force behind why the association exists. It defines the association in regard to its members and other constituents, its programs and services, its roles and functions, and the value it brings to its members and other constituents. A mission is long standing and is at the heart and soul of what the association does. A mission provides direction for making strategic decisions, developing a plan of action, defining ways to measure success, searching out important opportunities, making choices about needed resources, and satisfying the association's members and other constituents.

Vision

A vision is a picture of a preferred future. It is positive and inspiring. A strong vision will shape the association's future. It will challenge individuals to stretch the boundaries of their usual creativity. A vision serves the interests of its members and must be real enough that progress toward reaching it can be achieved. A vision guides decision making and aligns the association's actions with its mission and values.

Values

Values are the association's beliefs and principles that guide its planning and operations. They provide an ethical framework from which behaviors and actions are judged. Values may include such things as honesty, integrity, accountability, family, compassion, and caring, to name a few. They serve as controls that informally allow or forbid our behaviors. They are deeply engrained and timeless. Shared values are one of the essential elements of a strong association.

Value Proposition

Although value proposition is not a term often found in a strategic plan, it is an important component and outcome of strategic planning. The value proposition is the benefit that members perceive to receive from the association. It is the reason they belong, their return on investment. The value proposition answers the questions: "What is my benefit from joining the association?" or "What's in it for me?" The value proposition is often embedded in the association's mission (Gallery & Waters, 2008).

Eight Steps of the Strategic Planning Process

The essential steps in the strategic planning process include the following:

1. Plan the process
2. Survey and collect data
3. Analyze data
4. Build consensus
5. Formulate strategic priorities, goals, and objectives
6. Develop strategies and tactics
7. Implement strategies
8. Evaluate progress and effectiveness

Step 1: Plan the Process

The key to effective strategic planning is the up-front time spent in planning for the entire process. Many associations today conduct their planning sessions every 3-5 years with an annual progress check and evaluation. During the year prior to the plan's intended expiration, the association needs to begin planning for the next strategic planning process. Often associations will contract with a consultant to assist with planning the process and facilitating it.

External facilitators skilled in strategic planning are often preferred because they bring a fresh, objective perspective to the planning process. Also, the association's leaders and staff can participate in the process rather than be charged with leading it. Facilitators can offer their expertise in several processes needed to organize and develop a plan such as skills in group process, conflict resolution, leadership development, questionnaire design, action planning, and performance measurement. These facilitators are most effective if they are involved early on when the planning efforts are being initiated. Hiring a facilitator at the last minute will not, in most instances, produce a quality strategic planning effort. Both the facilitator and the association lose the benefits of the prior planning that is essential to the strategic plan's success.

> ***"The board chairperson and staff executive, or other designated volunteer leaders, should begin the planning process by outlining who needs to be involved, what needs to be done within time frames, what outcomes are anticipated, and how the planning process will be carried out."***

Can strategic planning be accomplished without a consultant or facilitator? Yes. Some boards have incorporated strategic thinking and planning as an ongoing process of governance. Other boards may determine that they are satisfied with their current goals and decide to tweak their strategies instead of reinventing the plan. The bottom line is that it doesn't really matter who leads the strategic planning effort as long as the organization uses a sound process for planning strategically for its future.

The board chairperson and staff executive, or other designated volunteer leaders, should begin the planning process by outlining who needs to be involved, what needs to be done within time frames, what outcomes are anticipated, and how the planning process will be carried out. Some associations charge a committee to work out the details of the planning process. Whoever does the planning needs to report its progress regularly to the board.

Stakeholders. One of the first steps in planning is determining who will be included in the strategic planning process and at what points they will be involved. The process of strategic planning will affect all the association's members and other constituents and supporters. These individuals are considered stakeholders because they have an investment in the association's future success.

Stakeholders may include members, potential members, employers, board members and other leaders, staff, programs and services recipients, associate organizations, subsidiaries, funding sources, suppliers, competitors, legislators, and colleagues from a related association. Many associations also include a representative from the consumer group that ultimately benefits from the association's product or service. For example, with professional nursing associations, a patient may be asked to participate in the association's strategic planning.

Step 2: Survey and Collect Data

The purpose of this step is to survey the environment to determine its current state and future possibilities. This step is often referred to as environmental scanning, and focuses on the environments both internal and external to the association.

Internal survey. It is important to look inward and realistically evaluate the association's strengths and weaknesses in its current state. Historical data are also beneficial because they help the association in realizing how far it has come. Valid strategic data may be gathered from various sources and through various methods including formal reports, focus groups, questionnaires, and interviews, to name a few. Information should be gathered in the areas of human resources, finances, technology, communication systems, management, leadership, programs and services, member recruitment and retention, member satisfaction, organizational structure, physical facilities, and public image/public relations. Information from potential saboteurs would also be important to gather.

"It is important to look inward and realistically evaluate the association's strengths and weaknesses in its current state. The external environment also impacts an association by forces that influence it, threaten it, provide it with stability, and provide it with opportunity."

The internal survey may also include forward projections and benchmarks comparing the association to similar associations. An assessment of progress on current goals is also important. Too often this component is neglected in strategic planning. Some planners try to wipe the slate clean and start from scratch, thereby missing out on the value of current goals and the positive feelings of accomplishment in having met the goals or in being in the process of meeting them.

External survey. Associations are affected by their external environments as well. To truly understand how an association functions, one must look at the larger picture created by the external environment. This external environment impacts an association by forces that influence it, threaten it, provide it with stability, and provide it with opportunity. An external survey helps the association focus on both the opportunities and threats posed by the external environment. In surveying the external environment, data are needed in the areas of economics, demographics, new legislation, changes in political leaders, social forces, environmental issues, funding and economic sources, competitors, current and potential collaborators, and new developments in the field or profession. It is also helpful to scan what other similar associations are facing and planning to do.

Step 3: Analyze Data

Once the data are collected from the previous step, they are analyzed and most often collapsed into a few broad categories. The analysis step is a vital component of strategic planning because it is in this phase that a large amount of information is brought together, sorted out, and summarized in a way that has meaning for the association and creates knowledge. An informative and concise documentation of the data makes it easier for the strategic planners to analyze and use this information. These data should be provided prior to the strategic planning meeting so participants can begin analyzing the data and formulating their thoughts for discussion.

"Determining strategic priorities is frequently the most difficult step in strategic planning because it is often hard to focus attention on one activity or function over others."

Step 4: Build Consensus

Many associations will bring identified stakeholders together to discuss, dialogue, and participate in creating the strategic direction. This meeting is the creative step in strategic planning because it envisions possible futures and generates energy among participants.

It is important to allow participants adequate time to think, analyze, and discuss options prior to developing the plan. The desire to get a document completed as quickly as possible often relegates thinking to simply filling in the space on a work sheet. The more participants are involved in creative and critical thinking, the more emotional and intellectual energy they will invest. This investment leads to a high probability that buy-in and successful implementation will occur.

Step 5: Formulate Strategic Priorities, Goals, and Objectives

After surveying the internal and external environments and analyzing the data collected, strategic priorities are then determined. The association's mission and vision are used as the guiding forces for determining the priorities. At this point, the mission and vision may be reviewed, revised, or the planners may choose to recommit to them. Decisions about the future are made by selecting a few strategic priorities.

This is frequently the most difficult step in strategic planning because it is often hard to focus attention on one activity or function over others. No step in the process is more important than concentrating on making the best use of the association's resources by determining a few vitally important priorities. When determining the strategic priorities, it is helpful to ask the questions found in Table 6-3.

Table 6-3
Questions for Determining Strategic Priorities

What are the most urgent or compelling issues that must be addressed?
For each of the issues, answer the following questions:

- What are the financial implications?
- What human resources (volunteers or staff) are required?
- Is there a group that is already working on this priority? If so, would we be duplicating its efforts?
- How will the members perceive value in this priority?
- What are the long-term implications of implementing this priority? What will be the consequences of not implementing this priority?

Source: Nowicki, 1998.

Selecting a small number of well-thought-out priorities or goals, usually between four to eight, helps the association focus on those items that are truly considered vital and will bring value to the members and the association. Once strategic priorities are determined, they need to be formulated into goal statements. Try not to get distracted by the terminology since each association uses its own set of terms. Keep in mind the strategic plan is a communication vehicle. What works for each association is what the association should use as long as the intent is clear to those who will implement and use the plan.

The following terms are consistent with those used in a study to determine consensus guidelines for strategic planning in associations conducted by Gallery and Waters (2008).

Goals. Developing goals will help the association in operationalizing the strategic plan. A goal is one step toward reaching the vision. It is a target point or stop along the way to the destination. The association needs to think about where it is today in regard to a specific topic or priority, then decide where it wants to be in 3 to 5 years. The association needs to decide what it should do to bridge that gap between now and then. This is the beginning step in setting a goal.

A goal is a desired outcome, a target, or a result. It states what we want to achieve. Goals must be realistic and challenging. They also must reflect the mission and strategic direction of the association. It is helpful to determine a few words to reflect the goal such as knowledge source, advocacy, education, or community. A goal statement would then be developed to further define the meaning of the goal:

> *"A goal is a desired outcome, a target, or a result. It states what we want to achieve. Objectives are key metrics that will affect the association's ability to meet the goals and the choice of direction in which to move."*

Goal Statement Example

Goal: Evidence-Based Practice (EBP) and Research

Professional Association will increasingly advance the art and science of the profession through evidence-based practice and research.

Strategic goal statements need to be written simply so they are clear and understandable to everyone. They should be written so there is little room for misinterpretation. If the goal is set today, one month from today any board member should be able to pick up the strategic plan and remember exactly what that goal means. If not, the goal statement is not clear enough and should be reworked.

Objectives. Once goals are established, objectives to achieve each goal are identified. Objectives are key metrics that will affect the association's ability to meet the goals and the choice of direction in which to move. They may begin with terms such as increase, decrease, expand, enhance, and develop. Objectives are measurable and realistic. There may be several objectives for each goal.

Using the above goal of Evidence-Based Practice and Research, the following objectives were developed to meet the goal:

Goal: Evidence-Based Practice (EBP) and Research

Professional Association will increasingly advance the art and science of the profession through evidence-based practice and research.

Objectives:

- Increase the availability of resources to promote evidence-based practice.
- Expand the association's capacity to support and conduct research.

The strategic plan often consists of the mission, vision, values, goals, and objectives. Once the plan is developed, it is helpful to share this phase of strategic planning with other leaders and staff to elicit their input and critique. Some associations share the plan with the membership and create opportunities for feedback from those who will benefit from the plan.

Step 6: Develop Strategies and Tactics

An annual plan (e.g., business or operational plan) will include more specific ways to achieve the goals and objectives such as strategies and tactics or action steps, along with the financial resources to support the goals. Most strategies are developed by the workforce such as committees, task forces, and staff.

"An annual plan will include more specific ways to achieve the goals and objectives such as strategies and tactics or action steps, along with the financial resources to support the goals."

Using the Evidence-Based Practice and Research goal example, the following strategies were determined to meet the objectives:

Objective 1. Increase the availability of resources to promote evidence-based practice.

Strategy: Enlist the Research Committee to develop an ongoing process to continually provide new and updated EBP information and resources.

Objective 2. Expand the association's capacity to support and conduct research.

Strategy: Enlist the Research Committee and Foundation to collaborate on offering a $5,000 grant for an EBP project related to the specialty.

Each strategy is developed or assigned to a workgroup (i.e., committee, task force, staff) to develop an action plan for implementing the strategy. The plan would include the strategic goal, objective, and strategy. The workgroup would determine the tactics or action steps, accountability, and timeframe. The workgroup would be held accountable for the action plan and would use the plan to evaluate its results and report it to the board.

Most associations have standard templates for action plans and board reports. These tools are used to demonstrate how the association's leaders are performing in the direction of the strategic plan. They also keep the strategic plan foremost in their minds.

Measuring Objectives and Strategies. When measuring objectives and strategies, it is important to keep in mind that not everything can be measured quantitatively (i.e. in numbers). Often the quantitative measurements provide only a partial indication of the true value of an outcome. Services offered to members, such as education and learning, are often things that cannot be measured with numbers alone. For this reason, it is a good practice to use a variety of performance measures to track progress on each objective. Excellent qualitative measures are provided in reports from members and other stakeholders regarding the quality and value they are receiving.

"The board should focus on the resources needed and available to implement the strategies. It needs to consider the overall operations of the association that often account for 80% of the association's work, and how the strategic plan objectives and strategies fit into the big picture."

Recap. Sometimes the terms mission, vision, strategic plan, goals, strategies, and tactics become confusing and jumbled. Here is a recap of what we just discussed.

- **Mission** is the association's purpose for existence.
- **Vision** is a picture of where the association should be at a given point in time in the future.
- The **strategic plan** guides the association in the direction of its vision.
- **Strategic priorities** are determined and worded into **goal** statements.
- **Objectives** are derived from the goals and provide metrics for achieving the goals.
- **Strategies** are developed as specific steps to meet the objectives.
- **Tactics** are the specific action steps that volunteer groups or staff would use to accomplish the strategies.

Step 7: Implement Strategies

Once the strategic goals and objectives are developed, the board looks critically at the plan to determine if all of the goals and objectives are compatible and not conflicting with each other and with the vision. All objectives need to be linked to the vision, mission, and goals. The board needs to ask the critical question, "If we implement these goals and objectives, will we meet or at least create a significant stretch toward our vision?"

The board needs to focus on the resources needed and available to implement the strategies. Budget planning needs to be linked to the strategic plan so there is monetary support for these strategic efforts. The board also needs to consider the overall operations of the association (e.g., existing programs and services, affiliates, etc.) that often account for 80% of the association's work, and how the strategic plan objectives and strategies fit into the big picture. Once these components are considered, the implementation phase begins.

In the implementation phase, the board's role in establishing direction is essentially complete. However, now the board is responsible for making sure the plan is communicated to all who will be involved in the implementation of the plan and contribute to its achievement. Aligning key individuals and holding responsible parties accountable for their portions of the plan are the next steps. Board members use the plan in guiding the workforce, inspiring them to achieve the association's mission and vision, and recognizing and rewarding those who contribute to goal achievement. They provide the tools and resources necessary for implementation of the strategic plan.

The plan is also communicated to the members and other stakeholders in a way that is meaningful and demonstrates the value that will be received as the plan is implemented. Suggestions for implementing the plan are provided in Table 6-4 (next page).

Table 6-4
Suggestions for Implementing the Strategic Plan

1. Establish an operating budget that provides the financial resources necessary to achieve the goals and objectives of the plan.
2. Communicate the strategic plan to all constituents through the association's publications at local and national meetings, and through other communication vehicles. Determine how to involve key local and committee leaders in achieving the strategic goals. Assist them in developing tactics and action plans.
3. Communicate the plan to other associations with a similar focus to determine potential collaborative efforts in achieving shared goals.
4. Communicate the plan to corporate and industry leaders who may be interested in contributing financial support for achievement of various aspects of the strategic plan.
5. Involve staff in all phases of strategic planning. Since staff will be responsible for implementing various phases of the plan, it is important to allocate resources so staff members will have the tools to accomplish their work.
6. Designate the board chairperson or other appointed volunteer leader to lead the implementation efforts and keep the strategic plan on track.
7. Use the plan to drive the leadership and management of the association including committee structure and activities, performance standards and appraisals, budget, staffing, recruitment and retention activities, the association's image, and programs and services.
8. The strategic plan is just that, a plan. While the goals and objectives remain fairly constant throughout the life of the plan, the strategies and tactics are fluid and can be changed as conditions change. As new opportunities arise, they should be evaluated as to their importance to the mission and their place in the strategic plan. If the new opportunities are determined to be strategically important, the strategic plan should be altered.

Source: Adapted from Nowicki, 1998.

Step 8: Evaluate Progress and Effectiveness

The strategic planning process is one of the most important activities in which an association engages. Table 6-5 provides a list of questions to evaluate the strategic planning process. If the planning process is based on data and knowledge, involves several levels of volunteers, members, staff, and other stakeholders, and is transparent in its development, it has a great chance of success. While the process can be lengthy and sometimes challenging, it can be extremely effective for ensuring the future of the association.

Table 6-5
Questions for Evaluating the Strategic Planning Process

- Was adequate planning done to prepare for the process?
- Did the internal and external survey provide helpful information on which to base the plan?
- Did we analyze the data appropriately?
- Are the strategic priorities and goals truly important?
- Are the goals clear and challenging?
- Will the objectives and strategies help us achieve the goals?
- Are we clear on how we will measure our goals and objectives?
- Are all goals and strategies compatible with each other?
- If we accomplish the goals, will we reach our vision and fulfill our mission?
- Does our implementation plan contain steps to communicate the strategic plan to our constituents, hold everyone accountable for their portions of the plan, inspire us to meet our goals, and recognize and reward all who contribute to achieving the plan?
- How and when will the strategic plan be evaluated? What reporting system have we established to document our results? Is it effective?
- If used, was the consultant/facilitator effective?
- What would we do differently next time?
- Did we develop a plan that is important and meaningful, makes sense to everyone, and will lead us in the direction we envision?
- Is the intended outcome of the plan to ensure that members will receive value that will enhance their business or practice?

Source: Adapted from Nowicki, 1998.

Progress toward accomplishing the association's strategic goals and objectives should be evaluated at least annually. Periodic reporting is very helpful to determine if implementation strategies are on track or if a reassessment is needed. Evaluation should be done especially during times of outstanding problems or as new opportunities present themselves. The board should be open to confront new opportunities and alter the plan if necessary. It should also evaluate components of the plan that may not be servicing the association as they were originally intended. While the plan provides direction and stability for the association, it is not rigid and unchangeable. The plan belongs to the association and only the association can determine its value and effectiveness.

"While the strategic plan provides direction and stability for the association, it is not rigid and unchangeable. The plan belongs to the association and only the association can determine its value and effectiveness. The board should be open to confront new opportunities and alter the plan as necessary."

An annual strategic plan evaluation provides an association with the following benefits:

- Determines if it is on the right path and if the plan is working
- Provides an opportunity to give feedback on the overall plan's progress to the volunteer and staff workforces
- Provides the basis for an annual report to the membership about how value is created for them
- Holds the workforce accountable since they are responsible for reporting their progress
- Holds the board accountable for its primary roles of setting direction, ensuring resources, and evaluating performance and outcomes
- Provides direction for next steps
- Validates the work of the association and creates opportunities to celebrate successes

A large component of the annual evaluation is focused on assessing if strategic goals and objectives are achieved. Current goals and objectives are evaluated according to whether they have been completed, are in progress, or have had no action taken to date. The board rewards and celebrates accomplishments and determines the impact of those achievements on the association. For objectives in progress, actions taken are summarized and future steps identified. For objectives with no actions taken, explanations are discussed along with factors that prohibited any action. Keep in mind that the purpose of the strategic plan is to be a living document over a period of time and it is not intended to be completed within one year. In some years, no intended action may be taken on various goals and objectives.

The last step in the annual evaluation is to determine the next steps. New objectives or strategies may be added based on new opportunities or issues. Other objectives or strategies may be deleted as they are completed or no longer relevant. Table 6-6 provides an example of questions for the annual evaluation of the plan (next page).

Table 6-6
Annual Strategic Plan Evaluation

Evaluate each goal of the plan according to the following questions.

1. General Status of the Goal
   Have all of the objectives been achieved?
   ☐ Achieved
   ☐ Partially Achieved
   ☐ Not Achieved

2. Progress Toward the Goal
   How satisfied are we with the pace of progress?
   ☐ Very Satisfied
   ☐ Satisfied
   ☐ Unsatisfied

3. What conditions in the internal and/or external environment have changed related to this goal (environmental scan)?

4. What has worked in executing the strategies and tactics related to the objectives of this goal?

5. What has NOT worked in executing the strategies and tactics related to the objectives of this goal?

6. Were adequate resources provided to achieve this goal?

7. What recommendations, if any, should be made to modify the strategies related to this goal? What are the next steps?

Source: Adapted from Frankel, 2008.

Strategic Management

Creating an effective strategic plan is one component of the governance and strategic management of an association. The strategic plan needs to be integrated into the operations of the entire association. The plan does not include everything the association does by any means. In fact, the plan may consume 20% of the association's resources while the other 80% of the resources involves the ongoing programs, services, and operations. With some associations, the strategic plan is so over-emphasized that the other components take a back seat.

Strategic management is a process that involves applying strategy to all aspects of the association. It includes strategic thinking on an ongoing basis, strategic planning, budgeting and financial management, operational planning and implementation, quality improvement, and continuous performance measurement. Strategic management involves a systems thinking approach where all components of the association that are systematically connected need to be considered along with the strategic plan.

Problems Experienced with Strategic Planning

The strategic planning process has its share of problems and pitfalls. Some associations think strategic planning is dead and archaic. In some instances, it can be. Usually the problems are related to inadequate preparation for the process, poor selection of individuals to lead and participate in the process, lack of creative energy and buy-in, negative prior experience, lack of adequate resources for implementation, inadequate communication and oversight of the plan, and certainly shelving the plan as soon as it is developed. Other plans are given so much priority that little emphasis is spent on the programs, services, and operations that are responsible for a majority of the association's current value proposition.

Gallery and Waters (2008) identify the following pitfalls with strategic planning:

1. Inadequate preparation prior to the planning process. Associations need adequate time, resources, and information to make important strategic decisions.
2. Validating the status quo. Some associations develop a plan that essentially contains what they are already doing as opposed to capitalizing on the planning to push the association out of its comfort zone.
3. No metrics or accountability. Some plans are very broad and don't contain measurable objectives, and therefore no accountability tracking.
4. Focusing on how to accomplish the objectives rather than ensuring that the right objectives are developed and clearly stated.

5. A broad plan without execution strategies. Plans must be carried out and monitored.
6. Capacity is not considered. Plans are developed without considering the resource allocation necessary to implement them.
7. The board does not buy into the plan. Perhaps the board does not understand the plan, has hidden agendas, or simply does not know how to execute it. Without active board support, the plan will fail.

"The creative energies and brain power at work during a strategic planning activity ultimately create a document that serves the association for several years."

Summary

Strategic planning is a process that attempts to create a visionary, yet realistic plan for a future that is full of change, uncertainty, and at times chaos. While it may sound like an impossible task, strategic planning can be one of the most interesting and rewarding opportunities in which a board member participates. It has many benefits both for the association and the individual. The planning process combines the collection and analysis of myriad pieces of information not normally collected at one time by an association. It brings together the creative ideas and dreams of various individuals who are committed to the association's future. It involves a thorough look at the various forces within society that can impact the association. The strategic planning process also creates a learning experience and team building activity for all the individuals involved.

Creating the future is exciting and fun. It is also hard work. The creative energies and brain power at work during a strategic planning activity ultimately create a document that serves the association for several years. The process builds the board's knowledge of the association and its internal and external environments. This knowledge assists the board in making future decisions on the important issues that impact the association's mission, vision, and goals.

The process also enhances strategic and systems thinking, key components of the board's role in leading the association. This chapter described the steps of the strategic planning process that will help the new board member prepare for, participate in, and oversee the implementation and evaluation of a multi-year strategic plan.

Learning Assessment

Chapter 6: Strategic Thinking and Planning

Reflect on the knowledge you gained from this chapter by responding to the following statements and questions. Some of the statements suggest topics for you to discuss with your mentor. This chapter may also have prompted other thoughts and questions to discuss with your mentor.

1. Based on what you read about strategic thinking, observe your board to determine the extent to which it engages in strategic thinking. Discuss with your mentor how you might learn more and contribute to the board's evolution to this level of thinking.

2. You are talking with one of your friends in the association who is not a board member. He refers to an item in the newsletter that states the board will conduct a strategic planning session six months from today. He does not understand strategic planning but is very interested in the process and how it will help the association. Based on what you learned about strategic planning, how would you describe the process to your friend?

3. Look at your association's strategic plan. If your association does not have a strategic plan, look at the association's goals. Is the information clear, understandable, and attainable? What questions do you have about the plan/goals? Discuss your questions or thoughts about the plan/goals with your mentor so you understand the plan in enough detail to communicate it to others.

4. How does your association implement its strategic plan/goals? How is it communicated, documented, and evaluated? Discuss this information with your mentor.

5. Become familiar with those areas of the plan that are most relevant to your role on the board. For example, you may have been assigned liaison responsibilities to a committee or task force. Discuss any questions you may have about these areas of the plan with your mentor.

6. Given your association's strategic plan/goals and your role on the board, write two goals that you feel you can focus on personally to assist the association in achieving its goals and vision. Write strategies for how you may accomplish these goals. How will you measure their achievement? Consider discussing your goals with your mentor and what type of assistance you may need in meeting them.

Chapter 7

Budget and Financial Management

Key Points

- ★ Board's Fiscal Responsibility
- ★ Treasurer's Role
- ★ Finance and Audit Committees
- ★ Budget Process
- ★ Financial Statements
- ★ Reserves
- ★ Investments
- ★ Financial Audits and Reviews
- ★ Tax Exempt Status
- ★ Signs of Financial Distress

Tables

- ★ Table 7-1 Annual Operating Budget
- ★ Table 7-2 Statement of Assets, Liabilities, and Fund Balances (Balance Sheet)
- ★ Table 7-3 Statement of Revenues and Expenses
- ★ Table 7-4 Interim Report
- ★ Table 7-5 Statement of Cash Flows
- ★ Table 7-6 15 Signs of Financial Distress
- ★ Table 7-7 Questions to Determine Sound Financial Position

Mentoring Opportunity

- ★ Learning Assessment

Download the Chapter 7 Tables and Learning Assessment online at www.ajj.com/mentoring — Use password MTS2E989

> *"It is the board's responsibility to work with the staff executive in developing a budget plan that coincides with and supports the strategic plan and the general operations of the organization."*

We deal with budgets and financial matters daily in our lives, yet many of us do not adequately understand the process very well. When it comes to budget and financial or fiscal management, there are two kinds of people:

- Those who really enjoy working with numbers and understand the process, and
- all others.

Many of us fall into the second category. While we know that managing budgets and other financial matters is important and vital to our financial survival, we would rather leave those functions to the people who fit into the first category.

Board members are responsible for the financial viability of an organization. Most likely, there will be some board members who fall into the first category of people who are good at numbers. We hope, at least, the treasurer will be one of those people! Whether board members fall into the first or second category, they will need to learn about how their specific board conducts its financial business. Each board and its financial processes and forms are unique.

This chapter will present basic information about budgets and finances that are applicable to all nonprofit boards. The forms and processes may differ, but the general concepts are the same across a majority of associations.

Board's Fiscal Responsibility

One of the board's major functions is to establish direction for the organization's future. While establishing direction involves developing a strategic plan with goals and objectives, it also involves ensuring that adequate resources are available to carry out the work. All plans need financial resources to some degree. It is the board's responsibility to work with the staff executive in developing a budget plan that coincides with and supports the strategic plan and the general operations of the organization.

Throughout the fiscal year, Berry (2008) states that board members are expected to:

- Receive timely financial statements—read them thoroughly and know what they mean
- Approve an operating budget for the upcoming year
- Approve an audit or review for the prior year
- Monitor the investment reports and ensure there are sufficient funds in reserves to cover unanticipated downturns

Board members must understand the organization's financial position to function effectively in their roles. It is the individual board member's responsibility to gain a sufficient level of comfort and understanding of the numbers. This takes time and new board members must ask questions of the treasurer and/or the staff executive until they feel comfortable in interpreting the financial picture. Often, after the budget report is given at a board meeting, there is a period of silence. Some interpret this silence as agreement with the report. However, many times board members simply do not fully understand the report; sometimes it is "over their heads." They are not sure what to say or what questions to ask. Members do not want to appear "dumb," so they do not say anything. This is fine if they do not have anything to say; however, if they do not understand the budget, they need to ask questions. Others in the room probably have the same questions on their minds. Remember, asking questions to obtain clarity is a board member's responsibility.

> ***"Board members must understand the organization's financial position to function effectively in their roles."***

The Sarbanes-Oxley Act, referred to as SOX, was passed in 2002 after the scandals and collapse of such companies as Enron, Tyco, and others. The act was intended to promote greater accountability, disclosure, and transparency to improve public trust in publicly traded companies. It essentially tightens the reigns on the disclosure and oversight of accounting practices, financial statements, audits, and internal controls related to reporting of financial information. While the act increases the responsibility of corporate boards in providing oversight of financial reporting, it has implications for nonprofit boards as well. Boards need to focus on accuracy in financial reporting, make sure they understand financial reports, ensure transparency in reporting financial information to members and stakeholders, ensure credible auditing practices, and be aware of internal controls.

> ***"There is a delicate balance that must be maintained between operating at a net gain and operating at a net loss."***

Financial statements are the major tools used by boards to exercise proper fiscal accountability and to assure that finances are in order. Order refers to financial integrity and financial performance. Integrity refers to the finances being sound, complete, and adhering to accounting standards. Financial performance, on the other hand, is satisfactory if, on average, the organization at least breaks even. In some years, the organization may generate a reasonable amount of revenue to provide the capital it needs to accomplish its work and provide a cushion for unanticipated circumstances. In other years, a net loss is tolerated, especially if the organization embarks on a major project that it anticipates would take significant capital. There is a delicate balance that must be maintained between operating at a net gain and operating at a net loss.

Associations that consistently generate a large surplus of revenues may be questioned as to whether they are providing the quality and quantity of services that the members or other contributors have a right to expect. Some members may think, if the organization is "putting away" so much money, either they are being charged too much for programs and services, or perhaps they are not getting enough for their investment. On the other hand, associations that consistently operate at a loss will undoubtedly go bankrupt. Again, it is a delicate balance that must be monitored.

While the board is ultimately responsible for ensuring the financial viability of the organization and its programs, there are usually several people involved in managing the organization's finances. The staff keeps the books and manages the day-to-day financial matters. The staff executive allocates budgeted funds in the most effective way possible according to the objectives set forth by the board. The executive also closely monitors the budget, oversees the preparation and accuracy of the financial statements, and works closely with the treasurer to ensure the integrity of these processes. The treasurer is the link between the board and the financial records, even if staff is keeping the books.

Treasurer's Role

The board's treasurer is responsible for ensuring the following:

- Appropriate financial records are maintained
- Actual revenues and expenses are compared with the approved budget, and variances are recognized, explained, and corrective action taken as necessary
- Periodic financial reports are given to the board and membership
- Required financial reporting forms are filed with the appropriate agencies

The treasurer presents the financial reports to the board using a common sense approach, explaining variances, and focusing on the most important components of the reports. Board members should understand the financial forms well enough to spot significant variances in the revenue or expense categories. A variance is a discrepancy between the dollars budgeted and the dollars received or spent. For revenues, a positive variance (over budget) is good if it means there are excess revenues as compared to the projected revenues. However, a positive variance (over budget) on the expense side is probably not good because more money was spent than what was budgeted.

"A variance is a discrepancy between the dollars budgeted and the dollars received or spent. The treasurer and/or staff executive should provide explanations of significant variances. Board members also should ask questions related to those items of significance."

The treasurer and/or staff executive should provide explanations of significant variances. Board members also should ask questions related to those items of significance. What variances are significant? Usually variances of eight to ten percent of the budgeted dollars are significant and should be explained. However, board members should not waste time on details and insignificant items. For example, a board is discussing a report on a $1 million budget at its board meeting and one category of the budget is contingency fund. A sum of $100 was recorded as expensed in this category. A board member asks what the $100 was spent on. Most likely, no one will know this answer off the cuff, even the staff executive who handles the day-to-day finances. Another board member asks if this information is really significant given the scope of the entire budget. The board member who asked the question realized she was stepping into micromanagement. The board needs to trust that the treasurer, board chairperson, and staff executive have done their jobs and have a handle on the finances, unless there are significant signs to the contrary.

Finance and Audit Committees

Many associations delegate certain financial duties to designated committees, such as budget and finance or audit committees. These committees have specific functions as determined by the board. They perform their functions and report directly to the board. Finance committees must exercise the same care as the board in refraining from micromanaging the organization.

"A budget is a guide to help the organization operate within its means. It is structured enough to provide direction, yet flexible enough to be changed as priorities and conditions warrant."

Budget Process

The operating budget is a plan for the financial direction of the organization, often a one-year plan. Since it concerns events that have not yet occurred, it makes suppositions, conveys intentions, and designs the flow of monies that are needed for the organization's operation. It is important to note that a plan does not mean a rigid, unchangeable document. Rather, a budget is a guide to help the organization operate within its means. It is structured enough to provide direction, yet flexible enough to be changed as priorities and conditions warrant.

Although the board has the ultimate responsibility for the budget, nothing dictates how a board should control the budget or its policies and processes. Each organization has a unique structure for its budgeting process. In some associations, the staff executive handles the largest share of drafting the budget. The executive then consults with the treasurer and together they develop drafts of the budget prior to its presentation to the board. In other associations, budget preparation is a joint process between the treasurer, president, staff executive, or other designated persons. Some associations assign this task to their budget committees. Whatever structure the board determines for its budget process, the people that should be involved are those who have the competence to prepare it.

Before any numbers are put down on paper, the board must consider its strategic direction and priorities. These goals drive the budget; the budget in most instances should not drive the strategic direction.

While it is true an organization cannot embark on new programs if it does not have the resources with which to do so, relying only on a projected budget could stifle any creative ideas for new revenue sources to support new projects. Also, before any numbers are put down on paper, many associations contact their constituents for their goals, projected activities, and projected budget needs. Historical trends and environmental changes are considered when preparing the budget. Some associations have separate budgets for individual programs, services, projects, or capital expenditures. Drafts of these budgets should be prepared before the operating budget is initiated.

Some associations prepare their budgets so that projected revenues balance out the projected expenses. In other words, the projected expenses equal the projected revenues. This is referred to as a balanced budget. The organization projects enough revenues to cover its expenses. It does not project a net gain or a loss. Other associations project a certain percentage of profit when developing their operating budget. This means the revenues component of the budget is projected to be a certain percentage higher than the expenses. Associations may also plan to contribute a certain percentage or specific dollar amount to its reserves, and reflect this as a line item in the operating budget.

Many associations include some type of legend to explain several of the line items in the budget. This is very helpful for the board to understand what the items represent and also for staff when they need to code revenues and expenses so they are categorized into the correct line item.

Once the budget draft is completed, the treasurer along with the staff executive, or other designated persons, present the budget to the board. Ideally, the board is given the budget with its legend prior to the meeting where the budget is being presented. Board members should thoroughly read and analyze the budget prior to the board meeting. This gives them the opportunity to flag questionable areas and prepare their questions for the budget presentation. During the presentation, attention should be drawn to the significant areas, particularly those numbers that have changed from the previous years. The budget presentation should not bury board members in detail; but highlight the significant areas.

Financial Statements

Financial statements are the major tools boards use to oversee the financial position of the organization. The board should insist that it receives timely and accurate financial statements so it can base its decisions on accurate, up-to-date financial data. The frequency of reports should be decided by the board and staff executive.

"Financial statements are valuable sources of data that tell a story about the organization's performance. They allow comparisons over time and provide a basis for measuring actual performance against expectations."

Financial statements should be prepared and presented as simply as possible. Complicated reports tend to make the budget reporting process much more confusing than it needs to be. Once the financial statements are explained to new board members and the individuals understand them, budget reporting becomes a process in which the board becomes increasingly competent. Board members are able to spot check the key budget areas and concentrate on the overall picture of where the organization stands financially, if it is on target as projected, and where it needs to go from there.

Most boards receive interim financial statements that cover a period of time in addition to the annual reports. A board may decide that it does not need a full set of statements monthly or quarterly, but it will determine which statements are most valuable on an interim basis. Interim may mean monthly or quarterly. Interim statements should be well prepared, preferably in the same format as the annual reporting statements. They should provide the board with the information it needs to fulfill its fiscal obligation to the organization.

Reading and interpreting financial statements will get easier over time. Financial statements are valuable sources of data that tell a story about the organization's performance. They allow comparisons over time and provide a basis for measuring actual performance against expectations. They allow board members to get a snapshot of the organization's financial status. It is important to ask questions about the budget and financial statements, especially if your gut is telling you something is not right.

There is no single standard for the types of reports boards must receive. Financial statements come in all sizes, shapes, and formats. However, most of them contain the standard information and language that will be discussed in this section. Refer to Tables 7-1 through 7-5 for more information and examples of financial statements.

Table 7-1
Annual Operating Budget

Explanation of Terms

Fiscal Year	This refers to the budget year. It may be the same as a calendar year, but it may be different. Each organization can determine its own fiscal year. The fiscal year includes a full 12 months, but the starting and ending months may be different from a calendar year that begins on January 1 and ends on December 31. For example, an organization may determine its fiscal year is July 1 to June 30, or April 1 to March 31.
Budget	The dollars projected or budgeted for the fiscal year.
Actual	The actual dollars received or spent for the fiscal year.
Revenues	Financial resources flowing into the organization. These income sources include such things as dues, programs, interest and dividends, sponsorships, and grants.
Expenses	Financial resources flowing out of the organization. These include such things as salaries, travel, supplies, and utilities.
Net Revenues/ Net Income	These terms indicate total revenues minus total expenses. *Net Income (or Net Revenues) = Revenues minus Expenses.* Other terms are profits or losses.

Professional Association, Inc.
2xx2 OPERATING BUDGET EXAMPLE
Fiscal Year January 1 - December 31, 2xx2

REVENUES	BUDGET 2xx1	ACTUAL 2xx1	BUDGET 2xx2
Membership Dues	$100,000	$ 98,175	$100,000
Corporate Membership	48,000	49,500	50,000
Annual Convention	315,000	325,000	326,000
Regional Meetings	25,000	26,400	26,500
Publications	63,000	65,400	65,000
Interest and Dividends	12,000	16,000	15,000
Mailing List Rental	4,500	3,180	3,500
Miscellaneous	500	1,440	1,000
TOTAL REVENUES	**$568,000**	**$585,095**	**$587,000**
EXPENSES			
Administration	$ 20,000	$ 18,000	$ 20,000
Central Office Management	73,000	72,500	73,000
Administrative Operations	58,000	57,600	58,000
Annual Convention	290,000	270,000	300,000
Regional Meetings	22,000	22,300	25,000
Publications	62,000	63,200	65,000
Committees	34,000	33,500	35,000
Professional Relations	8,000	8,755	9,000
Miscellaneous	1,000	1,460	2,000
TOTAL EXPENSES	**$568,000**	**$547,315**	**$587,000**
NET REVENUES	**0**	**37,780**	**0**

Source: Adapted from Nowicki, 1998.

Table 7-2
Statement of Assets, Liabilities, and Fund Balances

This statement summarizes the assets and liabilities of an organization at a given point in time. The difference in assets and liabilities determines the organization's net worth or equity. Assets of the organization must be balanced by the liabilities and the equity.

Explanation of Terms

Assets — Items owned by an organization that can be converted into cash. These are things of value to the organization. *Current Assets* is a term given to those assets that are easily convertible to cash. Examples include cash on hand, bonds, accounts receivable, furniture, and supplies. *Fixed Assets* such as real property and the land on which it sits are valuable but they are not readily converted to cash.

Accounts Receivable — An amount of money owed to the organization. Accounts receivable will be converted to cash at some time in the near future, therefore it is considered an asset.

Prepaid Expenses — Monies paid in advance of their use. An example would be upfront partial payment for a supply order.

Liabilities — Obligations, debts, things owed to others. Liabilities may include such things as accounts payable, long-term debts, and deferred revenues.

Accounts Payable — An amount of money that the organization will pay out at a future time for the purchase of an item. An example would be the use of a purchase order for new equipment. It is a liability because the funds will be expended some time in the future.

Deferred Revenues — An amount of money received in advance of the organization using it for a service or product. An example would be a grant or sponsorship of a book. This is a liability since the funds are obligated and will be used in the future.

Fund Balance — Net worth of the association; total assets minus total liabilities.

Professional Association, Inc.
STATEMENTS OF ASSETS, LIABILITIES, AND FUND BALANCE
December 31, 2xx1

ASSETS		
Current assets:		
Checking Account	$ 32,650	
Money Market	42,000	
Accounts Receivable	4,620	
Prepaid Expenses	1,560	
Other assets:		
Stocks	$247,000	
Bonds	236,540	
TOTAL ASSETS		$564,370
LIABILITIES and FUND BALANCE		
Liabilities		
– Accounts Payable	$ 5,492	
– Deferred Revenues (Textbook)	6,000	
TOTAL LIABILITIES		$ 11,492
FUND BALANCE		$552,878
TOTAL LIABILITIES AND FUND BALANCE		$564,370

Source: Adapted from Nowicki, 1998.

Table 7-3
Statement of Revenues and Expenses

This statement summarizes all revenues and expenses for a period of time and year-to-date. It helps the board to monitor its budget for any given period of time for each line item by comparing the actual results with the current budget. It helps the board determine if there are expense areas that are more than the budgeted amount. These areas may prompt the board to make a decision about whether to justify this spending or limit further spending. The opposite is also true. This statement may also identify areas in which the revenues are under what was budgeted. The board may need to justify the decrease in expected revenues, look for alternate revenue sources, or limit spending.

This statement provides a bottom line summary of the Revenues in Excess of Expenses or the Expenses in Excess of Revenues. This is helpful to determine the status of the total budget (over or under) at any given period in time. In the following example, Professional Association, Inc. had an increase in net assets for 2xx1 of $37,780. This indicated a profit or revenues in excess of expenses.

Professional Association, Inc.
STATEMENT OF REVENUES AND EXPENSES
For the Year Ended 2xx1

REVENUES	**2xx1**	**2xx0**
Membership Dues	$ 98,175	$ 96,240
Corporate Membership	49,500	45,000
Annual Convention	25,000	306,020
Regional Meetings	26,400	32,510
Publications	65,400	59,450
Interest and Dividends	16,000	11,500
Mailing List Rental	3,180	3,500
Miscellaneous	1,440	250
TOTAL REVENUES	**$585,095**	**$554,470**
EXPENSES		
Administration	$ 18,000	$ 17,500
Central Office Management	72,500	71,250
Administrative Operations	57,600	56,050
Annual Convention	270,000	262,500
Regional Meetings	22,300	22,000
Publications	63,200	63,000
Committees	33,500	29,400
Professional Relations	8,755	7,700
Miscellaneous	1,460	750
TOTAL EXPENSES	**$547,315**	**$530,150**
REVENUES IN EXCESS OF EXPENSES	**$37,780**	**$24,320**
FUND BALANCE, JANUARY 1	**$515,098**	**$490,778**
FUND BALANCE, DECEMBER 31	**$552,878**	**$515,098**

Source: Adapted from Nowicki, 1998.

Table 7-4
Interim Report

Following is an example of the 2nd Quarter Report for Professional Association, Inc. It reflects the budgeted and actual numbers for 2xx1, the budget for 2xx2, and the actual dollars generated and spent for the first half of 2xx2. The column labeled "variance" depicts the variance from the budgeted dollars to the actual dollars generated and spent. When board members receive this type of report, they should analyze the significant variances and determine the reasons for them. Remember, significant variances are those that are 8-10% over or under the projected budget. To get a true reflection of variances for the second quarter of the year, it would be helpful to have the previous year's (2xx1) 2nd Quarter Report for comparison.

Let's do an analysis of the quarterly budget report that follows and see what we can learn about Professional Association's financial status. Keep in mind it reflects the revenues and expenditures for one-half of the fiscal year. We'll begin with revenues. Almost all of the budgeted revenues for membership dues have been received and there are six months remaining in the year. This most likely indicates that the association has an annual membership renewal period and it has already occurred in the first half of the year. It is a good practice to have the membership renewal period and other major sources of revenues at the beginning of the fiscal year so the association has a good idea early on of where it stands financially for that year.

Corporate memberships are up by 10%. This indicates a significant variance—the actual dollars are over what was budgeted. This is a positive occurrence when it happens in the revenues portion of the budget. The budget also indicates the annual convention, the major source of non-dues revenues, has already been held. Since no dollars have been received for the regional meetings, we can assume the regional meetings have not yet occurred or perhaps they were canceled.

Publication sales have a significant variance. The board would need to discuss whether or not this was an expected occurrence for the second period of the year. The remaining items under revenues also indicate significant variances. These variances and their rationales would be discussed by the board.

Let's now look at the expenses. Expense items such as administration and central office management are often spread fairly evenly over the fiscal year. Therefore, at 6 months into the fiscal year, we would expect about half of the monies to be spent in these categories. The annual convention was a success financially since revenues were over the projected budget by $6,000 and expenses were under budget by $13,000. Again looking at the regional meetings, it is obvious they have not yet occurred, however $5,000 has been spent on them. Perhaps these are development or marketing costs. There is a significant variance of $25,000 in committee expenses. The board would need to ask some questions such as: Why? Has new technology decreased expenses? Are the committees doing their jobs?

Also looking at the expense items, the miscellaneous item shows a variance of $3,000. Since these dollars are significantly over budget, the board would need to determine and justify how this money was spent. Perhaps an opportunity surfaced that was not part of the strategic plan, however it was determined to be important.

To summarize this analysis, it appears that Professional Association, Inc. has done very well for the first six months of the fiscal year. If the board and staff are able to explain and justify the variances to everyone's satisfaction, it could be concluded that the association is operating in a fiscally sound manner at this period of time.

Table 7-4 (continued)
Interim Report

Professional Association, Inc.
2nd QUARTER REPORT (Interim Report)
January 1 - June 30, 2xx2

REVENUES	BUDGET 2xx1	ACTUAL 2xx1	BUDGET 2xx2	2nd QUARTER ACTUAL-2xx2	VARIANCE	PERCENT OF BUDGET USED
Membership Dues						
(based on 2,000 @ $50)	$100,000	$ 98,175	$100,000	$ 96,500	$ 3,500	96.5%
Corporate Membership	48,000	49,500	50,000	55,000	(5,000)	110%
Annual Convention	315,000	325,000	326,000	332,000	(6,000)	102%
Regional Meetings	25,000	26,400	26,500	0	26,500	0%
Publications	63,000	65,400	65,000	30,000	35,000	46%
Interest and Dividends	12,000	16,000	15,000	6,500	8,500	43%
Mailing List Rental	4,500	3,180	3,500	1,500	2,000	43%
Miscellaneous	500	1,440	1,000	100	900	10%
TOTAL REVENUES	**$568,000**	**$585,095**	**$587,000**	**$521,600**	**$ 65,400**	
EXPENSES						
Administration	$ 20,000	$ 18,000	$ 20,000	$ 11,000	$ 9,000	55%
Central Office Management	73,000	72,500	73,000	36,000	37,000	49%
Administrative Operations	58,000	57,600	58,000	25,000	33,000	43%
Annual Convention	290,000	270,000	300,000	287,000	13,000	96%
Regional Meetings	22,000	22,300	25,000	5,000	20,000	20%
Publications	62,000	63,200	65,000	30,000	35,000	46%
Committees	34,000	33,500	35,000	10,000	25,000	29%
Professional Relations	8,000	8,755	9,000	4,000	5,000	44%
Miscellaneous	1,000	1,460	2,000	5,000	(3,000)	250%
TOTAL EXPENSES	**$568,000**	**$547,315**	**$587,000**	**$413,000**	**$174,000**	
NET REVENUES	**0**	**37,780**	**0**	**$108,600**	**$108,600**	

Source: Adapted from Nowicki, 1998.

Table 7-5
Statement of Cash Flows

This statement is prepared in a format that identifies where cash came from and how it was used. An ongoing cash flow analysis will help to forecast periods of excesses and shortages of cash. The statement usually categorizes revenues and expenditures according to operating, investing, and financing activities. Although this statement is a requirement for accountants to generate, it is not one that merits much use by the board. It is included here because board members will see this statement and have a general understanding of its purpose.

Professional Association, Inc.
STATEMENT OF CASH FLOWS
For the Year Ended December 31, 2xx1

CASH FLOWS FROM OPERATING ACTIVITIES	
Revenues in Excess of Expenses	$ 37,780
Adjustments to Reconcile Net Income to Net Cash Provided by Operating Activities:	
Accounts Receivable	(4,620)
Accrued Interest Receivable	(0)
Prepaid Expenses	4,250
Accounts Payable	3,540
Deferred Revenues	(14,200)
Net Cash Provided by Operating Activities	**$ 26,750**
CASH FLOWS FROM INVESTING ACTIVITIES	
Proceeds from Redemption of Investments	53,895
(Purchase) of Investments	(35,475)
Net Cash (used in) Investing Activities	18,420
(DECREASE) INCREASE IN CASH AND CASH EQUIVALENTS	**$ 45,170**
Cash and Cash Equivalents - January 1, 2xx1	**$ 29,480**
Cash and Cash Equivalents - December 31, 2xx1	**$ 74,650**

Source: Adapted from Nowicki, 1998.

Reserves

Boards monitor their financial positions to be certain they can continue to operate and provide programs and services to their members. One way to gauge financial strength is the level of reserves of the organization. Reserves can be defined in different ways. For this chapter, reserves are defined as those unrestricted assets that are reasonably liquid, minus those liabilities that must be paid off fairly soon.

> ***"Boards monitor their financial positions to be certain they can continue to operate and provide programs and services to their members. One way to gauge financial strength is the level of reserves of the organization."***

The level of reserves that is appropriate varies from one organization to the next. One benchmark for determining strong financial position is having 50%-100% of one year's operating expenses in reserves. Other benchmarks are available such as one year's dues in reserves. There does not seem to be consensus in the association world on one specific benchmark; therefore, most associations choose a benchmark that works best and use it consistently to measure their financial position.

Associations can build their reserves by running at surplus or having more revenues than expenses at the end of the year. Having a healthy amount of dollars in the reserve account allows the organization to have funds available to invest in equipment, apply to programs, take more risks, and protect the organization during times when revenues fall short of expenses. Not all associations are in the position of having a healthy level of accumulated reserves. Each organization should evaluate its circumstances, consider its strategic goals, and set a reasonable reserve level. Building reserves is an evolving process that may take 5 to 10 years to achieve the desired goal. One way to commit to building the reserves is to target a fixed dollar amount as a line item in the expense section of the budget.

Investments

Typically, an organization will keep enough cash in its account to pay its expenses for a few months. The rest of the monies should be placed in short-term and long-term investments. Some monies should be designated to short-term investments such as certificates of deposit or money market accounts. These investments pay a higher interest rate than if the money was simply left in a savings account, but they also allow the organization the flexibility of readily converting the funds to cash if there is insufficient cash to cover expenses.

"Most board members do not possess the knowledge to govern the investments of an association. Therefore, the selection of an investment firm and financial advisor is critical."

Other reserve monies should be invested in longer-term investments such as stocks and bonds because of their higher yields. The board's responsibility with handling investments is different from dealing with budgets and other finances. The board's investment responsibilities include the following:

1. Define the investment policies and guidelines.
2. Select an independent investment firm to handle the investments in accordance with the policies and guidelines set forth in #1.
3. Monitor the return on investment.

Most board members are not investment savvy. They may know a little about their own personal investments, but do not possess the knowledge to govern the investments of an association. Therefore, the selection of an investment firm and financial advisor is critical. The board must select a firm that is credible and works with similar nonprofit associations.

The selection of the financial advisor from the investment firm is also important. The board should select a person who will explain in simple, understandable terms what the investments mean and provide guidance that will balance conservative with higher risk investing and advise the board when changes in the investment strategy are warranted. The advisor also needs to provide guidance in reading and understanding investment reports. Since most reports are not written for the average person to understand, it is important to have an advisor who is willing to take the time to help the board understand the status of its investments.

Financial Audits and Reviews

As part of their fiscal accountability, many boards employ the services of an external or independent auditor to audit or review the financial transactions of an organization. An audit is a lengthy and thorough process in which a certified public accountant (CPA) studies the organization's financial records and procedures. The CPA looks not only at the numbers, but also at whether appropriate accounting principles are used and if they are consistently applied. An opinion is formed about whether the organization's financial statements fairly reflect its financial position, the results of its operations, and its cash flow.

The board must realize its role in contracting with an auditor. The auditor is the agent of the board and reports directly to it, not to management. An auditor will prepare a letter to the board stating whether the financial statements conformed to generally accepted accounting principles. In addition, the report should highlight any major weaknesses in internal controls and other significant operational deficiencies. To perform as accurately and as fairly as possible, auditors must be absolutely independent of management and must resist any potential pressures from management to alter their opinion.

"An audit is a lengthy and thorough process in which a certified public accountant (CPA) studies the organization's financial records and procedures."

Is an audit necessary? Not always. Some state laws and association's bylaws require an audit. Associations that receive funding from various sources may be required to have an audit as a condition of receiving the funds. Some boards may want verification from an external evaluator that the association is sound financially. Other boards believe an audit is a way to demonstrate to the membership that their financial contributions are going to an association that is well-managed financially.

Some associations are too small or simply do not have the funds for an annual external audit. They may use one of the following alternatives to an audit:

- Have an external audit performed every two years instead of annually. This would cut the cost in half.
- An external auditor could conduct an annual review of the financial records. The review process is less thorough than an audit, but it does ensure that the financial statements have been prepared appropriately and the year's numbers make sense as compared to those of previous years. This review is less costly, not as thorough as the audit, but an acceptable method of demonstrating fiscal accountability.
- The association may ask a small group of financially astute members to undertake a members' audit in which the members visit the association's headquarters and examine the appropriateness of the financial activities and records. Some associations employ an external auditor to accompany and guide the members through this type of audit.

Tax-Exempt Status

Many volunteer leaders think their nonprofit associations are totally exempt from paying taxes. Is this true? In some cases, but not all. Board members are likely to hear references to the 501(c) designations that were created by the Internal Revenue Service. Two designations that professional associations will hear most often are 501(c)(3) and 501(c)(6). The 501(c)(3) is the designation for religious, charitable, scientific, and public safety associations, education institutions, some professional associations, and foundations. To qualify, an association must not be involved in substantial activities to influence legislation (i.e., lobbying) and they cannot participate in political campaigns. The 501(c)(6) designation refers to professional and trade associations, chambers of commerce, and business leagues that are not organized for profit reasons.

> ***"Nonprofit means the association is established to promote a profession, not necessarily to perform services for individual members. Nonprofit does not necessarily mean the association is exempt from paying property tax, state sales tax, withholding tax, and tax on unrelated business income."***

The above designations determine the tax requirements and status for each association. Nonprofit means the association is established to promote a profession, not necessarily to perform services for individual members. Nonprofit does not necessarily mean the association is exempt from paying property tax, state sales tax, withholding tax, and tax on unrelated business income. Taxes for nonprofit associations vary at state and local levels.

Whether a nonprofit organization is exempt from taxes or not, it is required to file a tax form (IRS Form 990). This form is an information return in which the organization documents its sources of income and various expenses. It also reports what it owns and what debts it has. In addition, the form asks numerous questions to ascertain whether the organization has acted appropriately under the laws that impact nonprofit associations. Since Form 990 must be made available for inspection and duplication to anyone who requests it, the association must ensure the information is accurately reported.

Most associations could not exist solely on dues income; thereby they create sources of non-dues revenues. These activities, which may or may not be subject to unrelated business income tax (UBIT), include tradeshows, exhibits, conventions, publications and advertising, corporate sponsorships, subsidiaries, and foundations. Nonprofit associations are permitted to engage in a certain degree of these activities as long as the activities are not a "substantial" part of the organization's portfolio. The organization may be required to pay taxes on the income from these activities. It is best to consult with an accountant to determine how any new activities might be viewed under the UBIT rules.

Signs of Financial Distress

While boards may have the best intentions and try their best to fulfill their financial responsibilities, there may be times that despite all of these efforts, financial problems occur. Mattocks (2008) identifies the signs of potential financial distress in Table 7-6.

Table 7-6 15 Signs of Financial Distress
1. Inadequate accounting skills
2. Board not focused on financial metrics
3. CEO not focused on finances
4. Frequent turnover of auditors
5. Lack of financial accountability throughout the organization
6. Too much trust, not enough skepticism
7. Internal borrowing from restricted funds
8. Lack of investment expertise and policies
9. Untimely financial reporting
10. Poor credit
11. Inadequate financial policies
12. Too much reliance on the audit
13. Spending down cash reserves
14. No management of product life cycles
15. No environmental scanning

Source: Mattacks, 2008.

A board needs to be watchful for potential signs of financial distress, but it should not become obsessed with them. Hopefully, they are the exception and not the rule. The board should establish certain internal controls that would protect the organization's assets and promote its efficient operations. These controls may take the forms of policies and procedures for accounting and reporting. While staff is responsible for implementing and maintaining the controls set by the board, the board must assure itself that staff is following board policies. The board also needs to periodically take a fresh look at its policies and procedures to make sure they are up to date, provide protection for the organization, and are not simply busy work for staff.

> ***"An organization in financial distress needs a board that does three things: clearly articulates the problem, determines its root causes, and commits to moving out of financal distress."***

Zone of Insolvency. Mattocks (2008) states that one third of nonprofits in the United States operate in financial distress. He defines the Zone of Insolvency as a period of organizational financial distress during which reasonable people could foresee total insolvency as a potential state. Associations in the zone experience such things as decreasing cash reserves, increased debt, aging product lines, and the inability to invest in the future. Boards that are governing in the zone have expanded legal responsibilities to protect all parties involved and ensure there is no inequality in benefits. Mattocks states there are only three ways out of the zone: restore financial strength, arrange a merger, or file for dissolution. A board in this situation needs to proceed with caution and seek legal advice so there is no violation of rights of any party in the zone, and the board is not sued for breaches in its fiduciary responsibilities.

An organization in financial distress needs a board that does three things: clearly articulates the problem, determines its root causes, and commits to moving out of financal distress (Mattocks, 2008). Building consensus and success in accomodating these three mandates will help the board avoid or move out of the Zone of Insolvency.

Summary

Boards have a critical role in assuring their fiduciary responsibilities. Board members can best perform their fiscal accountability role by understanding and overseeing budgets, financial statements, and investments without micromanaging. Boards should ask the right questions to determine the financial position of the organization, even if the questions sound simple or "dumb." No question is "dumb" unless it is not asked. The questions in Table 7-7 will be helpful in evaluating financial position.

Table 7-7
Questions to Determine Sound Financial Position

1. What are the association's strategic goals? Is our financial plan consistent with the strategic goals? Does the association have the financial resources to accomplish these goals? If not, what are some creative sources of additional revenues? Do priorities need to be shifted? How flexible are we to change when unanticipated circumstances arise?
2. Are we operating at a net gain or loss? How will this affect our future?
3. Is our cash flow adequate?
4. Where are we compared with our budget? Over, under, or on target? Are there reasonable explanations for variances?
5. Are we overseeing the fiscal management of our association or micromanaging it?
6. Are the major sources of revenues increasing or decreasing?
7. Are the major expense items rising without adequate rationale?
8. Are we filing our required reports in a timely manner?
9. Are we complying with our IRS tax-exempt status?
10. What do our audits show? What are we finding when reviewing our financial policies?
11. Do we have sufficient reserves? If yes, are we providing enough services and at affordable costs to our members? If no, what is our plan to increase our reserves?
12. How are we doing with our investments? What is our percent of return on our investments? How does the return compare with the standard indexes? Is our investment advisor complying with our investment policy?

Source: Adapted from Nowicki, 1998.

While boards have the responsibility to be fiscally accountable in performing their fiduciary duty to the organization, they must not lose sight of the bigger picture. Boards need to remember that fiscal accountability is no more important than accountability for what the organization accomplishes in actual results and the value these results bring to the members. Budgets and finances are the board's job, but not the most important one. The good that is done for the members and at what cost is the board's most important job. Missing this target by even a small percentage costs the organization more than most budgetary errors (Carver, 2006).

Learning Assessment

Chapter 7: Budget and Financial Management

Part I-Matching

Match the descriptions in Column B with the appropriate terms in Column A. Place the letter of the description in Column B on the line preceding the correct term in Column A. The correct answers may be found on the next page.

Column A

______ 1. Audit

______ 2. Accounts Payable

______ 3. Accounts Receivable

______ 4. Assets

______ 5. Deferred Income

______ 6. Expenses

______ 7. Fiscal Year

______ 8. Fund Balance

______ 9. Liabilities

______ 10. Net Revenues

______ 11. Prepaid Expenses

______ 12. Revenues

Column B

A. Revenues minus expenses
B. The budget year
C. Money received in advance of using it
D. Financial resources flowing into the organization
E. Money owed to the organization
F. Items owned that can be converted to cash
G. Financial resources flowing out of the organization
H. Thorough process that studies the association's financial records and procedures
I. Money the organization will pay at a future date
J. Money paid in advance of use
K. Assets minus liabilities
L. Obligations, debts, things owed to others

Part II - Short Answers

Reflect on the knowledge you gained from this chapter by responding to the following statements and questions. Some of the statements suggest topics for you to discuss with your mentor. This chapter may also have prompted other thoughts and questions to discuss with your mentor.

13. Obtain the financial statements for your association. Review each financial statement thoroughly and compare it to the types of statements described in this chapter. Write down the questions or thoughts that you have. Then talk with your mentor, the treasurer, and/or the staff executive to answer your questions and clarify your understanding of the budget and other financial statements.

14. Review your association's investment policy and compare it to the latest investment report so that you understand the investment strategy. Prepare your questions and talk with you mentor, the treasurer, the staff executive, and/or the investment advisor.

15. Determine the financial status of your association by answering the questions in the table, "Questions to Determine Sound Financial Position." Discuss your answers with your mentor, the treasurer, and/or the staff executive.

Answers to Part I - Matching: 1. H 2. I 3. E 4. F 5. C 6. G 7. B 8. K 9. L 10. A 11. J 12. D

Chapter 8

Effective Meetings

Key Points

- Reasons for Holding a Meeting
- Pre-Meeting Considerations
  • Meeting Purpose • Agenda • Consent Agenda • Participant Selection • Choosing a Meeting Time • Arranging a Meeting Site • Electronic Meetings • Standing Meetings
- Conducting a Meeting
  • Ground Rules • Role of the Chairperson • Role of the Participant • Consensus Decision Making • Parliamentary Procedure • Handling Challenging Situations • Groupthink
- Executive or Closed Session
- Components of Meeting Minutes
- Evaluating a Meeting
- Concluding a Meeting
- Tips for New Board Members

Tables

- Table 8-1 Sample Board Meeting Agenda
- Table 8-2 Sample Agenda Item Form
- Table 8-3 Conference Call Tips
- Table 8-4 Meeting Ground Rules
- Table 8-5 Tips for the Chairperson
- Table 8-6 Tips for Meeting Participants
- Table 8-7 Information to Include in Minutes
- Table 8-8 Questions for Evaluating Meetings

Mentoring Opportunity

- Learning Assessment

Download the Chapter 8 Tables and Learning Assessment online at www.ajj.com/mentoring — Use password MTS2E989

"This chapter will provide you with the essentials you will need to participate in and conduct meetings."

Have you ever participated in a truly effective meeting? If so, why was it effective? Many people cannot describe an effective meeting because they have never attended one. Meetings have gained a less than positive reputation because often times they are seen as a waste of time, and participants do not see outcomes from the meetings to justify the time spent. As Milton Berle once said, "A committee is a group that keeps minutes and wastes hours." Meetings have had their share of jokes also. In spite of all the negative things we say about meetings, they are essential to what we do and they can be very positive and effective.

As a new board member, you will have numerous opportunities to participate in a wide array of meetings. In addition to board meetings, you will most likely participate in task forces, committee meetings, problem solving meetings, and planning meetings, to name a few. Meetings can be very productive and time efficient, if everyone who participates is committed to their success. The purpose of this chapter is to discuss ways to plan, conduct, and participate in effective meetings. The chapter is written generically to describe all types of meetings, in addition to board meetings. Specific information about board meetings will be interspersed throughout the chapter. The information will be helpful to you as you plan to participate in a board meeting and will serve as a valuable resource when you are asked to chair a meeting or coach others in chairing their meetings.

As a board member, you are looked upon as a role model. When it comes to leading and participating in meetings, members and other individuals expect you to be knowledgeable and skilled. While the information in this chapter is simple, it is amazing how many people do not know these simple things or perhaps do not realize their importance. Using the information in this chapter will provide you with the essentials you will need to participate in and conduct meetings.

Reasons for Holding a Meeting

Meetings are important if they are called to accomplish a specific purpose. Some reasons for meetings include:

- Conducting business that cannot be conducted effectively by other means such as a board meeting
- Information sharing, such as a meeting of the membership

- Solving a problem or decision making, such as determining how to solve a problem that affects the entire membership
- Planning, such as a strategic planning meeting or planning an education program
- Gathering feedback to solicit opinions and ideas about programs and services, such as a focus group meeting

> *"Planning is one of the essential keys to an effective meeting. Time invested in advance of the meeting will save time during the meeting and help to assure the meeting's productivity."*

Before deciding to have a meeting, it is important to ask the following questions:

- Is a meeting necessary?
- What is the outcome we need to achieve?
- Is a meeting the best way to achieve the outcome?
- Are there other ways to achieve the outcome such as by phone (conference call), written means, electronic mail, or a virtual meeting via the Internet?

Answering the above questions will help to determine if a meeting is necessary. If so, planning for the meeting needs to begin as soon as possible. Planning is one of the essential keys to an effective meeting. Time invested in advance of the meeting will save time during the meeting and help to assure the meeting's productivity.

Meeting participants feel meetings are effective when (a) they start and end on time, (b) the time is well spent, (c) there is an equal opportunity for everyone to participate, and (d) they are productive, progress is made, and the outcome is achieved.

Pre-Meeting Considerations

Meeting Purpose

Some meetings such as board meetings are considered standing meetings. The purpose is clear and the meeting occurs regularly. For other types of meetings, one of the first considerations in planning them is to determine the purpose for the meeting. The purpose will help to decide who needs to participate in it.

Agenda

An agenda is an essential element of a meeting. It serves as a plan or blueprint for the meeting. The quality of the items placed on the agenda will determine whether or not the meeting will be productive, meaningful, and meet the intended outcomes.

Participants will work on what is in front of them; therefore, the agenda items must be important, meaningful, mission and strategic plan-driven, and within the group's authority to handle.

The agenda is jointly developed between the chairperson and the participants. The chairperson should ask participants for their contributions to the agenda and the participants should also feel free to add items to it. The agendas for board meetings are often jointly developed among the board chairperson, staff executive, and board members. Most boards have a standard format for submitting board reports and for submitting agenda items.

"Agenda items must be important, meaningful, mission and strategic plan-driven, and within the group's authority to handle."

An agenda can take any format and contain any information that is necessary for the meeting. Some agendas are very traditional such as the sample board meeting agenda included in Table 8-1. Committee agendas, for example, may be structured according to the strategies or action steps that the committee is working on. Some boards structure their agendas according to the goals of the strategic plan. Others plan the agenda so that all decision items are placed first on the agenda followed by those items requiring only discussion.

Table 8-1
Sample Board Meeting Agenda

Professional Association, Inc.
BOARD MEETING AGENDA
February 21, 20xx
Tampa, FL

I. Call to Order and Introductions - President (10 minutes)
II. Appointment of Timekeeper - President (1 minute)
III. Business
  A. (topic, person presenting, and timeframe)
  B.
IV. Consent Agenda - ALL (15 minutes for questions/comments)
  A. Committee/Task Force Reports (list of reports)
  B. Approval of Minutes
V. Meeting Evaluation
VI. Announcements
VII. Next Meeting - Date, Time, Place
VIII. Adjournment

Source: Adapted from Nowicki, 1998.

Agenda items of critical importance should be placed at the beginning of the agenda so there is adequate time devoted to these items. Like-items should be grouped together on the agenda. Housekeeping items and minutiae or operational details, if necessary, should be placed at the end of the agenda. Those items that are anticipated to generate much discussion and/or emotion should be separated by lesser-fueled items. It is also a good idea to schedule those items after breaks so participants are refreshed. Speaking of breaks, they should be scheduled throughout an all-day meeting at least every 1-1/2 to 2 hours.

All participants may submit agenda items. It is up to the chairperson to determine if these agenda items will be accepted for a meeting. The decision is often based on the importance or urgency of the item, how it fits with the purpose of the meeting, whether it needs to come to the group for a decision or can be handled in another way, and if there is available time on the agenda. For many boards, supporting documentation is often required when submitting an agenda item. This information provides a background of the item, the time needed, whether it requires a decision or discussion, the recommendation, rationale, and any fiscal implications. Refer to Table 8-2 for an example of an agenda item form (next page).

"The decision to place an item on the agenda is often based on the importance or urgency of the item, how it fits with the purpose of the meeting, whether it needs to come to the group for a decision or can be handled in another way, and if there is available time on the agenda."

An agenda should be sent to participants before the meeting if possible. This identifies the meeting as important and worthy of advanced planning. It is a reminder of the meeting and allows members to incorporate the meeting into their schedules. An agenda also helps to remind participants of what will be discussed at the meeting.

Table 8-2
Sample Agenda Item Form

Professional Association, Inc.
AGENDA ITEM FORM

NAME OF AGENDA ITEM:

DATE SUBMITTED:

SUBMITTED BY:

DESIRED ACTION:
[ ] Approval [ ] Information/Discussion

ESTIMATED TIME NEEDED:

INTRODUCTION:

RECOMMENDATION (include financial implications if applicable):

RATIONALE:

Many boards send out a packet or notebook of information that accompanies the agenda. This is referred to as the board packet or board book. It often contains the agenda, the previous meeting's minutes, committee, task force, and staff reports, supporting documents/proposals for business items, and other background information on issues to be discussed at the meeting. While a well-planned agenda is essential, the success of a meeting depends on the participants having the information in advance, and their commitment to reading it in preparation for the meeting.

The lack of planning for a meeting is the major cause of wasted time. The difference between a good meeting and a poor meeting is often determined by how the meeting time is used. An agenda is essential for keeping the meeting focused and on track. The quality of the meeting process and the dynamics that occur are the responsibility of the chairperson and the participants. They share the responsibility of making the meeting a success.

"The consent agenda is a time-saving tool because it saves the board from having to discuss and vote on/approve each item or report separately. It frees members to focus on major issues."

Consent Agenda

The action part of a meeting is the real reason for the participants to come together, not simply to report what could be read at leisure. Standing items such as committee and staff reports and other background information should become part of a consent agenda. The items listed within the consent agenda should be read by the participants prior to the meeting. Participants are expected to come to the meeting prepared with their thoughts and questions to deal with those items, if necessary.

When the chairperson presents the consent agenda, participants are asked if they have any questions or comments regarding the items within the consent agenda. Discussion ensues, if necessary, usually for an agreed upon time period. This part of the agenda is called "consent" because the participants consent to accept the items contained within it. If there are any components of the consent agenda that require additional action or approval, those items should be pulled out of the consent agenda and placed under the "business" section of the agenda. The consent agenda is a time-saving tool because it saves the board from having to discuss and vote on/approve each item or report separately. It frees members to focus on major issues.

Participant Selection

- How many? Choose the smallest number of participants and only those individuals who have the appropriate knowledge to contribute to the meeting.
- Who? Select those individuals who (1) have the authority to make decisions, (2) will carry out the decisions, and (3) have information to contribute to the decision making process. If the purpose of the meeting is information sharing, invite only those individuals who need to learn about the information.

> ***"When inviting meeting participants, select those individuals who (1) have the authority to make decisions, (2) will carry out the decisions, and (3) have information to contribute to the decision making process."***

Choosing a Meeting Time

The first consideration in determining a meeting time is the amount of preparation that must be done prior to the meeting. Then it is important to choose a time when the meeting participants will be available. If a meeting space is needed, this will also need to be considered in choosing the time.

In this day of time poverty, selecting a date and time for a meeting is no easy task. It is best to select a few dates and times and circulate them to the invited meeting participants to determine availability. Be creative! A meeting can be held at any time that is convenient or selected by the participants. Scheduling the first meeting for a group should usually be limited to one hour. If subsequent meetings are necessary, the group can decide how much time to allow. Different types of meetings require different time frames.

Arranging a Meeting Site

The choice of a meeting room depends on group size and the room set-up that is needed. The room should be arranged to accomplish the type of meeting that is being held. For example, if the meeting will involve discussion and decision making, the room should be set up so people will face each other. A round, rectangular, or U-shaped set-up works best.

A room should be chosen in which participants will feel comfortable and at ease. Other considerations include a place that is convenient and accessible to participants, and one that is well-lit and well-ventilated. If refreshments or audiovisual equipment are needed, space must be available to accommodate them.

Electronic Meetings

Given the various types of technology available, meetings will continue to take on new looks and formats in addition to the onsite venues. Conference calls or teleconferences, video conferences, and Internet-based meetings help us communicate information in a timely fashion instead of or in addition to face-to-face meetings. As with any meeting, order and productivity are important. Tips for getting the most out of a conference call are found in Table 8-3.

Table 8-3
Conference Call Tips

1. Decide in advance the purpose of the call. Is it informational, decision making, reporting, or other?
2. Determine who needs to be present on the call. Is a quorum needed for a vote? Check the bylaws. Does the staff executive need to be present?
3. Schedule the call. Keep in mind the time zones of the participants. Ask participants for their preferred times and dates. When scheduling the call with participants, notify them of the method to access the conference call. Conference calls should rarely be scheduled for more than one hour.
4. Make sure everyone knows the purpose of the call and what they need to do to prepare for it.
5. Have an agenda and stick to it. If possible, draft an agenda and send it to everyone for further input prior to the call. Then form the final agenda and send it to the participants along with the supporting materials. The agenda, if followed, will keep the meeting on track. When the agenda includes multiple items, time frames should be assigned to each item. During the call, a timekeeper may be appointed to keep the group on track.
6. Assign someone to record minutes. If business is conducted on the call, minutes should be taken. Taping the meeting is rather questionable due to the laws of various states regarding taping phone calls. It might be better not to tape conference calls.
7. Speaker and cellular phones. Confidentiality may be questionable when a participant uses a speaker phone. The meeting participants need to keep this in mind when determining the purpose of the call and the agenda items. Also, when speaker phones are used, the participant should state to the group if there are other persons participating on the call such as a secretary. Attendance by these individuals should be recorded in the minutes.
8. When participants speak, they should first state their name so everyone is clear who is speaking. Once all participants are familiar with each others' voices, this may not be necessary.
9. Since time is dollars, participants should state their issues and opinions as concisely as possible and limit interactions only to the matter at hand. The conference call is not the place to get side-tracked on irrelevant issues.

Source: Lockwood, 1996.

Standing Meetings

If the group plans to meet on a regular basis, it is a good idea to determine a regular day and time so participants can schedule other activities around this time. Some groups develop a meeting schedule for the year.

"A good meeting involves everyone. In the best of meetings, everyone participates, no one monopolizes, and everybody is somebody."

There are a couple of things to keep in mind with standing meetings. Just because a meeting is scheduled does not mean it has to occur. Some boards that meet monthly may run into this situation. All standing meetings need to be questioned each time they are planned. Is the meeting really necessary? Is there a purpose for it? Are there enough agenda items to constitute a meeting or can the items be handled in another way or during a subsequent meeting?

When standing meetings are scheduled for a specific time frame, the work/agenda usually expands to fill up the time allowed. For example, if a meeting is routinely scheduled for one hour and the business actually takes only 15 minutes, the group usually finds things to talk about to take up the entire hour. Sometimes this may be good, but usually it is just filler information and not really necessary. When participants look back on the meeting, they usually do not feel their time was well spent. Some participate only because they feel compelled and do not want to seem rude by excusing themselves from the remainder of the meeting.

Conducting a Meeting

Ground Rules

It is helpful to establish ground rules for conducting and participating in meetings. These rules will help to keep the meeting on track, provide order, and help the board arrive at good decisions. Table 8-4 includes a list of ground rules for effective meeting behavior (next page).

Table 8-4
Meeting Ground Rules

- Be prepared and complete assignments for meetings.
- Start and end the meeting on time.
- Stay focused and adhere to the agenda and time allocations.
- Listen attentively and ask questions.
- Be open minded and visionary.
- Avoid side conversations.
- Actively participate in discussions, but avoid monopolizing them.
- Only one person speaks at a time, and that person will be recognized to speak by the chairperson.
- Place all issues on the table, not under it.
- Decisions will be made by consensus and they will be based on the best interests of the members and the association.
- Committee/board business stays in the meeting room. Avoid carrying on the meeting in the hallway, lounge, or restroom where all participants may not be present.
- Support decisions made, especially when you leave the boardroom.
- Outside of the meeting, present a positive image of the group and its work.
- Take notes on decisions made so you can verify the information in the minutes when you are asked to approve them. Also, your notes will remind you of your assignments.
- Turn off all electronic devices prior to and during the meeting.

Role of the Chairperson

Good meetings rarely just happen. They require thoughtful planning along with appropriate information and leadership. The leader of the meeting, or chairperson, is responsible for prior coordination of the meeting as well as facilitating the process and content during the meeting. The chairperson makes sure the important information (content) is discussed and action is taken. But that is only half the role. The chairperson also handles the way participants work together to meet the goals of the meeting (process). It is important for the chairperson to keep the meeting moving along and to provide opportunities for everyone to participate.

A good meeting involves everyone. The chairperson's role is to facilitate discussion, not to do all the talking and dominate the meeting. Often, the chairperson remains neutral on the topics that are discussed. Remaining neutral helps the chair to be objective and concentrate on the process of facilitating the discussion. In the best of meetings, everyone participates, no one monopolizes, and everybody is somebody. Table 8-5 provides tips to help the chairperson lead a meeting.

Table 8-5
Tips for the Chairperson

At one time or another, most of us will have the opportunity to lead a meeting. When the challenge comes, the following tips will help in conducting a successful meeting. These tips assume all of the preparation for the meeting has been completed.

- Arrive early to the meeting. If the meeting occurs on site, check the room arrangement and room temperature. Pass out any written materials. Greet participants when they arrive.
- Begin the meeting with an introduction of all participants and tell everyone why they are part of this meeting. Explain the importance of everyone's roles to the success of the meeting. Thank them for their time and expertise.
- Ensure that a quorum is present, if required. If a quorum is not present, the meeting may continue, but decisions cannot be made.
- Respect all participants.
- Create win-win situations.
- Trust that people will come up with good ideas.
- Allow differences to be aired. Let all opinions be expressed.
- Don't hesitate to use your power to keep the meeting moving. Participants expect this of the chairperson.
- Try to see others' points of view with an open mind.
- Move the meeting along with well-timed summaries about what has been discussed and decided.
- Before moving on to the next agenda item, make sure everyone understands the action taken on the current item and any related follow-up that is needed. Follow-up assignments should state who will do the follow-up and by when.
- Be confident. This may be your first time chairing a meeting, but no one will know that unless you tell them or act nervous! Pretend you are a pro.
- Concentrate all of the time. It is your job to know what is going on.
- Use and encourage humor.
- Encourage discussion and analysis of problems. Do not rush into solutions before the problem has been well defined and analyzed.
- Seek consensus on decisions. Get everyone's opinion on important matters. Do not interpret silence as agreement. Ask to be sure.
- Prevent the meeting from turning into a gripe session. Restrict comments to behaviors that can be changed or situations within the group's control.
- Never make participants feel threatened.
- If a guest is invited to the meeting, prepare him/her in advance. Inform the guest about the group and the purpose of the invitation. Be clear of the time allotted on the agenda and for how much of the meeting the guest may attend. Some informal time may be scheduled outside of the meeting for other participants to talk with the guest.

Source: Adapted from Nowicki, 1998.

Role of the Participant

Meetings are the ultimate team sport, and winning requires more than a good quarterback. Too often we will leave a meeting and say, "That was a waste of my time" or "We did not accomplish anything." It is easy to blame an unproductive meeting on someone else, however a successful meeting is the responsibility of all the team players.

> ***"A successful meeting is the responsibility of all the team players."***

One of the most important responsibilities of a participant is to come prepared for the meeting. Reading materials prior to the meeting is essential. If you are responsible for an agenda item, come prepared to share highlights of your item, not to present it or, worse yet, read it. Participants should have done their homework in reading the information you prepared for them. The meeting time for your agenda item can focus on discussion, problem solving, and decision making (Nadler et al, 2006).

Tips for being an effective meeting participant are found in Table 8-6 (next page).

Table 8-6
Tips for Meeting Participants

- Prepare for the meeting. Review the agenda and read any other information distributed before the meeting. Jot down questions or points for clarification. If you have placed an item on the agenda, be well prepared with enough facts and information to present and discuss the item.
- Consider it a compliment when you are asked to participate in a meeting. You and your position/expertise are important.
- Use the meeting as an opportunity to develop your image and interpersonal skills.
- Arrive on time.
- Listen. Active listening involves an open posture, eye contact, and facial expressions that show interest.
- Know what you are talking about when you speak.
- Treat others fairly during the discussion.
- Stick to the matter at hand — the agenda. Help the chairperson keep the meeting on track.
- Be a part of the solution, not the problem.
- Express your opinion on issues raised for discussion.
- Take notes. Your memory may not be up to par after the meeting.
- Ask relevant questions.
- Ask for clarification or an explanation if you do not understand.
- Tell yourself you are going to get at least one good idea from the meeting. You will spend your time listening for that idea.
- Avoid disruptive behavior. Evaluate your meeting behavior. Are you one of the causes of "challenging situations?"
- Avoid side conversations.
- Avoid bringing hidden agendas to the meeting. If you have something to say, put it on the agenda.
- Support the decisions of the group, especially outside of the meeting room.
- Participate in establishing ground rules for meeting behavior, then do your part in adhering to them. Tactfully confront your fellow participants who may violate the ground rules.
- Participate in evaluating the meeting by identifying the meeting's strengths and also providing suggestions for improvements.
- After the meeting, follow up on your assignments and report back.

Source: Adapted from Nowicki, 1998.

Consensus Decision Making

Decisions made in meetings should be given careful consideration before conclusions are reached. In most meetings today, voting has gone by the wayside. Instead, decisions are reached by consensus. Unfortunately, while people know the word, not everyone understands what consensus means.

Consensus decision making involves all meeting participants contributing their opinions and ideas, discussing situations and alternatives, and determining a solution and plan of action that everyone can support. During the process of coming to consensus, the chairperson will summarize the trend of the discussion at intervals to see how much agreement is surfacing with the group. Once the group arrives at a decision, it is important to ask if there is any hesitation to accept the decision. If someone is unable to accept the decision, further discussion needs to occur. That person should be asked to provide other alternatives, which are then discussed, and jointly the group arrives at a decision that is acceptable to everyone.

Consensus is a process that creates win/win situations. The solutions do not compromise any strong convictions or values of those involved. Consensus is not compromise. No one should have to give up something to gain something in return. While all participants may not agree totally with the decision, or they may not think it is the ideal solution, everyone is willing to give it a try and they agree to support it. This means when participants leave the meeting, they do not sabotage the decision.

If consensus cannot be reached, at least the group has given it their best effort. The issue may need to be tabled until another time when more information or other alternatives are available. The experience of consensus building can be a powerful way for individuals to learn how to work thoroughly through situations and explore alternatives. It is much different from voting. With voting, usually some win and some lose. With consensus, no one must lose in order for someone else to win. The interaction is collaborative. When individuals experience success with consensus building, they feel good about the process because they know they have been heard, their ideas have been given a chance, and all options are considered.

Can voting and consensus decision making be combined to arrive at a decision? In some cases, voting may be appropriate.

"When individuals experience success with consensus building, they feel good about the process because they know they have been heard, their ideas have been given a chance, and all options are considered."

There are times when a board thoroughly discusses an issue and everyone arrives at a consensus decision except one or a few members. These members may be very passionate about the topic at hand and they will never agree to go along with the board's decision, nor are they likely to offer acceptable alternatives. In these cases where a decision must be reached, the chair may call for a vote. While this may not be the ideal way to make decisions, it may be the best alternative, given the circumstances.

> ***"The chairperson's role encompasses dealing with challenging situations that may, and usually do, arise during a meeting."***

Parliamentary Procedure

Robert's Rules of Order have for years been the traditional guide used for adhering to parliamentary procedure during board meetings. Given the culture of today, fewer and fewer associations are using Robert's Rules to guide their actions at board meetings. While they may continue to be used at large business meetings of the associations, only a few boards adhere to the rigidity of these rules at board or committee meetings. Robert's Rules have a tendency to create confusion and intimidation when trying to use the proper terminology and proper order. The rules tend to stifle the creative and fluid dynamics that are characteristic of the boards of today. Some boards may continue to feel compelled to use the rules because that is the way the meetings have always been conducted. Other boards have done away with the rules except for situations when a vote is required for any issues with a financial impact.

Handling Challenging Situations

Being a chairperson is a very important position. Since the chairperson is responsible for the process of the meeting, the role encompasses dealing with challenging situations that may, and usually do, arise during a meeting. Each meeting has participants who rarely talk and those who will not stop talking. The chairperson's job is to maintain a balance. Here are some examples of challenging situations and how they can be handled effectively.

The Talkers. Participants who dominate the meeting by talking often have good ideas but go into too much detail and get sidetracked. Or, they have something to say about every topic or issue that is raised. Talkers can actually ruin a meeting.

Techniques to Handle Talkers

- Be subtle at first. Close the topic by saying, "Thank you, I understand."
- Use direct questions to draw out other people.
- State, "I'd like to hear what others think about..."
- Avoid looking at the talkers when asking a question.
- A private conversation with talkers after the meeting or during break may help.
- If the above fail, tape the meeting and ask the talkers to listen to the tape.

The Neighbors. Participants talking to their neighbors (side conversations) is something that will happen in a typical meeting. Usually these conversations are brief. However, they can become a problem if they happen often or for an extended length of time. They interrupt the meeting and distract other participants.

Techniques to Handle Neighbors

- Invite the neighbors to share with everyone what is being said.
- Politely ask the neighbors to turn their attention to the group's discussion.
- Stop the group's discussion and look at the persons talking. The silence will usually end the side conversation.
- Speak to the persons outside the meeting and inform them that the behavior is disruptive.

The Non-Talkers. Quiet individuals may feel intimidated or lack the confidence to speak up during the meeting. They may not think they have ideas that are important to contribute. Often these individuals are introverted and need time to think first about what they are going to say.

Techniques to Handle Non-Talkers

- Encourage the non-talkers to speak. Give them eye contact while asking for a response from the group.
- Ask a question about an area in which the non-talkers are knowledgeable and can speak with confidence. Usually this is an ice breaker.

- During a discussion, ask the non-talkers if they have anything further to contribute. While the response can be a one-word answer, they will at least feel involved in the discussion.
- Use a round robin approach so everyone is encouraged to participate when it is their turn.
- When non-talkers do talk, listen attentively and reinforce the importance of their contribution. Creating a positive experience for them will encourage future contributions.
- Avoid ridiculing the non-talkers for not talking.

The Hecklers. Hecklers disrupt the meeting with snide remarks or simply want to argue. Often, hecklers irritate the group.

Techniques to Handle Hecklers

- Do not argue or reprimand hecklers. Beat them at their own game. Ask for positive suggestions.
- When hecklers speak with an inappropriate remark, ask the group to join in the discussion by stating what they think of the remark.
- If hecklers are insensitive to the problems they are creating, directly point out that the behavior is disrupting the progress of the meeting. Then turn to another person with a question to get the meeting back on track.
- Speak to the hecklers outside the meeting, inform them the behavior is disruptive, and ask for cooperation in eliminating the disruptive behavior.

The Squashers. Squashers say NO to everything. People who are against change or who may be negatively affected by a decision may squash ideas.

Techniques to Handle Squashers

- Rephrase the negative comments in a positive way to help participants define problems.
- Ask the questions, "Do things need to be this way? How can we make them a positive experience?"
- Ask the question, "Does anyone feel differently about this?"
- If you know the squashers will be negative about an issue, talk with them privately before the meeting, ask for their opinions, and allow them to air their views on a one-on-one basis.

The Busybodies. These individuals believe their work is more important than the work of the group. Busybodies often arrive late, leave early, take personal messages or talk on their phones during the meeting, and leave the room for brief periods. This behavior disrupts the group and there could be a delay if the busybodies need a briefing upon return. The continuity of the meeting is broken, participants forget their ideas, and valuable time is wasted.

Techniques to Handle Busybodies

- Establish ground rules to address these behaviors. Confront the busybodies if their behaviors continue and state they are in violation of the ground rules.
- Talk to the busybodies outside of the meeting and inform them that their behaviors are disruptive. Ask for cooperation.

The Experts. These people are usually knowledgeable but do not know when to be quiet and let others contribute their knowledge also. The experts have something to say about everything and eventually other participants stop listening because they have simply heard enough.

Techniques to Handle Experts

- Talk to the experts privately about their behavior and its effects on the other participants. Acknowledge the expertise offered, but state that others need to contribute also. Ask the experts to listen and encourage others to contribute.
- Since the experts can intimidate others in the group, try to ask the experts to serve as resources and ask for their opinions when needed. Also, ask the experts to listen to others' opinions first, then offer their opinions, if appropriate.
- Ask the experts to be special recorders of certain discussions since their expertise will help to record the important points on this topic.
- Try not to alienate the experts.

The Directors. Directors think that they should be chairing the meeting. Perhaps they have been previous chairpersons of the group or another group and they know everything there is to know about facilitating a meeting. While the directors may be very knowledgeable of the role, the situation becomes competitive with the current chairperson's role in the meeting.

Techniques to Handle Directors

- Invite the directors to lead a segment of the meeting, record minutes, or lead a subgroup.
- Talk with the directors privately, acknowledging their expertise in leading a meeting, but state it is not their role in these meetings. Ask for the directors' cooperation in being effective participants by not competing with you and letting you run the meeting.

The Coroners. There will often be those who leave the meeting and provide others with a devastating postmortem of the meeting. Sometimes participants take turns in playing the role of the coroner. The coroners remember the negative things that happened, even if they were few, and somehow forget about all of the positive things that occurred during the meeting.

Techniques to Handle Coroners

- Establish ground rules that state the business that is discussed at the meeting remains among the participants of the meeting. Also, the image of the group is important to everyone, so all participants are expected to present a positive image of the group and its work. If participants take on the coroner role, they should be confronted about violating these ground rules.
- Avoid getting caught up in the aftermath of the coroner's ruling!

Handling Other Challenging Situations

No one is talking. Sometimes it is difficult to get a discussion going. For whatever reason, participants are quiet. The chairperson could handle the silence in various ways such as stating:

- "Let's not all talk at once." This usually generates some humor and breaks the ice.
- "It is pretty quiet...I am not sure what the silence means..." This is almost always effective in getting participants to respond. Sometimes, they will state that they simply need time to gather their thoughts before they respond. Allow them time to do this.

- "What if (suggest an idea) ...., How many of you would agree with that?"
- "Who hates the idea?" This gives permission to the group members to dissent, if that is the case.

Getting Off Track. There are times when participants are so engaged in a discussion that they steer off track. It is easy for this to occur when a group gets together, especially a group of individuals who knows each other well and has not communicated with each other in a while. The chair must be attentive to these situations and help corral the group back to the relevancies of the agenda item being discussed. This can occur by simply saying, "We are getting off track" or "We have gone over our time allotment for this item and need to move on." This usually serves as a reality check for participants and they willingly agree.

> *"Members may feel that loyalty and approval of other participants are more important than expressing an opinion that is different from the team. This is called 'groupthink.'"*

Dealing with Deadlock. Another situation that occurs is an impasse or deadlock. After much discussion, a group simply cannot reach consensus. Suggestions for dealing with this problem include the following:

- Realize that deadlock may be okay, and move on to the next agenda item.
- Ask participants to reverse roles to get a fresh perspective on the situation.
- Discuss the consequences of each position.
- Assist the opposition in determining what needs to happen for them to move ahead with the idea(s) on the table.
- Take a break so people may refocus.
- If the issue remains unresolved, table it for a future discussion.

Groupthink

While cohesiveness is necessary for effective group functioning, meeting participants can become too cohesive. Cohesiveness can be carried to an extreme where participants feel pressured to conform to ideas and decisions with which they may not agree. Members may feel that loyalty and approval of other participants are more important than expressing an opinion that is different from the team, or they may think they are off target and are unwilling to express their thoughts. This is called "groupthink." To avoid groupthink, participants need to state their positions and ask questions when they do not understand or when things just do not seem right. The only dumb question is the one that is not asked. Additional information on groupthink is provided in Chapter 5, Teamwork.

"It is essential that the information recorded in the minutes be accurate. The minutes need to contain the actions of the meeting, not necessarily the discussions."

The first line of defense in handling all of the above situations is the chairperson. This person has tremendous responsibility and needs the support of all participants. The chairperson needs the courage and tact to correct, corral, and sometimes ask unruly participants to retire from the group. No group can survive a toxic culture for very long, and good volunteers will not continue to devote their time to an association where the culture is not meaningful and enjoyable.

Executive or Closed Session

Most board meetings are open to any members to attend. However, there are special circumstances when the board determines that the information to be discussed at the meeting is confidential in nature. The board will call an executive or closed session. This session is open only to the individuals that the board deems appropriate. Executive sessions may be held when the board is conducting a performance evaluation, discussing the renewal of a contract, or holding a disciplinary session. Individuals attending an executive session are bound not to discuss or disclose anything that occurred in the session. The minutes of an executive session must be read and acted upon only in executive session.

Components of Meeting Minutes

Minutes are a way of briefly stating in writing the actions that occurred at the meeting. For board meetings, the minutes serve as the legal record of the meeting. Therefore, it is essential that the information recorded in the minutes be accurate. The minutes for each board and each meeting will most likely look different. There are several formats to record minutes. The important thing to remember is the minutes need to contain the actions of the meeting, not necessarily the discussions. It is not important to know who said what and why. The actions or decisions, follow up assignments, and persons responsible are the essentials to be recorded. Generally, minutes should include the information found in Table 8-7.

Table 8-7
Information to Include in Minutes

1. Name of the group/committee and the kind of meeting (e.g., board, closed session).
2. Date, time, and place of the meeting.
3. Those in attendance, including the chair, secretary, and any guests.
4. Acceptance of previous minutes, if applicable.
5. Agenda items, decisions, follow-up, person(s) assigned, and timeline. Brief points of discussion may be included if they are important to the understanding of the decision. Minutes record what was done, not what was said. They should be factual and not contain personal opinions. Avoid adjectives and adverbs.
6. Titles of the reports provided in the consent agenda, if applicable.
7. For motions, the maker of the motion along with the actual wording of the motion are transcribed.
8. Each agenda item is transcribed separately and numbered for ease in reading and locating the item.
9. The time of adjournment and the recorder's signature.

Source: Adapted from Nowicki, 1998.

With most meetings, the minutes are distributed to meeting participants as soon after the meeting as possible. The participants are responsible for reading the minutes and making any corrections. It is best to do this as soon as you receive the minutes while the meeting is still fresh in your mind. At the next meeting, the minutes are not read. The chair will ask if there are any corrections or additions to the minutes. The minutes will be amended as needed or they will "stand as written." Approval of minutes may also be included in the consent agenda. Another option is to approve the minutes electronically while they are still fresh in everyone's mind. If minutes are approved outside of the meeting, the next meeting's minutes need to reflect that the minutes were previously approved.

Evaluating a Meeting

Practice makes perfect–but only if we are practicing the right things. Just because we have attended meetings for years does not necessarily mean we are doing it right! There is always room for improvement; therefore, a group should evaluate its meetings.

Some groups do a "process check" at the end of their meetings to determine what worked, what did not, and what needs improvement. Other groups may use a written evaluation tool composed of questions such as those in Table 8-8. The tool can be distributed at the end of the meeting and completed individually by each participant. In a round robin fashion, each participant summarizes their evaluation of the meeting by stating the strengths of the meeting and recommendations for enhancing future meeting effectiveness.

Table 8-8
Questions for Evaluating Meetings

- Did the meeting accomplish its purpose?
- What percentage of the meeting focused on strategic direction vs. planning and administrative details?
- Did the meeting begin and end on time?
- Did everyone contribute to forming the agenda?
- Did the agenda clearly define the work to be done?
- Were all the agenda items covered?
- Was the time for the meeting adequate? Was the time well used?
- Were issues discussed thoroughly or were decisions made too quickly?
- Did the chairperson keep the meeting moving along so the agenda items were covered?
- After each agenda item, was there a summary of the action to be taken? If so, did the summary include to whom assignments were given and a deadline?
- Were the location and time convenient?
- Was the room set-up and work space adequate?
- Was the meeting process effective and efficient?
- Did everyone have a voice in decisions made at the meeting?
- Were there members who dominated the discussions?
- Did some members seem quiet and not contribute to discussions?
- Were some members negative? Did they squash ideas?
- Were there side conversations going on?
- Were some members arguing and heckling?
- Were there some members too busy to pay attention to the meeting?
- Were challenging situations handled appropriately?
- Was everyone prepared for the meeting?
- What behaviors facilitated group process?
- What behaviors hindered the group's functioning?

Now summarize what worked and what didn't. Develop strategies for improving the next meeting.

Source: Adapted from Nowicki, 1998.

Concluding a Meeting

After all agenda items are discussed, the meeting is summarized. The summary may include the highlights of the meeting and a restating of assignments and deadlines. Minutes should be distributed as soon as possible to refresh everyone's minds about assignments that were made. As the meeting concludes, the agenda for the next meeting begins to be prepared. Any items that need follow-up should be put on the upcoming agenda.

Successful meetings end on a final note of achievement. Individuals are thanked for their participation and commended for the accomplishments made. It is helpful to talk about where the group began, where it went, and where it finished. Doing so leaves participants with a positive feeling about the meeting and about their roles in the process. Once these notes are made and business is concluded, the meeting is adjourned. Those individuals who would like to talk about other issues may remain. Those who need or want to leave also are free to do so.

"New board members should do their homework so they can contribute effectively during the meeting. They should be familiar with the association's bylaws, minutes of previous meetings, and other documents that pertain to meetings."

Tips for New Board Members

New board members may have attended their association's board meetings in the past as observers. This is a good opportunity to learn about the culture of these board meetings and the rules to follow. If you have not had that experience, discuss with your mentor or a current board member the culture and the politically correct things to do and those to avoid. Be familiar with the association's bylaws, minutes of previous meetings, and other documents that pertain to meetings. Do your homework so you can contribute effectively during the meeting. Bring more information than you will need, and use it if necessary.

During your first board meeting, the board will most likely be very cordial and willing to help you understand both the content and the process. Be kind to yourself; it is acceptable to feel a bit anxious and expect to be somewhat overwhelmed. Most board members can remember their first board meetings and how novice they felt. Try to present your best image by being enthusiastic and willing to learn. Pay attention to others when they speak. Show your interest by asking questions to obtain more information and for clarity. Contribute information in a positive manner when you are ready. Find out the dress code for the meeting and dress accordingly. Last, but not least, be yourself. You know you have something to contribute or you would not be sitting at the board table!

Summary

> *"Board members are looked upon as role models and are expected to be well-skilled in conducting and participating in meetings."*

An effective meeting involves planning, both by the chairperson and the participants. New board members must possess or develop effective meeting skills not only for their roles on the executive board, but also for their roles in leading other meetings and groups throughout the organization. Board members are looked upon as role models and are expected to be well-skilled in conducting and participating in meetings. Since most of the board's work is accomplished through some form of a meeting, it is important to learn and practice effective meeting skills.

Each person who attends a meeting takes back positive or negative reactions from that meeting. An effective meeting can have great benefits. Participants can return home or to their jobs rejuvenated, excited, and motivated. Their good feelings can be contagious if they are spread to others. The opposite can also be true if negative feelings are taken away from the meeting. There will always be portions of the meeting that are very positive, but there will be portions that are frustrating or negative. What we remember about the meeting, whether positive or negative, is our choice.

Good meeting skills can provide participants with positive feelings about the content and process of the meeting and their roles in contributing to a successful meeting. Effective meetings result in improved team work, interpersonal relationships, morale, and productivity.

Meeting skills can be learned, and if practiced, can make meetings productive and fun. They can be enhanced by following this chapter's tips for both the chairperson and participants. Further improvement can occur by evaluating meetings and getting feedback about your own behavior in meetings. Remember, meetings are the ultimate team sport – winning requires the quarterback and all the team players.

Learning Assessment

Chapter 8: Effective Meetings

Reflect on the knowledge you gained from this chapter by responding to the following statements and questions. Some of the statements suggest topics for you to discuss with your mentor. This chapter may also have prompted other thoughts and questions to discuss with your mentor.

1. What have you learned from this chapter that you plan to use to enhance your skills as a meeting participant?

2. What have you learned from this chapter that you plan to use to enhance your skills in chairing a meeting?

3. After your first board meeting, ask your mentor to give you feedback about your performance at the board meeting. Was the feedback consistent with your self-assessment?

4. Based on your own assessment and feedback from others, what will you do to enhance your meeting skills at future board meetings?

5. After your first board meeting, ask your mentor to evaluate the meeting with you using the Questions for Evaluating Meetings (Table 8-8) found in this chapter. Address what went well, what did not go very well, and what challenging behaviors you witnessed at the meeting. How was the meeting handled by the chairperson and how did the participants contribute to a successful meeting? What needs to improve?

References

Mentoring the Stars: A Program for Volunteer Board Leaders

American Society of Association Executives. (2006). *Seven measures of success: What remarkable associations do that others don't.* Washington, DC: Author.

Ancona, D., & Bresman, H. (2007). *X-teams: How to build teams that lead, innovate, and succeed.* Boston, MA: Harvard Business School Publishing Corporation.

Benner, P. (1984). *From novice to expert: Excellence and power in clinical nursing practice.* Menlo Park, CA: Addison-Wesley Publishing Company.

Bennis, W., & Nanus, B. (2003). *Leaders: Strategies for taking charge.* (2nd ed). New York, NY: Harper & Row.

Berry, K. (2008). What do your financial statements tell you? *Associations Now: The Volunteer Leadership Issue Supplement, 5*(1), 72-73.

Carver, J. (2006). *Boards that make a difference* (3rd ed.). San Francisco, CA: Jossey-Bass Publishers.

Chait, R., Ryan, W., & Taylor, B. (2005). *Governance as leadership: Reframing the work of nonprofit boards.* Hoboken, NJ: John Wiley & Sons, Inc.

Chang, R., & Kelley, P. (1993). *Step-by-step problem solving.* Irvine, CA: Richard Chang Associates, Inc.

Cohen, N. (1995). *Mentoring adult learners: A guide for educators and trainers.* Malabar, FL: Krieger Publishing Company.

Covey, S. (1990). *The 7 habits of highly effective people: Powerful lessons in personal change.* New York, NY: Simon & Schuster, Inc.

Darling, L. (1985). What to do about toxic mentors. *The Journal of Nursing Administration, 15*(5), 43-44.

De Cagna, J. (2007). The ungovernance model. *Associations Now, 3*(8), 36-40.

DePree, M. (1992). *Leadership jazz.* New York, NY: Doubleday.

Fields, W. (1994). Coaching and mentoring. *Nursing Standard, 8*(30), 105-110.

Frankel, J. (2008). Annual strategic plan evaluation. Yardley, PA: Tecker Consultants.

Gallery, M., & Waters, S. (2008). The development of consensus guidelines for strategic planning in associations. *Journal of Association Leadership, 4*(3), 48-67.

Hardy, J. (1990). *Developing dynamic boards: A proactive approach to building nonprofit boards of directors.* Erwin, TN: Essex Press.

Harper, A., & Harper, B. (1992). *Skill-building for self-directed work team members.* New York, NY: MW Corporation.

Hersey, P., Blanchard, K., & Johnson, D. (2001). *Management of organizational behavior: Utilizing human resources.* Upper Saddle River, NJ: Prentice Hall.

Hockman, J. (2008). Conversation that counts: Engaging in the right dialogue at the board table. *Associations Now, The Volunteer Leadership Issue, 5*(1), 66-67.

Ingram, R. (2003). *Ten basic responsibilities of nonprofit boards.* Washington, DC: BoardSource.

Jacobs, J. (1997). The Volunteer Protection Act of 1997: How the new law will affect associations. *Association Management, 49*(8). 39-41.

Jacobs, J. (2008). Your legal responsibilities. *Associations Now, 4*(1), 70-71.

Kirk, W.A. (2007). *Board members: Governing roles and responsibilities.* Lanham, MD: University Press of America, Inc.

Knowles, M. (1980). *The modern practice of adult education: From pedagogy to andragogy.* Englewood Cliffs, NJ: Cambridge Adult Education.

Kotter, J. (1990). *A force for change: How leadership differs from management.* New York, NY: The Free Press.
Lindeman, E. (1961). *The meaning of adult education.* Eugene, OR: Harvest House Ltd.
Lockwood, M. (1996). Calling all participants: How to ensure a productive conference call. *Association Management, 48*(1), L-61-L-62.
Mattocks, R. (2008). *Zone of insolvency: How nonprofits avoid hidden liabilities and build financial strength.* Hoboken, NJ: John Wiley & Sons.
Nadler, D., Behan, B., & Nadler, M. (Eds.). (2006). *Building better boards: A blueprint for effective governance.* San Francisco, CA: Jossey-Bass Publishers.
Navran, F. (2006). Doing right while doing good. *Associations Now, 2*(1), 16-19.
Nowicki, C.R. (1998). *Mentoring the stars: A mentorship program for new board members.* Pitman, NJ: Anthony J. Jannetti, Inc.
Park, D. (1990). Strategic planning and the nonprofit board. Washington, DC: National Center for Nonprofit Boards.
Rogers, C. (1979). *Freedom to learn.* Columbus, OH: Charles E. Merrill Publishing Company.
Senge, P. (1990). *The fifth discipline: The art and practice of the learning organization.* New York, NY: Currency-Doubleday.
Tecker, G., Frankel, J., & Meyer, P. (2002). *The will to govern well: Knowledge, trust, and nimbleness.* Washington, DC: American Society of Association Executives.
Tecker, G. (2007). Accountability cuts both ways. *Associations Now: The Volunteer Leadership Issue, 3*(1), 82.
Zachary, L. (2005). *Creating a mentoring culture: The organization's guide.* San Francisco, CA: Jossey-Bass Publishers.

Suggested Readings

Brown, J. (2006). *The imperfect board member: Discovering the seven disciplines of governance excellence.* San Francisco, CA: Jossey-Bass Publishers.
Constantine, G. (1997). The Volunteer Protection Act of 1997: How landmark legislation evolved. *Association Management, 49*(8), 37-38.
Dalton, J. (2007). Strategy management. In J. Cox (Ed.), *Professional practices in association management* (pp. 47-56). Washington, DC: ASAE and the Center for Association Leadership.
DePree, M. (2001). *Called to serve.* Grand Rapids, MI: William B. Eerdmans Publishing Company.
DePree, M. (2003). *Leading without power: Finding hope in servicing community.* San Francisco, CA: Jossey-Bass Publishers.
Flynn, O. (2007). Whose interests are you serving? *Associations Now: The Volunteer Leadership Issue, 4*(1), 77.
Garvey, R., Stokes, P., & Megginson, D. (2008). *Coaching and mentoring: Theory and practice.* Thousand Oaks, CA: Sage Publications.
Gelatt, J. (1992). *Managing nonprofit organizations in the 21st century.* Phoenix, AZ: Oryx Press.
Grace, K.S. (2008). *The ultimate board member's book.* Medfield, MA: Emerson & Church Publishers.

Haines, S., & McKinlay, J. (2007). *Reinventing strategic planning: The systems thinking approach.* San Diego, CA: Systems Thinking Press.
Herold, A. (1997). Avoiding antitrust problems. *Association Management, 49*(1), 80-82.
Hopkins, B. (2003). You and UBIT. *ASAE Executive Update.* May, 2003.
Hurley, G. (1996). Understanding the job of director: Directors who know their limits can help the board operate at the optimum. *Association Management, 48*(1), L-49-L-51.
Jacobs, J. (2007). *Association law handbook: A practical guide for associations, societies, and charities* (4th ed.). Washington, DC: American Society of Association Executives.
Katzenback, J., & Smith, O. (1993). *The wisdom of teams: Creating the high performance organization.* Boston, MA: Harvard Business School Press.
Kouzes, J., & Posner, B. (2007). *The leadership challenge.* (4th ed). San Francisco, CA: Jossey-Bass Publishers.
Kriegel, R., & Patler, L. (1991). *If it ain't broke...break it! And other unconventional wisdom for a changing business world.* New York, NY: Warner Books.
Maginn, M. (2004). *Making teams work: 24 lessons for working together successfully.* New York, NY: McGraw-Hill.
Maxwell, J. (2007). *The 21 indispensable qualities of a leader: Becoming the person others will want to follow.* Nashville, TN: Thomas Nelson.
Maxwell, J. (2008). *Mentoring 101.* Nashville, TN: Thomas Nelson.
Merlevede, P., & Bridoux, D. (2004). *Mastering mentoring and coaching with emotional intelligence.* Norwalk, CT: Crown House Publishing Company.
Murray, M. (2001). *Beyond the myths and magic of mentoring: How to facilitate an effective mentoring process.* San Francisco, CA: Jossey-Bass Publishers.
Parsloe, E., & Leedham, M. (2009). *Coaching and mentoring: Practical conversations to improve learning.* Philadelphia, PA: Kogan Page Publishers.
Robinson, M. (2001). *Nonprofit boards that work.* New York, NY: John Wiley & Sons, Inc.
Senge, P., Kleiner, A., Roberts, C., Ross, R., & Smith, B. (1994). *The fifth discipline fieldbook: Strategies and tools for building a learning organization.* New York, NY: Currency-Doubleday.
Shenkman, M. (2008). *Leader mentoring: Find, inspire, and cultivate great leaders.* Franklin Lakes, NJ: Career Press.
Wellins, R., Byham, W., & Wilson, J. (1991). *Empowered teams: Creating self-directed work groups that improve quality, productivity, and participation.* San Francisco, CA: Jossey-Bass Publishers.
Zey, M. (1984). *The mentor connection.* Homewood, IL: Dow Jones-Irwin.

A Must Read:
An excellent source for board members' continuing education and board development is the *Associations Now: The Volunteer Leadership Issue* published each January by the American Society of Association Executives (ASAE) and the Center for Association Leadership. The publication may be accessed from ASAE at www.asaecenter.org.

Index

A

B

C

D

E

N

O

P

Q

R

S

T

U

V

W

Z